On That Windswept Plain

The First One Hundred Years

of

East Fife Football Club

James K. Corstorphine

Text Copyright © 2003 James K. Corstorphine

All rights reserved

No part of this publication may be reproduced, stored in a retrieval system or transmitted in any form or by any means without the prior permission of the publisher.

Paperback edition first published in 2003

Revised and adapted for electronic publication in 2015

Second Paperback Edition published in 2018

Please be aware that any opinions expressed within the pages of this book are entirely those of the author and not necessarily the views of East Fife Football Club or any individual connected with East Fife Football Club.

By the Same Author:

East of Thornton Junction, the Story of the FifeCoast Line
James K. Corstorphine, Leven, 1995. (ISBN 0-9525621-0-3)

Peter Smith, the Fisherman Poet of Cellardyke
James K. Corstorphine, Leven, 2000. (ISBN 0-9525621-2-X)

Scottish football's greatest prize! East Fife won the Scottish Cup in 1938 by beating Kilmarnock 4-2 in the final at Hampden Park, Glasgow, on 27th April 1938 following a 2-2 draw at the same venue four days earlier. The Methil club are the only Second Division side to lift the cup in the history of the competition, a feat that will probably never be repeated. (Author's Collection)

When East Fife brought the Scottish Cup home to Methil in 1938, the trophy was taken around several local businesses and displayed in shop windows. One Methil shop proprietor's wife, it is rumoured, took the famous cup to bed with her at night for safekeeping! (Author's Collection)

Contents

Introduction 1
Chapter One: On That Windswept Plain...................................11
Chapter Two: Ring Up the Curtain!......................................17
Chapter Three: The Eastern and Northern Leagues 27
Chapter Four: Into the Central League 49
Chapter Five: A New Beginning! 60
Chapter Six: The First Major Trophy................................73
Chapter Seven: Into the Scottish League! 81
Chapter Eight: A Remarkable Achievement 91
Chapter Nine: First Division Football Comes to Methil!..........107
Chapter Ten: Their Finest Hour 131
Chapter Eleven: War and Peace 151
Chapter Twelve: Halcyon Days................................163
Chapter Thirteen: The Dawson Years................................193
Chapter Fourteen: From Bad to Worse 207
Chapter Fifteen: Jimmy Bonthrone Returns 219
Chapter Sixteen: Back in the Big Time 239
Chapter Seventeen: Dark Days Again 271
Chapter Eighteen: Pushing for the Premier 285
Chapter Nineteen: Down in the Doldrums...................307
Chapter Twenty: Enter Steve Archibald................................331
Chapter Twenty-One: A Fresh Start in a New Stadium..........351
Acknowledgements 373
Sources and Bibliography 374

6

Introduction

"Ahm no' gaun back!"

How often have you heard that phrase whilst standing at your local football ground, having just watched your local team suffer a humiliating defeat at the hands of a club from the lower reaches of the league? Probably more often than you'd care to remember!

At the next home match, however, the disgruntled spectator who uttered these very words will no doubt be seen in his usual spot on the terraces. The embarrassingly poor performance of the previous game will be forgotten and, with the eternal optimism that is ever present in the mind of the loyal football supporter, he will be looking forward to the forthcoming match with eager anticipation.

There are exceptions, however, and my father is a prime example.

A keen follower of the men in black and gold, my dad travelled far and wide to watch East Fife during the early 1950's. Then, on January 30th 1954, East Fife lost 3-0 to Queen of the South at Bayview in the first round of the Scottish Cup. The previous Saturday he had watched his favourites beat the mighty Glasgow Rangers in a League match. The very fact that East Fife, League Cup holders at the time, could defeat one of the best teams in the land one week then crash out of the Scottish Cup to an un-fancied side the next was too much to take. He never went back.

I don't know if the absence of my father's vocal encouragement had anything to do with the club's demise, but shortly after he made his resolution never to set foot in Bayview again, the club began to slip down the league. Only five seasons later, East Fife were a second division club. The halcyon years were over.

As a result of my dad's decision to turn his back on football, visits to football matches were few and far between during my early years. Living in Cellardyke, it simply was not possible for a young lad to travel the sixteen miles to Methil on his own. I had to make do with watching the local amateur side, Anster United.

The first senior match I ever attended was in the early 1970's, when I was fortunate enough to be allowed to accompany a school friend and his father to a game, even though my own father had initially voiced his disapproval at the idea.

"Ye'll get hit on the heid wi' a bottle", was his reply to my first request. It was his view that all football grounds had become dens of violence since he had last attended a match almost two decades earlier. Eventually he relented and I was allowed to go.

Before long I was hooked. Soon, most of my spare time would be taken up with studying results, fixtures, league tables and so on. Every Saturday night I would make the two-mile round trip on foot to Anstruther to buy the *Sporting Post* in order to satisfy my craving for football facts and figures.

"Ye're jist fillin' yer heid fu' o' useless information", was one of my father's more commonly used expressions at that time. His attempts to get me to spend less time studying football and more time on my schoolwork, however, were fruitless. My rebellious nature caused his demands to have exactly the opposite effect.

I continued to fill my head with 'useless information' and, over the years, I eventually gained enough knowledge to enable me to write this book about the history of one of the most successful provincial Scottish football clubs of all time. East Fife were founded in 1903. After several years of playing in local and regional leagues, the club was eventually admitted to the Second Division of the Scottish Football League in 1921. Incredibly, just six years later, the Fifers played in the 1927 Scottish Cup final at HampdenPark, where they lost 3-1 to Celtic.

The club's greatest hour was undoubtedly when, in 1938, they won the Scottish Cup by defeating Kilmarnock 4-2 at

Hampden in a replayed match following a 1-1 draw. In doing so they became the only side ever to win the cup whilst playing in the Second Division, an achievement that will probably never be repeated.

The ten years following the Second World War must, however, be regarded as the most successful period in the club's history. During this time, East Fife won the League Cup no fewer than three times and made yet another Scottish Cup final appearance in 1950.

Their league record during this same period is also impressive. After gaining promotion to the top league in 1948, the club twice finished their league campaign in third place and twice in fourth place over the next five seasons. In season 1952/53, two defeats and a draw in their last three league matches denied them the League Championship, the team having maintained pole position for most of the campaign. This book covers the first hundred-year history of East Fife Football Club, from its formation until the end of the 2002/2003 season. I can only hope that the reader will gain as much pleasure from this book as the writer has gained during many enjoyable years of research.

Leven Thistle, the most prominent football club to operate in the local area before the formation of East Fife, pictured in season 1901/02 (Author's Collection)

Chapter One: On That Windswept Plain

The year 1903 is significant in world history for a variety of reasons, but one event in particular stands out from the rest. Probably the most notable event of the year was the first manned flight in a motor powered aeroplane at Kitty Hawk, North Carolina, USA, where the Wright Brothers, Wilbur and Orville, achieved their much renowned feat on 17th December.

On a much smaller scale, however, 1903 was also the year when there was an exciting new development in Fife football circles; an occurrence which would lead to shock waves surging through the world of Scottish football in the years to come. Although this event would do nothing to shape the future of civilisation, it would prove to be no less significant to the residents of Methil and its environs and to future generations of football followers throughout the east of Fife and beyond. East Fife Football Club was founded.

Interest in football had been growing steadily in the area during the late 1800's, fuelled in part by the growth of the east of Fife's only senior club at that time, Raith Rovers. Raith were founded in Kirkcaldy some twenty years earlier and, by 1903, interest in football in the county was such that Raith were just one of five senior clubs playing in Fife, the others being Cowdenbeath, Dunfermline Athletic, Lochgelly United and Hearts of Beath.

For the first mention of football in the Levenmouth area, however, we must go back almost a quarter of a century before the formation of East Fife, to the year 1879. It was in this year that Cameron Bridge Football Club came into existence. The club was formed by a group of local football enthusiasts in March of that year, who played matches amongst themselves at Cameron House, permission having been granted for the use of the grounds by Mr Haig, owner of the local distillery. The playing members of Cameron Bridge F.C. would appear to have entered into the venture with great enthusiasm, not content with confining games to Saturday afternoons. When the hours of daylight became shorter and the nights became chillier, the sounds of football matches could still be heard after dusk coming from the grounds of Cameron House as the winter of 1879 approached, as is evident from this report taken from the *East of Fife Record* in October of that year:

"Several matches between the members of Cameron Football Club have recently been played. One came off on Saturday last, when the close of play showed the sides to be 3 goals and 2 goals respectively. This week, under Luna's fair light, some interesting play has taken place".

The formation of Cameron Bridge F. C. did not, however, initiate the immediate formation of other football clubs in the area during those early days. Most of the inhabitants of the towns and villages in the eastern part of the county were content to play cricket on summer Saturdays and amuse themselves with indoor pastimes throughout the winter months. Competitive football matches were to be confined to the west of Fife for the next two to three years. Nevertheless, by 1885 the game had gradually started to spread to the east of Fife, with clubs being formed along the course of the developing railway network. Improved rail travel and its associated communication facilities were key factors in the development of football clubs and football competitions in the district. In Leven, several football teams were founded during the mid 1880's, with Star of Leven being one of the first clubs to be formed in the town. This club, however, had no connection with the Star of Leven club that was prominent in the early years of the Scottish Cup, who hailed from the Dumbarton area.

East Neuk of Fife side Cellardyke Bluejackets, formed in the late 1800s, pictured with the Martin White Cup in 1901. The fact that the team hailed from a local fishing community is evident from the hand knitted fishermen's jerseys worn by the players! (Photo: Courtesy of Peter Smith)

The game also spread to the East Neuk of Fife around this time with Anstruther and Cellardyke Association Football Club, the first club to be formed in the East Neuk, inaugurated in September 1885.

As the game grew in popularity, several junior and amateur football teams were founded in the Levenmouth area during the 1890's. Buckhaven, in particular, had a successful and well-respected junior side playing at TollPark on the north side of the town adjacent to Wellesley Road.

It was rumoured late in 1902 that the Buckhaven club were planning to turn senior, a move which brought the following comment from the local press:

"Some people talk of running a senior team in Buckhaven, but older heads view this as beyond the resources of the town itself; they hold, and rightly we think, that such a team could only be done by amalgamation with Wemyss or Leven".

It must be remembered that, in 1902, Buckhaven, Methil and Leven were all separate towns and not one built up area as they are today.

Speculation was further fuelled on Christmas Day 1902, when Buckhaven played host to a 'Leven Select' in a friendly match. The Leven side fielded a number of senior players in a game which finished 3-0 to the home side. The reason for this match, apart from festive season entertainment, remains unclear, but indications are that the Leven Select was a trial senior side put together to see if such a football club was a feasible proposition.

Throughout January 1903, local feeling that the Levenmouth area could support a senior side grew stronger almost daily. The local newspaper, the *Leven Advertiser*, was of the opinion that a more organised football club was much needed for the district to replace the poorly run local junior outfits. Referring to local side Leven Thistle, the newspaper observed:

"Had Leven's been a professional team these recent failures of players to attend would not have twice troubled the committee. A strong feeling in favour of having a senior team has grown up and in Buckhaven especially the idea has supplanted all delight in the junior team"

The general opinion, however, still remained that the fishing community of Buckhaven could not support a senior side on its own. A more realistic venture would be the formation of a football club representing Leven, Methil and Buckhaven, with the team playing in a location geographically central to the three towns. The established population centres of Leven and Buckhaven coupled with the population expansion associated with the growth of the mining industry in and around Methil suggested that a senior football side representing the district would be a worthwhile venture.

With these factors in mind, a group of local 'football enthusiasts' decided to call a public meeting to discuss the idea, which was held in Suttie's Hall, Methil, on 9th March 1903. Mr J Waddell, Junior, from Leven, who made a short speech about how the formation of a local senior football club could benefit the area, chaired the meeting. Several similar speeches followed, all in favour of the project.

There then followed much discussion and debate, which resulted in the agreement that a new senior club would be formed with the name 'East of Fife Football Club'.

A Representative Committee was then formed, with Councillor Suttie from Methil installed as Chairman, Thomas Neill from Leven as Secretary and Mr J. Campbell from the Steamboat Tavern in Methil appointed treasurer.

Funding for the club was to be raised by offering 400 shares to the public at the price of five shillings per share.

Applications were to be made to join the Scottish Football Association and the Northern League as well as other senior organisations.

It was proposed that the new club should take up tenancy of Town Hall Park, a vast stretch of open ground situated high above Methil and currently the home of junior side Leven Thistle. The park was exposed to the elements due to the complete absence of buildings in the vicinity and was often referred to in Thistle's match reports as *"that windswept plain above Methil"*.

Fife's five other senior clubs warmly welcomed the formation of a new football club representing the east of the county and all shared the opinion that a Fife League could be formed between the six teams.

The decision to form a senior club playing in Methil did not, however, entirely satisfy the Buckhaven football public. After the decision had been taken to form East of Fife F.C., talk was rife of forming a rival senior club from the fishing community. The *Leven Advertiser* reported on the matter and referred to the proposal as *"penny wise, pound foolish caper"*. It would appear that the organisers behind the rival venture eventually realised that the local communities didn't have the resources to support two senior clubs and the idea was dropped. Developments then took their course and applications were made to join the various associations as planned.

The name East of Fife F.C. was considered to be too much of a mouthful, however, and was shortened to East Fife F. C. The official colours were stated as green and white hooped jerseys with white knickers.

East Fife Football Club officially became members of the Scottish Football Association in April 1903. Their application to join the Northern League was rejected, however, and for the first year of the club's existence they would have to be content with playing in the newly formed Fife League, the Wemyss Cup and the Scottish Qualifying Cup, as well as organising challenge matches against other senior clubs of similar standing.

After much negotiation, the club secured tenancy of Town Hall Park for home matches. The park was then given the more appropriate name of BayviewPark due to its elevated and open position overlooking LargoBay. The enclosure was *"the largest and finest in Fifeshire"* according to the Leven Advertiser, with the actual playing surface measuring 126 yards by 84 yards.

Less than happy with the agreements concerning the park, however, were Leven Thistle. The local junior outfit, who had moved into Town Hall Park only the season before, now found themselves without a home. With nowhere to play and facing the likelihood that their regular patrons would defect to the newly formed senior club, Thistle decided to call it a day. The East Fife Committee, on the other hand, set about the business of preparing their club for the forthcoming season with great enthusiasm. The Methil Men were about to take their first faltering steps on the road to success!

Chapter Two: Ring Up the Curtain!

The earliest known photograph of East Fife Football Club, taken at half time during the friendly with Falkirk on 12th September 1903. Back row, left to right: J.Adamson (President), D.Ednie, H.Allan (Capt.), P.Miller, W.Moffat, J.Waddell, T.Drummond, D.Melville, A.Brunton, J.Lawrie. Middle row, left to right: T.Turnbull (Match Secy.), R.Smith, J.Jarvie, D.Wilson, W.Wilson, J.Nangle, T.K.Neill (Hon. Secy.) Front row, left to right: A.McArdle, T.Middlemass. (Author's Collection)

With the basic essentials in place, the East Fife Committee set about the task of raising a team in preparation for the first match against Heart of Midlothian, who agreed to send a side to Methil on 15th August 1903 in return for the princely sum of £15.

Initially, the committee decided that the best combination would consist mainly of experienced seniors blended with one or two players recruited from the local junior ranks.

One of the first players to sign for the club was Harry Allan, the experienced Hearts right-back and former Scotland internationalist, who was appointed Captain of the side. Tom Drummond was signed from Cowdenbeath to fill the left-back position and goalkeeper Moffat was signed from Lothian side Broxburn Athletic.

For the position of centre-half, the club put its faith in Melville from Buckhaven and the position to his right was filled by Peter Middlemass, another Cowdenbeath lad.

For the left-half position the club had a choice of players; Adams from Newtongrange and local lad Willie Bell from Buckhaven.

Houston, a player who had seen service with Hearts and Tottenham Hotspur, was signed as a centre-forward, but could also be played in either of the inside-forward positions and on the left wing. Houston was well known in football circles as the player who scored the winning goal when Hearts beat Celtic in the 1901 Scottish Cup final. Competing for the position of centre-forward was the lanky figure of McArdle, signed from Leith Athletic.

Manson, an outside-left, was signed from St Andrews and Willie Wilson joined the club from Dundee to fill the position of inside-left.

For the opposite wing, the club secured the services of Nangle from Lochgelly. A third Cowdenbeath player, Davie Wilson, was signed up to play at inside-right. The wage that the first East Fife players were paid was rumoured to be 7/6 (37½p) per week.

Saturday August 15th 1903 dawned dull and overcast, but this did nothing to dampen the spirits of the spectators heading for BayviewPark. Despite the popular counter attractions of a band performance in Kirkcaldy, Largo Flower Show and a quoits match at Methilhill, a crowd of just under 1,000 turned up to witness the event.

One of the main attractions for local followers of the game was the inclusion of former Buckhaven player Roderick Walker and Leven lad Tom Collins in the Hearts eleven.

As rain threatened, the East Fife players lined up with the tall figure of Moffat in goal. Allan and Drummond were at right and left-back respectively, with Middlemass, Melville and Bell filling the half-back positions. The forwards who were chosen to pull on the East Fife jerseys for the first time were Nangle, Houston, McArdle, Wilson and Manson.

Captain Harry Allan won the toss and decided to defend the east goal for the first half.

Any hopes that the rain would hold off were dashed midway through the first period, when the heavens opened up. The ball soon became saturated with water and difficult to control. Hearts were first to adapt to the wet and slippery surface and they took the lead with a goal from left-winger Bell. Back came East Fife and Nangle and Houston thrilled the crowd with their 'rattling style' on the right wing. The pair were causing all sorts of problems for the Hearts defence and it was no surprise when Nangle slipped the ball past goalkeeper Moir to score East Fife's first ever goal. The joy was short lived, however, and Forrester regained the visitors' lead just before the interval.

During the second half, the home side began to play more as a team and soon began to pile the pressure on the Hearts defence, bringing out the skills of the full-backs Walker and Collins, much to the delight of the crowd. Eventually, the Fifers' pressure paid off and Nangle scored again to tie the match at 2-2.

Delighted with what he had witnessed during the inaugural match, the reporter from the *Leven Advertiser* commented:

"The result was full value for the play. Considering everything, the new team did splendidly. Take any eleven players, total strangers, and dump them down on a field at the start of a season and they would do no better. Given another match together and we will be prepared to see East Fife meet the County cracks and beat them".

The press report went on to paint pen pictures of the East Fife team.

The height and ability of goalkeeper Moffat was reckoned to be a great asset, although the player looked to be short of match practice. In defence, the past experience of team

John Nangle, scorer of East Fife's first-ever goals

Captain Harry Allan was apparent and would be of invaluable benefit to his partner, left-back Drummond. Drummond's passing style was said to be 'pleasing', and the player was sure to become popular with the spectators
With the exception of the 'brilliant' centre-half Melville, the midfield was thought to be the weak part of the team. Although it was possibly a little early to judge right-half Middlemass, there was certainly a lot of room for

improvement in this position. On the opposite flank, the reporter was of the opinion that Willie Bell had had a tough debut against Hearts' best wing, although he had played to the best of his ability.

With the exception of one forward, there was nothing but praise in the run down. McArdle was reckoned to be a 'crack centre' who 'did a power of useful work'.Right-winger Nangle, scorer of both East Fife goals, did more than enough during the match to guarantee a regular place in the side. Although inside-right Houston was also reckoned to be a quality player, it was thought that he was being played out of position and would be better suited to his familiar place on the left wing. Inside-left Willie Wilson was praised for his positioning and, despite being a stranger to the area, had already won over the spectators. Outside-left Manson, however, appeared to lack confidence and experience and, although the player had ability, the report concluded that he would benefit from another season in the junior game. BayviewPark also came in for praise:

"This was the first time the newly laid out pitch has been lined and the congratulations of the public go to the men who planned the enclosure", commented the report, before concluding: *"BayviewPark is one of the finest adapted fields in Fife. It is early yet to speak of what the club has to do to improve it, but a pavilion and stand must be among the first things once the club has recovered from the heavy outlay it must have incurred"*.

On the following Saturday, 22nd August 1903, East Fife made the short journey west for another friendly match against Kirkcaldy United, a recently formed senior club which had previously been known as Kirkcaldy Amateurs. United played at OvertonPark, a football pitch that still exists adjacent to the residential area known as Overton Mains. Before the East Fife team could take to the field, however, there was a serious problem to overcome. It was discovered that the green and white hooped jerseys worn in the Hearts match had not stood up well to their first wash and were unfit to wear. The Methil men had no choice but to borrow a spare set from United and return the inferior jerseys to the manufacturer!

The match itself had a happier outcome, with East Fife recording their first ever win. First half goals from debutant inside-right Dave Wilson, who had filled the vacancy caused by Houston moving to the left wing, and centre McArdle, were just enough to overcome the Kirkcaldy side by two goals to one.

It is interesting to note the sporting comments of the Kirkcaldy spectators, who voiced the opinion that East Fife were 'a crack team'. The match report that appeared in the local press concluded with the opinion that East Fife's next visit to OvertonPark was likely to be a big crowd puller!

The first home victory came seven days later in the club's first competitive match, a Fife League fixture against Hearts of Beath. Resplendent in their new replacement green and white hoops, the home side easily overcame their visitors from west Fife with a 3-1 win. The *Leven Advertiser* reckoned that a further five goals for the Methil side would have been a fairer reflection of play!

At the beginning of September, East Fife returned to Overton Park to face Kirkcaldy United in the Scottish Qualifying Cup and returned east with a 1-0 win and a place in the second round.

Next came a friendly with Falkirk reserves at Bayview, which finished 1-1. At half time in this game, local photographer Mr Mayor of Leven took the first East Fife team photograph.

The second round of the Qualifying Cup paired East Fife with Hearts of Beath. After two drawn matches, the Methil Men finally succumbed to the Hill of Beath side by two goals to one at the neutral venue of Reid's Park, Lochgelly, where a crowd of 1,200 paid a total of £30 to see the action.

Unfortunately, once the initial enthusiasm for the new football club had waned, attendances dropped, which in turn caused apathy amongst the players and club officials.

At the beginning of November 1903, the East Fife Committee, through the medium of the *Leven Advertiser*, voiced their disappointment at the support shown for the club during its early days.

"What young club ever had a bed of roses?" commented the same newspaper a few weeks later. *"Why do none of the old workers rally to its aid? The club seems to be understaffed, upon a very few does all the work devolve".*

The opinions voiced in the local press had little effect and the prevailing lack of enthusiasm amongst the players resulted in a farcical Fife League meeting with Raith Rovers on New Year's Day 1904.

First to call off was Harry Allan, who claimed that an old injury had re-asserted itself. Willie Walker was absent as he had been hit by a fall of debris down the pit and goalkeeper Moffat was unavailable as he was on a trip to the south of England. With Lawrie, Adams and Smith all claiming to have "missed the train", only five regulars, Dave & Willie Wilson, Kennedy, Houston and Melville, were available. The club tried to secure the services of goalkeeper Jack Smith to replace Moffat, but the player "couldn't make up his mind" whether he wanted to play or not!

Eventually, the club secured the services of some local men to make up the numbers and the match went ahead in front of a crowd of over 3,000. Not surprisingly, the Rovers dominated that first New Year Derby and ran out comfortable 3-0 winners.

In mid-January, following a 4-0 drubbing at Bathgate, Lawrie announced that he was unhappy playing for East Fife and asked to be released. This announcement was quickly followed by a report that Harry Allan was unlikely to be seen back at Bayview.

At the end of January, players Ness, Johnston and Smith failed to turn up for a home friendly against the Civil Service. The referee delayed the kick off by ten minutes but, when there was still no sign of the men, the game started with East Fife fielding with only eight players. Not long after the match started, three men were recruited from the crowd to fill the vacant positions. Only a week later, failure to raise a team to play Hearts of Beath at Keir's Park in a Fife League match caused forfeiture of the points.

With the club on the verge of folding less than a year after being formed, the Committee desperately tried to recruit players from the junior ranks so that the already arranged fixtures could be fulfilled.

The plight of the club prompted the following letter to the *Leven Advertiser* on 18 February 1904:

Sir – What has become of the lovers of football in Leven and Methil? When the East Fife club was first mooted, every second man one met was quite jubilant over the prospect of a strong club being organised and associated with the district. But it is a matter of regret to many that since the inauguration of the club it has not received the support that was expected or, indeed, it deserves. Anyone looking at the field on Saturday could not fail to be struck with the poor turnout of spectators. It must have been disappointing to those who had to finance the match and most depressing to the players themselves. It is hardly fair to those who both give their time and money to maintain this game not to get more sympathy and support from those interested in football. I think it was perhaps only an overlook rather than any lack of interest in the success of the club, and I write this as an appeal especially to our Leven friends to rally round East Fife and at the remaining matches help them to have 'record gates'. The club's greatest recommendation for admission to the Northern League will be good gates and I trust the public will see to it that this will not be an objection when East Fife make an application to that body.

I am, &c. Observer

Fortunately, sufficient enthusiasm was drummed up to keep the club going, and the rest of the 1903/04 season was played out with Fife League fixtures and a series of challenge matches.

The Fife League comprised of seven clubs who were scheduled to play each other on a 'home and away' basis, with the other six teams in the competition being Cowdenbeath, Dunfermline Athletic, Raith Rovers, Lochgelly United, Kirkcaldy United and Hearts of Beath. The final league table was never printed in the local press, but East Fife must have finished up pretty near the bottom if not actually in last place. Of the eleven matches played (it would appear that the fixture against Hearts of Beath at Keir's Park was not fulfilled), the Methil Men won only twice. Both Cowdenbeath and Hearts of Beath were beaten at Bayview, but home defeats were suffered at the hands of Dunfermline Athletic and Kirkcaldy United. The points were shared in the home fixtures with Lochgelly United and Raith Rovers. As for the league fixtures played away from home, all five games were lost, with the biggest reverse a 5-0 defeat from Cowdenbeath at NorthEndPark.

The only other competitive match played was the semi-final of the Fife Cup against Raith Rovers at Stark's Park, which the home side won 4-0.

Out of the sixteen friendly matches that were played during that first season, all but three were played at Bayview. Home victories were recorded against Edinburgh Adventurers, Black Watch, St Mirren 'A', Civil Service and Bathgate. The honours were even in the home challenge matches against Hearts 'A', Falkirk 'A', Hearts of Beath, Dundee Wanderers and Kirkcaldy United, with only Dundee 'A' and St Bernard's managing to beat the Fifers on their own soil. As for the three friendly matches played away from home, the victory against Kirkcaldy United at OvertonPark was followed by heavy defeats from Bathgate at MillPark and Aberdeen 'A' at Pittodrie.

On a more melancholy note, there was one other match played during season 1903/04. On Boxing Day 1903, East Fife played host to a Buckhaven/Wemyss select in order to raise money for the families of four local fishermen who were drowned in the Firth of Forth when their boat, the *Welsh Prince*, was lost. A crowd of 800 paid a total of £20 to see East Fife beat the select side 4-1.

The main concern amongst the people associated with the club, however, was whether or not the Fifers had a future in the game. Would the apathy that had dogged the Methil Men during their first season prevail? Only time would tell!

Chapter Three: The Eastern and Northern Leagues

In June 1904 the Northern League decided at its Annual General Meeting to increase its membership by one club, and applications were duly received from East Fife, Kirkcaldy United and Bon Accord from Aberdeen. The successful applicants were Kirkcaldy United, who received eighteen votes compared to East Fife's four. Bon Accord failed to attract any votes at all.

Disappointed at being rejected for a second time, East Fife desperately tried to find a ways to fill the fixture card rather than confine themselves to Fife League matches, cup competitions and challenge games. Always keen to offer advice, the *Leven Advertiser and Wemyss Gazette* printed an article in which the Sports Editor advised that the best way forward would be to resign from the Fife League and compete in the East of Scotland Cup Competitions, stating that:

"A team of East Fife's calibre could make its mark in these. A league is a good supplementary thing, second only to a cup tie".

East Fife thought otherwise. After investigating other possibilities, Chairman Gray called a meeting of clubs he thought would be interested in forming a new league for Fife and the Lothians. The clubs who were represented at the meeting were East Fife, Hearts of Beath, Edinburgh Adventurers, Bathgate, Bo'ness, Broxburn, Broxburn Shamrock, Dykehead and West Calder.

All nine clubs who attended the meeting were in favour of the new combination and, at a further meeting held in August 1904, the Eastern League was born. The Fifers' first Eastern League match was played at West Calder on 3rd September, where they lost 5-1.

The heavy reverse at West Calder was followed by a 4-1 defeat in the East of Scotland Qualifying Cup against Broxburn

Shamrock and, on 17th September, a disappointing 3-0 home defeat to Lochgelly United in the Scottish Qualifying Cup.

The first victory in the Eastern League came at the beginning of October when Adventurers were beaten by a single goal at Bayview. A week later Hearts of Beath were put to the sword at the same venue, but the joy was short lived.

A run of nine Eastern League defeats was to follow before the Fifers finally managed to take both points against Hearts Reserves (who had replaced Hearts of Beath in the competition) on 18th March 1905!

The run of defeats was not, however, without incident. On 12th November 1904 the East Fife squad set out for Bo'ness by train in order to fulfil an Eastern League fixture. The arrangement was that the players would meet up with club officials James Gray and Jock Mann (who had travelled earlier with the team hamper) at Polmont Station, where it was intended they would all board the train for Bo'ness. Unfortunately, some of the players boarded the Glasgow express instead of the local train, and went flashing through Polmont Station, past James Gray and Jock Mann, who were standing helpless on the platform. After the rest of the team had arrived on a later train, the depleted party continued to Bo'ness, where the match eventually started with East Fife fielding a number of local volunteers!

The Fifers fared a little better in the Fife League during season 1904/05, finishing fourth out of the seven competing clubs. One other match worth mentioning was a 3-1 home victory over Partick Thistle in a friendly arranged as part of the transfer of East Fife half-back Joe Melville to the Glasgow club.

In May 1905, proposals were put forward to disband the Eastern League and form a new league called the Central Football League, which would take its member clubs from the counties of Fife, Clackmannan and the Lothians. The clubs expected to take part were Adventurers, Alloa Athletic,

Bathgate, Bo'ness, Broxburn Shamrock, Cowdenbeath, Dundee Reserves, Dunfermline Athletic, East Fife, Hearts of Beath, Heart of Midlothian Reserves, Hibernian Reserves, Kirkcaldy United and Lochgelly United.

At a meeting held in Dunfermline on 6th May, it was decided to proceed with the formation of the Central League, but with a slightly depleted membership after the three Scottish League clubs withdrew their reserve sides from the competition and Kirkcaldy United decided to remain in the Northern League. Broxburn were added to the original number, but Cowdenbeath then withdrew after their application to join the Scottish League was successful, which meant that the proposed new combination would have ten members.

The effect this scenario had on the Northern League was that they would now have to start the new season with only nine clubs as Lochgelly United and Dunfermline Athletic had defected to the new competition, Cowdenbeath had joined the Scottish League and Stenhousemuir had resigned due to travelling difficulties. In order to keep their competition running, the Northern League had no option but to offer a place to East Fife in the hope that the two Fife clubs that had defected to the Central League would stay with the Northern combination. East Fife were unanimously elected to the Northern League in June 1905 and Lochgelly United and Dunfermline Athletic were persuaded to stay, which meant that in season 1905/06 the teams who would be travelling to Methil on league business were Aberdeen Reserves, Arbroath, Dundee Reserves, Dundee Wanderers, Dunfermline Athletic, Forfar Athletic, Kirkcaldy United, Lochee United, Lochgelly United, Montrose and St. Johnstone.

Season 1905/06 opened with defeat in a Wemyss Cup match against Raith Rovers at Stark's Park on 17th August and was closely followed by a home win over re-formed local juniors Leven Thistle in a benefit match for Thistle's Sandy Jarvie. On Saturday 19th August East Fife played their first match in the

Northern League against Montrose at Links Park, but it was not to be a happy baptism with the 'Gable Endies' triumphing 3-1. The following week Kirkcaldy United made the short journey through to Methil for the second league game and this time East Fife emerged victorious with a single goal win. United were the visitors for the second Saturday in a row on Saturday 2nd September when a record crowd of 2,000 lined the ropes at Bayview for a Qualifying Cup first round tie. There was to be no repeat of the previous week's result, however, as the Kirkcaldy side progressed to the second round with a 2-0 win.

Northern League victories against St. Johnstone and Montrose then followed and the points were shared with Lochee United and Dundee Wanderers as the Fifers justified their membership of the competition. The reasonably good league form was maintained until the end of the season, during which time they recorded convincing victories over Aberdeen Reserves and Dundee Wanderers; the seven goals to one win against the latter setting a new club goal scoring record. Their first season in the Northern League finished with the Fifers in fifth place, having played 22 games of which 8 were won, 7 were drawn and 7 were lost. League goals scored numbered 41, with 36 goals conceded. The league winners were Aberdeen Reserves, closely followed by Arbroath in second place.

In January 1906 the Penman Cup Association came into being. The association was formed with a view to holding an annual cup competition for clubs from Fife, Clackmannan, Stirling, and the Lothians. The clubs present at the inaugural meeting were Edinburgh Adventurers, Alloa Athletic, Bathgate, Bo'ness, Broxburn Athletic, Broxburn Shamrock, Cowdenbeath, Dunfermline Athletic, East Fife, East Stirlingshire, Hearts of Beath, King's Park, Kirkcaldy United, Raith Rovers, St Bernard's and Stenhousemuir. East Fife were drawn at home to Cowdenbeath in the first round, but bowed out of the new competition at the first hurdle with a 2-0 defeat.

In the Wemyss Cup, a competition that alternated annually between league and knockout format, East Fife emphasised that they were now a side to be reckoned with by finishing runners-up to Raith Rovers.

Towards the end of the 1905/06 season, BayviewPark was completely enclosed with a wooden fence. This allowed the club to charge an admission fee rather than rely on 'passing the hat' around the assembled spectators on match days.

"Rapid progress has been made with the barricading", observed the *Leven Advertiser and Wemyss Gazette* in March 1906, who concluded: *"by Saturday anyone wishing to see the game will have to pay"*.

There was one other event during season 1905/06 that is worthy of mention. Late in December 1905 a Kennoway gentleman, Mr Ferrie, acquired the lease of the whole of BayviewPark, although East Fife retained tenancy of the pitch. Although this development passed almost without notice at the time, it was to have far reaching effects on the club over the decade that was to follow, which will be explained later in this chapter.

Overall, East Fife regarded 1905/06 as a most successful season, both on and off the park. Attendances at Bayview had increased steadily as confidence in the team's ability grew and, by the end of the season, crowds were considered to be equal to, if not larger than, attendances at senior games in other parts of the county. Income at the gate was by now almost equalling expenditure for the first time in the club's history.

The Fifers now considered themselves to be in a position worthy of playing in the Scottish League and duly applied for membership during the summer of 1906. Their application was turned down, however, as the two clubs who had finished season 1905/06 at the bottom of the Scottish Second Division, Vale of Leven and East Stirlingshire, were both re-elected. The decision was then taken to increase the size of the Scottish Second Division by two clubs for season 1906/07 and East Fife made their second application to join, the other applicants being Alloa Athletic, Ayr Parkhouse, Beith, Dumbarton, Dundee Wanderers, Dunfermline Athletic, Lochgelly United, Renton, Royal Albert and Stenhousemuir. The successful clubs were Ayr Parkhouse with 14 votes and Dumbarton with 12 votes. East Fife, along with Dundee Wanderers, gained only one vote each.

Just visible in front of the smoking chimneys of Fife Coal Company's Leven No.1 Pit in this 1906 photograph is a newly fenced-in BayviewPark. The first grandstand can be seen on the far side of the ground. Note the completely unmade Wellesley Road carrying the newly opened Wemyss and District Tramway! (Photo: Courtesy of Alan Brotchie)

Bearing in mind the healthy position regarding crowd figures, the club made plans to erect a 400-seat grandstand on the north side of the pitch during the summer of 1906. Improved travel to and from Bayview was promised with the opening of the Wemyss and District Tramway along the south side of the ground and, with the influx of labour associated with the building of Methil No.2 Dock, the club expected crowds to double over the coming season.

Construction of the new grandstand started in June and it was complete in time for the Methil Highland Games on 19th July. Reporting on that event, the *Leven Advertiser and Wemyss Gazette* observed:

"The Grandstand was liberally patronised and came in for a fair test, which ought to establish public confidence in its stability"

The Fifers looked forward to season 1906/07 full of confidence for the future. BayviewPark, now fully enclosed with a wooden fence and boasting a grandstand, a re-furbished pavilion with separate referee's room and a playing surface that was second to none, was the envy of many less fortunate clubs. The confidence of the club rubbed off on the general public and by mid-August it was reported that sales of season tickets had exceeded all expectations.

Perhaps one of the reasons for the encouraging sales figures was the new fence and the location of the new grandstand. Spectators who had until now been accustomed to watching the games perched on coal wagons in the railway sidings on the north side of Bayview would find their view severely restricted. They would have no option but to pay for entry into the ground in future!

On the down side, however, concern was raised at the state of the green and white-hooped jerseys, which had been worn since the club's inception in 1903. The colours had now become so faded that some spectators were of the opinion that opposing teams could well lodge a protest. The local press campaigned for East Fife to kit themselves out in new strips, claiming that *"all black, with white collars and cuffs would be a most effective costume"*.

Contrary to popular belief, East Fife did not change to all-black outfits at this time. The green and white hoops were retained and continued to be the first choice colours until the start of season 1909/10, although there is evidence to suggest that their second choice colours during this period were black and white.

On the playing side, the club were happy to report that long serving player Peter Middlemass had signed up for the 1906/07 season despite interest from west Fife clubs. Local man Tom Collins, however, had decided to return to Hearts and brothers Tom and John Adams also decided that their futures lay elsewhere.

Defender Archie Grant, a former Leven Thistle player who had seen service in London with CrystalPalace and Chelsea, was signed up before the start of the season along with another player with a London connection, forward J. McGhee from Woolwich Arsenal. Other newcomers were half-backs Rougvie from Thornton, Taylor from Dundee and Penman from Leith Athletic along with forwards Downie from Lochee United and local lad W.Smith who was signed from Aberdeen. Players re-signed from the previous season were half-backs Dewar and White and forwards Andrew Horne, Andrew Nairn and Willie Wilkie. Trainer Jack Mann announced that he would no longer be able to devote his time to the club as he had a new occupation 'away from the pit' and was replaced by Buckhaven man James Bathgate.

On 18th August 1906, the first game was played at the new-look BayviewPark. BrechinCity were the visitors for a Northern League match which also marked the Angus club's first competitive outing in senior football. City proved no match for an enthusiastic East Fife eleven, however, who ran out 4-1 winners. One disappointing factor surrounding the match was that the new grandstand was not as popular as had been expected, with the *Leven Advertiser and Wemyss Gazette* observing:

"It is one of the little indulgences the visitors to Bayview have not yet acquired the taste for. A rough day will likely send them flocking in. The warm sun made it a pleasure to be around the line".

The win over Brechin was followed by a 3-0 victory over Hearts of Beath, which saw East Fife take an early lead at the top of the Northern League. The following Saturday, 1st September, it was down to Qualifying Cup business at Lochgelly, where the Methil Men lost narrowly and exited the competition. This defeat prompted a correspondent calling himself simply 'H.B' to write to the *Leven Advertiser and Wemyss Gazette* requesting that the £20 recently received from the transfer of Wilkie to Partick Thistle be used for signing up and coming young players rather than 'stiff old men'!

Keir's Park, the home of former Fife senior club Hearts of Beath. East Fife were regular visitors to Keir's Park during the early 1900's for Eastern and Northern League matches as well as Qualifying Cup ties. Today the ground is the home of the successful Junior side Hill o' Beath Hawthorn, winners of the Scottish Junior Cup in 1990. (Jim Corstorphine)

Since its recent improvements, BayviewPark was becoming a highly respected ground in local football circles and was chosen as the venue for the Scottish Qualifying Cup second round second replay between Raith Rovers and Lochgelly United at the beginning of September 1906. A crowd of almost

5,000 attended the match, realising gate receipts of £116, a record for a football match in Fife!

Following their bright start to the Northern League campaign, the Fifers hit a slump following the Qualifying Cup defeat and lost three league games in quick succession. There was little improvement in form before the end of the year, by which time only six matches had been won from fifteen played, six had been lost with the honours shared in three fixtures. An early exit was also made from the Fife Cup at the end of October when Cowdenbeath came to Methil and won by a single goal.

The first game of 1907 was a league fixture against Montrose on 5th January, which was abandoned due to poor light after 75 minutes. It was 19th January before the second game of the year was played, which ended in yet another defeat, this time from Kirkcaldy United at Scott's Park. Despite four changes to the side, the local press were so unimpressed with the team's latest performance that they printed the headline 'Bernard 0 Kirkcaldy United 2', claiming that the only decent player in the side was the goalkeeper! It wasn't just the local press who rated the custodian highly, however, with Falkirk keen to land Bernard's signature after impressive trials against Raith Rovers and Rangers.

In the first round of the Penman Cup, on 16th March 1907, the Methil Men recorded an impressive 2-0 victory over a strong Cowden side in a match that was not without incident. East Fife's Bob Stalker and Cowdenbeath's Savage collided when challenging for the ball and the Cowden man was knocked unconscious. He was carried to the pavilion where, after lying unconscious for 20 minutes, the decision was taken to send for Doctor Caskie. Before the doctor arrived, however, Savage regained consciousness and, after being helped out on to the park, played on to the end of the game. The referee later stated that he had been on the verge of abandoning the match when the player came round!

After league victories over Montrose and Forfar Athletic, the eagerly anticipated Penman Cup second round tie was due to be played against King's Park in Stirling on 13th April. This posed a great problem for the Fifers, as the Northern League was adamant that the return fixture between East Fife and Montrose had to be played at Bayview that day. In order not to upset the Northern League or the Penman Association, East Fife took the bold decision to play both matches on the same Saturday. The recognised first eleven played in the cup-tie and a scratch side, containing 10 juniors, fulfilled the league fixture. Both East Fife teams fared well. The cup-tie against King's Park was drawn 2-2 and the honours were also shared in the league match in Methil, which finished 1-1.

The replay of the Penman Cup tie was scheduled to take place at Bayview on Saturday 27th April but, unbelievably, the Northern League once again insisted that the scheduled fixture between St Johnstone and East Fife in Perth had to be played, which meant that the Fifers would again have to field two sides. Seeing the Penman tie as the more important of the two games, the stronger eleven remained in Methil to face King's Park whilst a scratch side travelled to Perth.

The Stirling side were defeated 2-1 at Bayview and East Fife progressed to the semi-final of the Penman Cup. The second string, despite putting up a fair fight against St Johnstone, went down 3-2 at the Recreation Ground. The Perth side were still in the running for the league title at the time and could well have won the competition had it not been for East Fife's 1-0 victory over the Saints in their final game of the season on 11th May.

As for the Penman Cup, the semi-final was played on 4th May at AlbionPark, Broxburn, in 'boisterous, showery weather', where the Fifers bowed out of the competition 2-1 to Broxburn Athletic.

The Fifers finished season 1906/07 ninth in the fourteen-team Northern League. Despite the relatively disappointing performances on the park, the crowds had, as anticipated, been favourable at Bayview all season. Had the football been more entertaining to watch, general opinion was that the attendances could well have been higher.

East Fife pictured in front of the original pavilion at BayviewPark during season 1907/08. Back row: W. McBeath (trainer), James Todd (secretary), McLean, Fitzpatrick, Mackie, Bell, Gray, Clark, J Campbell (treasurer). Front row: Scott, Beveridge, Peggie, Horne, Menzies. (Photo: Courtesy of Stephen Mill)

East Fife made their third application for admission to the Scottish League towards the end of the 1906/07 season along with Dunfermline Athletic. At the same time both Raith Rovers and Cowdenbeath, already Scottish League members, applied for promotion to the First Division, there being no automatic promotion and relegation at this time. All four clubs were unsuccessful.

The Fifers prepared for season 1907/08 with a pool of seventeen signed players. Despite regular 'keeper Bernard having departed for Dundee, the club still had two custodians to choose from, with the previous season's second choice goalie Stewart joined by new signing Campbell from Townhill. For the positions of left and right-back, the long serving Peter Middlemass would now have to compete for his place in the side with new signings McDonald from Lochgelly and Nairn from Raith Rovers.

For the half-back positions, the Fifers had a choice of four players: Robertson, McKinlay, Bell and McLean.

In the front line, Scott from Cowdenbeath, Peggie from Lochgelly, Wilkie from Partick Thistle and Nairn from Kirkcaldy joined Marr, Horne and Stewart. In addition, amateur player Stalker agreed to assist the club when required during the coming season.

As all the players with the exception of Campbell, Middlemass and Stalker were resident in the district, new trainer Macbeth could look forward to the coming season in the knowledge that most of the players would be able to train and practice together.

It was at this time that secretary Jim Todd attempted to pull off what would have been a sensational signing when he just failed to bring 'Dod' Wilson to Bayview. A product of junior side Lochgelly Rangers, Wilson had played for Cowdenbeath before moving to Hearts where he, along with brother Dave, won a Scottish Cup winners medal in 1903. He then signed for Everton, where he played in their record 9-1 victory over ManchesterCity, which was also City's record defeat. Wilson was then supposed to sign for Portsmouth, but Everton wouldn't let him go. As the player was determined to leave the Merseyside club, East Fife tried to tempt him to Methil, but instead Wilson opted to move to Belfast.

To say that the 1907/08 season got off to a poor start was an understatement. The only practice match held before the first league fixture was at Bayview on Thursday 15th August against local junior side Buckhaven United, who won 2-0.

Two days later Brechin City were the visitors to Methil for a Northern League match, but anyone expecting a repeat of the previous season's corresponding fixture was to be seriously disappointed as the Angus side triumphed 4-2.

Seeking revenge for their humiliation the previous week, East Fife took on Buckhaven United at their home ground of TollPark on Thursday 22nd August. Unfortunately for the senior side, however, only nine players turned up and even then some were 30 minutes late! United were 2-0 up before East Fife managed to recruit local players Chalmers from Leven and Turpie from Buckhaven Our Boys to make up the numbers. Alas, despite managing to pull a goal back, the junior side recorded yet another win over their more fancied neighbours.

After losing their second league fixture at Arbroath, East Fife recorded their first win of the season at home to Hearts of Beath, who had by this time dropped out of the Northern League, by four goals without reply in a Wemyss League match.

In the Qualifying Cup, the Methil Men bowed out to Cowdenbeath 3-1 in their first round fixture at NorthEndPark. There then came a series of eight Northern League fixtures which saw a distinct turnaround in the Fifers' fortunes, and resounding victories against Dundee Wanderers, Lochee United, Arbroath, Dundee Reserves and Dunfermline Athletic resulted in a rise to second place in the table by the end of October. The run of good form set the Methil Men up nicely for their home Fife Cup semi-final against Kirkcaldy United on 2nd November 1907. The Fife Cup was then considered to be a major tournament and a record crowd lined the Bayview ropes to witness a 2-0 win for the home side.

Despite their impressive league form, the Fifers still couldn't get the better of Buckhaven United. With no fixture scheduled for Saturday 14th December, a match was arranged with the local junior club at Bayview, where once again the seniors were humbled by a 3-1 defeat.

The impressive league form continued into the New Year, during which time the first two rounds of the Consolation Cup were safely negotiated with home victories over Forfar Athletic and Inverness Caledonian. The competition then produced a remarkable marathon run of matches against both Cowdenbeath and BrechinCity in rounds three and four. On 22nd February 1908, East Fife and Cowdenbeath fought out a no scoring draw at Bayview. The following Saturday the tie was replayed at NorthEndPark, Cowdenbeath, and ended in a draw of two goals apiece. The second replay was staged in Lochgelly, where again the honours were shared with another 2-2 draw. For the fourth and decisive match, both sides travelled to Stark's Park, Kirkcaldy, where the Methil Men eventually triumphed 2-0.

In round four, the quarter-final, the Fifers fought out a 1-1 draw against BrechinCity at NurseryPark on 14th March, before both sides served up a no scoring draw at Bayview in the replay. ClepingtonPark, Dundee, (later to become Tannadice) was chosen as the neutral venue for the second replay on Saturday 28th March, where again the teams could not be separated and the match finished all square at 1-1. With the end of the season fast approaching, and with a backlog of fixtures to be fulfilled, the third replay was scheduled for the following Wednesday at DensPark. Unbelievably, the sides again fought out a no scoring draw and were instructed to return to the same venue the following day, when an exhausted East Fife side eventually settled the tie with a 2-0 win.

The semi-final of the Consolation Cup against Dumbarton was played at Bayview just two days later on Saturday 4th April and, not surprisingly, the tired home side succumbed to their west of Scotland opponents by three goals to one.

The following week, Saturday 11th April, East Fife travelled to the neutral venue of NorthEndPark, Cowdenbeath, for the final of the Fife Cup against Lochgelly United. This was the first final of any competition that the Methil Men had taken part in and their large travelling support were not disappointed as the two sides served up an entertaining 3-3 draw. The replay was arranged for the following Saturday at the same venue and this time the travelling supporters were left celebrating at the end of the match following a 4-2 win. In lifting the Fife Cup, East Fife had won their first ever trophy! Although nowadays the Fife Cup is considered to be a minor

NorthEndPark, often referred to as 'The Colliers' Den', was home of Cowdenbeath F.C. from 1888 until 1917 and hosted Scottish League matches between 1905 and 1915. East Fife were regular visitors to North End Park and it was here, on 18th April 1908, that the club won its first trophy, the Fife Cup, by beating Lochgelly United 4-2 after a 3-3 draw. (Jim Corstorphine)

tournament, back in 1908 it was considered to be a major prize. After being presented with the trophy, team Captain Tommy Fitzpatrick was carried shoulder high by a euphoric band of East Fife supporters, around 500 having made the journey to Cowdenbeath by special train.

Once back in Methil, the cup was taken to the Steamboat Tavern, where it was filled to the brim and passed around the ecstatic assembly. When the curtain was raised later that evening at the local Gaiety Theatre, the large audience were pleasantly surprised to find that in place of the cast of the evening's entertainment stood the victorious East Fife players and Officials proudly displaying the Fife Cup! The team soaked up the applause before the curtain was finally lowered, allowing the celebrations to continue in one of the local drinking establishments.

Each and every player was rightly proud of the achievement, but none more so than Captain Tommy Fitzpatrick, who wore his Fife Cup winner's medal at family gatherings and social events for the rest of his days!

Due to their marathon run in the Consolation Cup, East Fife were unable to fulfil their Northern League fixtures, and finished in eighth place. The Penman Cup tie against Alloa Athletic, which had finished 2-2 at RecreationPark on 8th February, was never replayed for the same reason and the Clackmannanshire side were allowed to progress to the next round of the competition.

As the Fifers were making a name for themselves on the field of play, however, matters off the park were causing great cause for concern as the season drew to a close. As was mentioned earlier, BayviewPark and its environs were now the property of Mr Ferrie, a Kennoway gentleman, who was slowly giving the land over to housing developers. By March 1908 the builders had almost encroached on the football park and, although it was anticipated that the pitch might be saved for one more season, many enquiries were being made about feus on BayviewPark. It was widely expected that East Fife would eventually have to re-locate to the west of Methil Brae. Commenting on how the local football clubs had, for many years, been forced to lead a nomadic existence due to the continuing expansion of the towns and villages which now constitute the Levenmouth area, the local press stated that:

Pictured wearing his Black Watch football jersey, East Fife Captain Tommy Fitzpatrick was so proud of his team's achievement in winning the Fife Cup in 1908 that he wore his winners medal at family occasions and gatherings for the rest of his days! (Photo: Courtesy of Stephen Mill)

"Footballers have shifted a few times since (Methil) Rovers had the pitch at SchoolPark, never dreaming twelve years ago that brick and lime would so completely block out the field. Bayview Park is coveted for building purposes, but it is possible a playing pitch will be preserved. For some time there has been talk of a recreation company in another part of the town but that scheme hangs fire. It is a big thing."

Due to the revenue gained from the marathon Consolation Cup run at the end of the previous campaign, the club started season 1908/09 on a sound financial footing. As well as retaining the nucleus of the team, the club signed Jack Ower from Perth as a back up for the defence along with half-backs J. Philp from Dunfermline and his brother Willie from Bowhill. To augment the forward line, 'veteran of sixteen seasons' W. Mercer was signed along with Lawson from Kirkcaldy and local lad Barclay, who had scored regularly for Lochgelly during the previous season.

As for the problems and uncertainty regarding the future of BayviewPark, the local press reported in early August that:

"More worry has come from the threatened feuing at Bayview than from any other source. Messrs Buchan & Duncan and Mr Robert Galloway have accounted for the whole frontage along the tramway and, this week, workmen are lifting the barricading back a fair breadth all the way. This carries it to within 3 yards of the touchline, just where the rope recently ran. Keeping this back five feet will leave a narrow passage for the spectators, but they will be sheltered behind the fence. A wire netting will be needed to protect the properties, however, from wildly kicked balls. The pitch is safe to football so long as there is no further outburst of feuing and a call for a new road at right angles to the tramway".

Fortunes in all competitions left a lot to be desired in the early stages of season 1908/09. Poor league form and an early exit from the Qualifying Cup at the hands of Raith Rovers brought an air of despondency to the club by the beginning of

September. It was to be the last day of October 1908 before the Fifers managed to record a victory in the Northern League, which came in the form of a 2-0 victory over Montrose at LinksPark. The first home victory in the competition was not recorded until 21st November with a 2-0 win against Dunfermline Athletic!

Meantime, success in the first round of the Fife cup arrived in the form of a pleasing 3-0 victory over Cowdenbeath at NorthEndPark following a no scoring draw at Bayview. The Fifers belied their poor league form in the Penman Cup too, with a 1-0 first round win against Bathgate.

The club's fortunes started to pick up towards the end of the year, with a 2-0 home win over Montrose followed up with a 3-1 victory over Dundee Wanderers at ClepingtonPark on Christmas Day.

The New Year saw the Fifers progress in the Penman Cup, the Fife Cup and the Consolation Cup, but it is the latter competition which proved to be the most interesting and exciting tournament of the season. After being awarded a 'walk over' against Raith in the first round, victory over Bathgate by a single goal on 23rd January saw East Fife paired with Berwick Rangers in round four. The long trip south of the border for the first ever meeting between the sides on 20th February 1909 resulted in a 2-2 draw and, in the replayed match at Bayview a week later, a large crowd saw the Fife progress to round five with a 1-0 win. The 'gate' amounted to £30, a considerable sum in those days, but the club should have taken at least another £10 according to the local press, the deficit being *"due to the absence of a couple of stretches of wire netting and two policemen"*!

Round five of the Consolation Cup saw Renton, the one time self-crowned 'Champions of the World' make the trip to Methil on 7th March. The spectators who turned up at Bayview to witness the match thought that their favourites had won a place in the semi-final of the competition following a 2-0 win, but the referee thought otherwise. Before the game started the match official took the decision to play a friendly between the sides rather than the scheduled cup-tie due to the inclement weather and the state of the playing surface. Neither the referee nor the club thought to inform the spectators of the decision, which resulted in an angry protest when the final whistle sounded and the truth came out! Renton returned to Methil the following week and this time the cup-tie was played, with East Fife finally managing to claim a semi-final place with a 2-1 win.

Before progressing, it may be worth considering the following point with regard to Renton's claim to have been one time 'Champions of the World'. The reason behind the Dunbartonshire club's claim was that, after they had landed the Scottish Cup for the second time in 1888, they challenged and beat English F.A. Cup winners West Bromwich Albion. As East Fife won (albeit 21 years later) the only two matches ever played against Renton, they can rightly claim to have a 100% record against former 'World Champions'!

The semi-final of the Consolation Cup saw the Fifers drawn to play Arbroath at Gayfield on 20th March 1909, where a crowd of 2,000 saw the match finish all square at 1-1. The replay was scheduled for Bayview Park the following Saturday, where a 2,500 crowd paid a total of £55 to see the action, but again the teams could not be separated and the game finished at two goals apiece. The second replay took place on 3rd April at NorthEndPark, Dundee, where a repeat of the previous Saturday's score meant that the two sides had to meet yet again the following midweek at RecreationPark in Perth. This time the 'Red Lichties' ran out winners by two goals to one and the Fifers' Consolation Cup marathon was over for another year.

Two days later, on 9th April 1909, a tired East Fife side went down 2-0 to Alloa Athletic in the semi-final of the Penman Cup at Recreation Park and, following a 3-1 defeat from champions Dundee 'A' in the final Northern League match of the season, the final of the Fife Cup was lost 3-0 to Raith Rovers at Stark's Park on 24th April.

It had been a disappointing season as far as the Northern League competition was concerned, with only three wins recorded out of the sixteen matches played along with eight defeats and five draws, resulting in a final league position of second bottom.

Towards the end of the season, developments elsewhere in the Scottish game signalled the end of the Fifers' involvement with the Northern League. In March 1909 the Scottish Football Association announced that it was prepared to sanction the formation of a 'Second XI League' for the benefit of the Scottish League clubs. As this new league would inevitably mean the withdrawal of Dundee 'A' and Aberdeen 'A' from the Northern League, the decision was taken by some of its member clubs to form a new competition covering a wider geographical area.

At a meeting held in Dunfermline during March 1909, a new twelve-team competition was inaugurated consisting of West Lothian clubs Bathgate, Broxburn Athletic and Bo'ness; Alloa Athletic and King's Park from the Stirling area; former Northern League clubs St. Johnstone, Arbroath, Dunfermline Athletic, Lochgelly United, Kirkcaldy United and East Fife with the twelfth place taken by Cowdenbeath's second string. The Central League, which was destined to have a huge impact on the Scottish game, had been born!

Chapter Four: Into the Central League

Many improvements were carried out at BayviewPark during the summer of 1909 in preparation for the club's participation in the new Central League. A bathroom was erected at the rear of the pavilion, where the players would be able to enjoy a 'spartan plunge', which, according to the *Leven Advertiser and Wemyss Gazette*, was *"a long advance on the public ablutions they had to make in front of the pavilion and hundreds of spectators"*.

Another improvement to the area adjacent to the pavilion was the construction of a small enclosure where club officials could meet 'without the crowd being around them'. President Farmer, Vice President Thomson, Secretary Neill, Treasurer Campbell and Committee members Stevenson, Mitchell, Telfer, Lawrie, Duffy, Robertson, Rutherford and Muir also decided that the area in front of the pavilion was to be out of bounds except for club officials.

The ground improvements were also to be of benefit to the spectators, however, with the erection of a partition in the grandstand to break the sweep of the wind through the seats. *"The place ought to be cosier on a breezy day"*, observed the local press.

A 'stout new wire' was erected around the park in order to stand the surge of a big crowd. In order to keep the new barrier in top condition, the common practice of crowds sitting on the wire would, in future, be discouraged.

As for the playing surface, it was reported to be *"improved beyond all recognition"*.

Meanwhile, at a meeting of the Central League on 5th June, it was decided to admit Stenhousemuir to the new competition at the expense of Cowdenbeath's second XI.

East Fife kicked off their Central League days with a home match against St Johnstone on Saturday 21st August 1909. The match finished all square at a goal apiece, but it is interesting to note that the East Fife goal was credited to both Mitchell and Murray as nobody could decide which player touched the ball last! Of greater concern was the fact that the Fifers had to finish the match with ten men due to a serious leg injury sustained by their recently signed centre-half Coull.

There was an amusing communication between East Fife and Bo'ness in the days prior to the league fixture at NewtonPark on 11th September. The West Lothian club, no doubt mindful of their opponents' apparent inability to find their way around the country on the rail network (the Fifers having 'got lost' on their last trip to Newton Park in 1904), offered to send a steam tug over the Forth to pick up the East Fife team! Unfortunately, the Fifers had to decline the kind offer as secretary Thomas Neill had already made arrangements for the team to travel by rail.

The Bo'ness match was lost 3-1, but the next trip across the ForthBridge a week later proved more successful when Broxburn were beaten 2-1 in a Qualifying Cup second round tie.

East Fife's first ever Central League win on 25th September 1909, a 4-1 victory over Broxburn Athletic, is also significant in that Wilkie's three goals for the home side was the first ever hat-trick scored at BayviewPark. As if the fact that it had taken over six years since the club's inception for the first hat-trick to materialise wasn't hard enough to take in, the same player repeated the feat just a week later when he scored all three goals in East Fife's 3-0 win over Aberdeen Harp at Bayview to safely see the Fifers through to the fourth round of the Qualifying Cup. More importantly, in reaching the fourth round of the qualifying tournament, East Fife won the right to play in the Scottish Cup for the first time in their history.

The fourth round of the Qualifying Cup saw the Methil Men drawn to face Kirkcaldy United at Bayview, a match which was billed as 'The Premier Event in Fife'. Interest in the game was such that a special train was laid on for United supporters to travel from Kirkcaldy and the Wemyss trams were reported to be 'out in force' on the day. A crowd of 3,000 were packed into Bayview like sardines for the match on 17th October, which United won by a single goal.

Disappointing though it was, the Qualifying Cup exit gave the team the opportunity to concentrate on the Central League, which occupied the fixture list for the remainder of the year with the exception of a 4-1 Penman Cup win against Broxburn on 27th November.

The first half of the Central League season saw the Fifers win just four of the eleven matches played, with three draws and four defeats, although the side lost by more than a single goal on only one occasion. All that was to change on the first day of January 1910, however, in a league match at Alloa. Now, whether it was all down to the previous evening's excesses is not documented, but the fact is that some of the regular team called off on the morning of the game and a mixture of reserves and juniors filled their places, including veteran Horne, who had to be 'called out of retirement'.

The result was a final score of 6-0 to the home side, an outcome which equalled the Fifers' record defeat. The East Fife supporters who made the journey through for the game found the performance hard to take, none more so than well-known Methil characters Jack Robertson and Joe Lawrie.

The pair were inseparable friends who, it has to be said, were a rather unlikely combination. Jack was only about four feet tall and around four stone in weight, whereas Joe, landlord of the 'Steamboat Tavern' in Methil, weighed in at eighteen stone! The East Fife players were all familiar with wee Jack, who they regarded as a mascot, and tried their best to oblige his vociferous demands from the touchline. The players drew the line, however, at the wee man's occasional shouts to "lay that fella oot"! When the sixth goal found the back of the net at Alloa, Jack turned to his big pal with a similar request.

"Will ye break in Joe?" Jack hoarsely whispered. Fortunately, the discretion of his chum averted that last desperate resort!

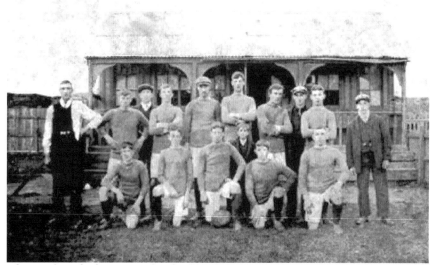

An undated photograph of a local Junior team, taken in front of the original Bayview pavilion around 1909. Jack Robertson, the 'East Fife Mascot', is the individual standing in the centre, behind the player with the ball. (Author's Collection)

The team got back to winning ways the following week with a 3-0 Central League win over Kirkcaldy United, which set them up nicely for the club's first ever Scottish Cup tie against Hurlford at Bayview on 15th January 1910. The cup tie should have been played the following week but was brought forward in order to avoid clashing with the Kirkcaldy United v Queen's Park match at Scott's Park on the same day. In the event, however, United accepted Queen's offer of £120 to move their match to Hampden, so the clash would have been avoided in any case.

The weather had been wet and blustery all week but on the morning of the match it brightened up a little. In the afternoon, however, the rain returned and the players were soaked to the skin as the Fifers won a place in the last sixteen of the competition with a convincing 4-1 win.

"Methil turned out in force on Saturday to cheer on East Fife in the Scottish Cup", reported the *Leven Advertiser and Wemyss Gazette*, who went on to add that Bayview had been in 'tip-top' condition despite the wet weather.

The next round of the competition provided East Fife with the first really big match in the club's history, when they were drawn to play Queen's Park in Methil on 12th February 1910. Now, this may seem a little puzzling for those more familiar with modern day football, but back in 1910 a match against Queen's Park was considered to be as attractive as a match against Rangers or Celtic. The Glasgow amateurs, who in 1910 fielded a host of well known players including the famous Scottish internationalist R.S.McColl, were founded in 1867 and had won the Scottish Cup no fewer than ten times before East Fife were even dreamt of! The 'Spiders' were also beaten Scottish Cup finalists on two occasions during this same period as well as twice finishing runners up in the English F.A. Cup. The *Leven Advertiser and Wemyss Gazette* were certainly justified in their article previewing the cup-tie to claim that *"In Scottish, or indeed the World's football history, there exists no greater name than that of Queen's Park"*

I will therefore make no further excuse in devoting almost four pages to this famous event!

Unlike the present day, Queen's Park could, in the early days of the Twentieth Century, boast crowds numbering tens of thousands rather than the paltry hundreds who now occupy the vastness of the National Stadium for home matches. It was no surprise then, when the Glasgow club offered East Fife first £75, then £100, then £150 (a lot of money in 1910!) to switch the game to HampdenPark. East Fife's officials, anxious that a first class match such as this should be played in the local district, refused to accept the tender, stuck to their guns and insisted that the game be played in Methil.

As the day of the match approached, East Fife set about the task of upgrading Bayview to the standard worthy of the occasion, with additional stands being erected and improvements made to the enclosures.

Special trains were arranged to transport spectators from Glasgow and other parts of Fife, as it was anticipated that the crowd would be enormous in the event of favourable weather. It was also anticipated that the Wemyss and District Tramway would carry record numbers of passengers.

The morning of the cup-tie dawned cold and frosty and, by lunchtime, rain began to fall. Despite the inclement weather, tramcars full of football supporters arrived at the gates in rapid succession from both east and west, and as kick off time approached throngs of pedestrians hurried along Wellesley Road heading for Bayview.

Inside the ground, despite the decision to double the entrance fee from 6d (2½p) to 1/- (5p), the crowd lined the ropes on all sides of the park, struggling to gain the best vantage point, there being no banking at BayviewPark in those days!

As the kick off approached, the weather conditions brightened somewhat, and the East Fife club officials busily made last minute adjustments to the playing surface. Other officials did their best to meet the demands for seats in front of the stand and pavilion.

The Methil Town Band entertained the crowd with 'some lively airs', before a pipe band entered the arena as the spectators, no doubt by this time in a great state of excitement, filled the old cigar box which was passed amongst them to overflowing in appreciation of the music.

After the music had died down, a Salvation Army officer took the opportunity to remind the huge crowd through a megaphone that it was 'self denial week'.

Just as the officer moved from the stand there was a deafening applause as the East Fife players left the pavilion, jumped the fence and sent a ball 'spinning to the west goal'.

Leven photographer Mr Patrick then lined up the players and photographed 'the cup tie eleven', resplendent in their dark blue jerseys.

Once the photograph was taken, the pipe band struck up once more and, while they played, the Queen's Park team arrived, discarded their overcoats and immediately leapt over the perimeter fence and on to the field.

East Fife won the toss and the match got under way.

After only 15 minutes play, Bayview erupted when Patrick Dougan rounded Queen's Park defender Thomson and fired the ball past 'keeper Adams into the corner of the net.

"The cheer might have been heard a mile away", commented the *Leven Advertiser and Wemyss Gazette.*

The Fifers lead was, however, short lived, as three minutes later the 'Spiders' equalised through McColl. The visitors then pushed forward and would have taken the lead but for a missed penalty. The next goal however, came once again from East Fife's Patrick Dougan, whose shot found the Queen's Park net via a post to put the home side 2-1 ahead.

When the half time whistle blew, general opinion amongst the crowd was that East Fife were worthy of a bigger lead. The players enjoyed their brief respite from the action by sipping mugs of steaming meat extract.

Realising that victory was within their grasp, the East Fife Directors increased the players' win bonus from £3 to £4 per man before play resumed.

In the second half the wind fell to a light breeze and, spurred on by their increased bonus offer, the Fifers relentlessly attacked the visitors' goal, but as is so often the case under these circumstances, the minnows' luck ran out and the 'Spiders' broke out of defence, charged up the park and equalised through Hamilton.

Having dominated the match for long periods, the breakaway goal knocked the confidence out of the Fifers and, almost straight from the re-start, Queen's Park regained possession and scored what proved to be the winner through McColl. Despite having lost, there was nothing but praise for the East Fife team after the match.

"It looked at times as if it was East Fife who were the big club such was their domination," commented the local press. The atmosphere as the spectators made their way home is perhaps best summed up with this extract from the *Leven Advertiser and Wemyss Gazette*:

"Lovers of genuine sport left the field feeling that they had seen one of the best exhibits of football ever seen in the Kingdom. With the rush to the exit gates the referee's whistle ceases and the crowd now responds to the whistle of tramway car conductors and of trains; the people who crowded the back stairs of the houses in Wellesley Road withdraw and, shortly after 5 o'clock, the field is deserted; over the tea cups men sit during the night and discuss football and the wonderful hold it has over big and small communities."

The Methil Men had certainly given their all in their unsuccessful bid to reach round four of the cup, and had won many friends in the process. As so often happens under such circumstances, however, euphoria is quickly followed by anti-climax. In the matches following the cup-tie, poor form prevailed and the Fifers failed to win another Central League match before the end of the season!

It is perhaps worth pointing out that the poor sequence of results that followed the cup exit coincided with the absence of two-goal cup hero Patrick Dougan, who had headed south for trials with Burnley. Although Dougan impressed the Turf Moor club, terms could not be agreed and the player returned to Bayview in mid-April.

On a happier note, the Fife progressed to the final of the Penman Cup following a 2-1 home win against King's Park; East Stirlingshire having scratched to the Fifers in the quarter-final. Due the fixture backlog, the final against Stenhousemuir was held over until the following season.

As the 1910/11 season loomed, East Fife became increasingly concerned about the uncertainty surrounding BayviewPark as plans for the new school at Aberhill were drawn up. Initially, it was hoped that the only change to the football ground would be a further reduction in the dimensions of the playing surface. Reporting on the matter in early August, the local press were of the opinion that:

"when the alterations are completed a more compact and tidy enclosure should be the result and one that may not be susceptible to the ravages of the young hooligans who continually take a delight in destroying the club's property".

It soon became apparent that the landlord and Wemyss School Board had other ideas.

When spectators arrived at BayviewPark for the first match of the 1910/11 season, they found that the whole playing surface had been moved several yards to the west. This meant that the grandstand, which had been situated in the middle of the north touchline, was now at the north-east corner of the ground. The pavilion, which had occupied a position between the grandstand and the north-west corner of the park, now found itself situated almost exactly on the half way line!

The main concern, however, was the condition of the playing surface. About one third of the pitch at the west end had been moved onto a rough field and, before the first game could go ahead, the ground staff had to repair the playing surface in order to eradicate the bumps and holes.

The *Leven Advertiser and Wemyss Gazette* commented following the opening match against King's Park on 20th August:

"The park was not like the old place. The pitch is elbowed west on to rugged ground and has left the stand and pavilion away on the east section of the enclosure. Almost crowding in on the goals look the barricading, above which gauntly rises the poles to carry nets to stay rugby and 'Dubbieside' goals. The staff continue to trim and patch away at the ground and hopefully, in a short time, the 'mantraps' should all be remedied out of knowing".

The Central League had also seen changes since the end of the previous campaign, with Broxburn Athletic dropping out and being replaced by Heart of Midlothian's second eleven.

On the playing side, most of the previous season's squad had been retained, with the addition of Wemyss from Hearts. The club were also negotiating terms with Kilmarnock's Douglas and Stark from Raith Rovers.

On the last day of August, the long awaited final of the Penman Cup against Stenhousemuir, held over from the previous season, was played at the neutral venue of NorthEndPark, Cowdenbeath. An evenly contested match resulted in a 1-1 draw, but owing to an already congested fixture list the replay had to be postponed until November.

The following Saturday brought an early exit from the Qualifying Cup when Lochgelly United came to Methil and won 2-1.

Back on Central League business, poor form once again haunted the side and it was not until the start of October that the first league success was recorded; a 2-0 home win over Stenhousemuir. This victory did not, however, signal a change in fortunes. By the end of the year there had been only three league wins from sixteen matches with five draws and eight defeats; a run which saw the Fifers sitting at the bottom of the league following a home defeat at the hands of Arbroath on 3rd December.

The replay of the Penman Cup final with Stenhousemuir eventually went ahead on 5th November at Lochgelly where, despite serving up a six goal thriller, the sides still could not be separated and the match finished all square at three goals apiece.

The doom and gloom was blown away early in the New Year when East Fife and Stenhousemuir contested the final of the 1909/10 season's Penman Cup for the third time at BrockvillePark, Falkirk, on 3rd January 1911. This time, despite the 'Warriors' having almost home advantage, the Fifers brought the Cup to Methil for the first time with a 2-1 victory. The trophy was presented to the jubilant players side on the following Saturday night, following the team's 2-1 Central League win against St Johnstone, in front of a large gathering at the White Swan Hotel in Wellesley Road.

Anyone connected with the club who felt that a complete turnaround in fortunes was imminent was to be sorely disappointed, however. Following the win over St. Johnstone, the Fifers managed just one more victory before the end of the season; a 4-2 home win against Lochgelly United in a Central League fixture. Indeed, as it turned out, the club was about to enter one of the darkest periods in its history.

The first indication that all was not well came in mid-February 1911, when it became apparent that the club was in a bad way financially. Poor gates during the season, no doubt brought about by poor form, meant that the club managed to break even on just a few occasions, never mind make a profit.

On 22nd February, an article appeared in the *Leven Advertiser and Wemyss Gazette* suggesting that the only way to save the club from folding was for it to become a Limited Liability Company, with an associated share issue, in order to raise much needed funds.

The club struggled on, but after two blank Saturdays in March when the financial situation forced the cancellation of two fixtures, doubt was expressed as to whether the Fifers could continue into the following season, with the local press commenting: *"Things are so unsettled in the domestic life of the club that the officials have little stomach for fixtures"*.

It seemed that East Fife were on the verge of extinction.

The 3-1 defeat at Stenhousemuir on 1st April confirmed that the Fifers could only finish bottom of the Central League and this, coupled with a dire financial situation, meant that the club would have to drop out of the Central League even if they did manage to stay in business.

Faced with the possibility that their beloved football club was about to cease operations, club officials, local businessmen and supporters rallied round and decided on a course of action.

Eventually, the decision was taken to float the club as a Limited Liability Company, with a share capital of £500 divided into 2,000 shares of 5 Shillings (25p) each. By mid-April the flotation was reported to be 'proceeding merrily' and, on 29th May 1911, East Fife Football Club Limited was incorporated as a Company under the Companies (Consolidation) Act 1908. The Fife had been saved!

Chapter Five: A New Beginning!

Everyone associated with East Fife Football Club looked forward to the 1911/12 season with fresh enthusiasm. Never before in the history of the club had the outlook been so promising. The re-birth of the club as a Limited Company with its associated cash injection meant that the 'old wood' could be cleared away and some fresh talent brought to Bayview. The opportunity was also taken to change the official team colours to black and gold, a choice that the club has retained to this day.

Of the eleven regulars who finished the previous season, only half-backs Ramsay and Sloggie were retained. The position of Goalkeeper was filled by Innes from Buckhaven, a player who carried the reputation of being the best junior 'keeper in Scotland. The full-back positions were occupied by new signings Allan from Hibernian and Welsh from Dundee Hibs. McCallum was recruited from Lochgelly to complete the half-back line along with retained players Ramsay and Sloggie. Thorburn was signed from Raith Rovers to play on the right wing, partnered by Rae from Denbeath Star. The position of centre-forward would be filled by Pat Currie and, to his left, were new signings Scott from Bo'ness and Ferguson from Cowdenbeath. Reserves would be selected from Baird, Barbour and veteran Horne. It was anticipated that new Manager Dave McLean would also, on occasion, take a place in the team.

Chairman of the new Limited Liability Company was Councillor Rolland, assisted by Secretary W.T.Nisbet.

On Thursday 17th August 1911, the first match played by the 'new' club, a Wemyss League fixture against Kirkcaldy United, was successfully negotiated with a 1-0 victory. Two days later, however, came a 3-0 reverse against the 'Warriors' of Stenhousemuir in the opening Central League fixture at Ochilview, although general opinion was that the

Fifers were the better side over the 90 minutes. A share of the points at home to Alloa Athletic the following week was followed by a shock early exit from the Qualifying Cup at the hands of Hearts of Beath at KiersPark.

The first Central League win of the season came on Saturday 9th September when Scott and McCallum netted three goals without reply against Lochgelly United at Bayview.

How did the local football enthusiasts react to the ambitious new organisation? Did they come along to Bayview in greater numbers than they had done in the past? The answer would appear to be yes, although not everyone was happy to pay their 'tanner' at the gate, according to an article which appeared in the *Leven Advertiser and Wemyss Gazette* following the Lochgelly match, when the following question was put to a certain group of spectators who regularly viewed the match from the adjacent railway sidings:

"When will the 'waggoners' have the decency to enter BayviewPark by the gate and pay their humble tanner? These individuals have more to say about the composition of the team than the man or boy who pays up every match!"

The report concluded with the opinion that a stretch of canvas should be erected along the full length of the ground to block the view from the railway wagons.

On the park the team were still blowing hot and cold and, by the end of the year, the sixteen Central League fixtures played had produced seven wins, four draws and five defeats. All things considered, however, it had been a fairly satisfactory first half of the season considering the club had nearly gone to the wall at the end of the previous campaign. The first match in 1912 was a 2-0 home win against Bo'ness at Bayview in the second round of the Penman Cup on 6th January. The following two weekends saw the first round of the Consolation Cup played out in which the Methil Men bowed out to Lochgelly United by the odd goal in five at Bayview following a 1-1 draw at Recreation Park.

At the beginning of February, the Central League programme resumed with a home fixture against Stenhousemuir. On a bitterly cold afternoon, snow started to fall as the match progressed and, with twenty minutes remaining, the referee decided to abandon the game as the lines were no longer visible. Much protest then ensued from both teams and some of the crowd came on to the pitch to surround the pavilion. In order to avoid an ugly scene, the referee decided that the game could be played out as a friendly! Strangely, there is no record of the league fixture ever being replayed.

The month of March 1912 was severely disrupted by a coal strike, the only fixture played resulting in a 3-1 home win over King's Park in the third round of the Penman Cup. Due to travel restrictions brought about by the strike, several Central League fixtures could not be fulfilled and the remainder of the season was taken up mainly with the local cup competitions, in which East Fife were crowned champions of the Wemyss League for the first time. The season was wound up with victory against Alloa Athletic in the semi-final of the Penman Cup at RecreationPark, but once again the final of the competition had to be held over until the following season.

A poor opening half of the Central League campaign for season 1912/13 saw just three games won from the fifteen matches played before the end of December, with six defeats sustained over the same period. The fourth round of the Qualifying Cup was reached following victories over BrechinCity and Clackmannan at the end of September and the beginning of October, which allowed the Fifers entry into the Scottish Cup for the second time in their history. A crowd of 3,000 turned out to see the Fifers exit the qualifying competition 2-1 to St. Johnstone at Bayview on 19th October. Also played during the first half of the season was the final of the Penman Cup against Raith Rovers, which had been held over from the previous season. The match was played on 7th October at Stark's Park, where neither side could find the net, so yet another date had to be found for the replay in an already congested schedule.

As for the 1912/13 Penman Cup competition, the Fifers went down at the first hurdle with a 2-0 defeat from Cowdenbeath at NorthEndPark.

With the club having received a bye in the first round of the Scottish Cup, the eagerly awaited second round tie against St. Johnstone, the Fifers' conquerors in the qualifying competition, was played on 8th February 1913 at RecreationPark, Perth. On a park that resembled 'a quagmire' according to the local press, the Fifers proved to be no match for their Scottish League opponents, who progressed to the third round with a comfortable 3-0 victory.

The remainder of the league season brought a mixture of results, but concluded with a four game run during which three games were won; the only defeat being against Alloa Athletic at RecreationPark as the Clackmannanshire side won the Central League Championship.

Despite their poor league form during the first half of the season, a final league position of sixth was attained, with eight wins recorded from the 22 matches played along with six draws and eight defeats. One other match worthy of note as the season drew to a close was the 10-1 victory against Hearts of Beath in the first round of the Fife Cup at the beginning of March, which smashed the club's previous record victory of 7-1 set over seven years previously.

After starting the 1913/14 season favourably with two wins a draw from the fixtures against Stenhousemuir, Falkirk Reserves and Forfar, East Fife faced Lochgelly F.C. at Bayview in the first round of the Qualifying Cup on 6th September 1913. This Lochgelly side, not to be confused with the more illustrious Lochgelly United, had been founded as a senior club only the previous year, having originated as Lochgelly

Juniors F.C. The club had decided to turn senior when it seemed that local rivals United would be unable to continue following the miners strike in March 1912 when they, like East Fife, were unable to fulfil their fixtures and suffered financially as a result. United survived, however, and the town of Lochgelly found itself in the farcical situation of having to support two senior clubs! Although the new club attempted to join the Central League, their application was rejected and instead they played in the Eastern League alongside near neighbours Hearts of Beath and Clackmannan. Lochgelly had actually been drawn at home in the cup-tie, but agreed to play the match in Methil in return for £25 and rail fares from Lochgelly! Surprisingly, the visitors returned home with a 1-0 win, which turned out to be their only victory over East Fife in the few meetings between the sides.

Inconsistent form in the Central League then ensued and the Fifers only managed to win a further two matches in the competition, against Lochgelly United and Falkirk Reserves, before the turn of the year. Some of the results made pretty depressing reading: a 4-1 hammering from Dundee Reserves at Bayview and away defeats at Forfar and Arbroath by 3-0 and 4-1 respectively.

A 2-1 home win against Bathgate in the second round of the Penman Cup, however, partly eased the gloom.

The year 1914 brought a complete turnaround in the club's fortunes on the park. Three days into January, both Central League points were taken from Bathgate at Bayview with a 1-0 win, which was followed seven days later with an impressive 3-1 win at DensPark against Dundee's second string. Revenge was then gained over Arbroath when the 'Lichties' were convincingly overcome 3-1 at Bayview in the second round of the Consolation Cup. The good league form continued with a home win against Kirkcaldy United at the end of January, before the third round of the Consolation Cup saw the Fifers paired with Crieff Morrisonians on the last day of the month.

The Perthshire side were no match for East Fife, who progressed to the fourth round courtesy of a 6-0 win.

After yet another Central League fixture was successfully negotiated with a single goal victory over Bathgate at MillPark, it was destination Edinburgh to face Scottish League members St Bernard's in the fourth round of the Consolation Cup at the Royal Gymnasium ground. In what was the Fifers' first-ever competitive match against the famous old Edinburgh club, the home side progressed to the fifth round with a narrow 1-0 win. The Central League fixtures were wound up with wins against Kirkcaldy United and Lochgelly United, a share of the points with Armadale and Bathgate and defeat in the return fixture with Armadale. Considering their poor form earlier in the season, the Fifers did well to finished their 1913/14 league campaign in the top half of the table, having completed all 26 fixtures of which ten were won, nine were drawn and seven were lost.

In the local cup competitions, revenge was gained in style over Lochgelly with a 5-0 home win in the first round of the Fife Cup. Progress was also made in the first round of the Wemyss competition with a home win against Raith Rovers, but the Methil Men fell at the next hurdle in both tournaments, against Lochgelly United in the Fife Cup and against Cowdenbeath in the final of the Wemyss Cup.

In the weeks following the conclusion of the football season, events elsewhere in Europe started to cause widespread concern; events which would rapidly make the game of football pale into insignificance. On 28th June 1914, Archduke Franz Ferdinand of Austria was assassinated in Sarajevo. As a direct result, unrest rapidly spread and, exactly one month later, Austria declared war on Serbia.

The 'knock-on' effect saw Germany occupy both Luxembourg and Belgium and declare war on France during the first four days of August. The day following the declaration of war on France, Britain declared war on Germany and immediately set about the task of landing troops in France. The Great War had started. By the end of August, Japan had declared war on Germany and the Russians had also joined in the conflict as the war became worldwide.

The call for volunteers was met enthusiastically by most local men of a fighting age, who answered Kitchener's call and flocked in huge numbers to the recruitment centres to join up. The glory and honour of fighting for their country was a far more attractive proposition than enduring the underground hell of the coalmines, and several thousand young men marched off to fight cheered on by their friends and families. Few would be fully aware of the circumstances behind the conflict. Even less would know the full horror of the bloody battlefields that lay ahead. Thousands would never return.

Strangely, as the conflict was brewing in Europe, the Scottish League decided to increase the size of the Second Division by two clubs to fourteen. East Fife duly applied for membership, along with Alloa Athletic, Bathgate, Clydebank, Forfar Athletic and near neighbours Lochgelly United. With the two clubs who had finished bottom of the league the previous season, Vale of Leven and Johnstone, having to apply for re-election, there were actually eight teams fighting it out for four available places. When the dust had settled, both clubs seeking re-election were successful, along with Lochgelly United and Clydebank.

To attempt to relate the history of a football club during the time of the Great War is extremely difficult, when one considers the fact that the local press rightly regarded current football affairs to be of secondary importance. There was so much to report from the Western Front during the early stages of the war that few column inches were given over to football, with the result that very little of East Fife's progress was recorded at the time. The club did, however, continue to play in the Central League during the 1914/15 season.

In the Qualifying Cup, East Fife were drawn to face Kirkcaldy United at Scott's Park, where the two sides battled out a goal-less draw on 19th September. The match was replayed at Bayview a week later, where the Kirkcaldy side were soundly beaten 4-0. Interest in the match was such that in the following edition of the *Leven Advertiser and Wemyss Gazette*, sufficient column inches were found to report that the crowd had been too large to collect money from and many spectators saw the game for free! The Fifers eventually exited the competition on 14th November at DensPark, Dundee, when they lost by a single goal to Forfar Athletic.

Fixtures during the remainder of season 1914/15 were few and far between for obvious reasons and, in August 1915, a meeting was held by club officials to decide if it was worthwhile keeping the club going.

Fortunately the Fifers decided to carry on, and entered the new twelve-team Eastern League which was created as a result of the Scottish League's decision to disband the Second Division for the remainder of the war.

The creation of the Eastern League meant that East Fife would be able to lock horns once again with Lochgelly United and there was also the added attraction of competing in the same league as near neighbours Cowdenbeath, Dunfermline Athletic and Kirkcaldy United. The forthcoming season would also see Dundee Hibernian (later to become Dundee United) and East Fife lock horns for the first time. With the rest of the league being made up from former Scottish League members East Stirlingshire, Leith Athletic and St Bernard's along with former Central League clubs Armadale, Bathgate and Broxburn United, it promised to be an interesting campaign. Although the Methil men started badly with a heavy defeat at the hands of Kirkcaldy United on 21st August before losing their first-ever meeting with Dundee Hibernian at the beginning of September, the team put in some good performances over the course of the season. The second round of the Penman Cup was reached by defeating Dunfermline Athletic by the odd goal in five on 18th September and former

Scottish League side East Stirlingshire were beaten 6-1 at Bayview at the end of the month. After further impressive outings which saw Dundee Hibernian beaten 3-0 on their own soil and Dunfermline Athletic dumped 4-1 at Bayview, the second round of the Penman Cup was successfully negotiated with a 3-0 home win against Lochgelly United at the beginning of December. The Methil Men eventually exited the Penman competition to Cowdenbeath at the semi-final stage. A 2-0 home defeat from St. Bernard's on New Year's Day 1916 signalled a downturn in league form, and the Fifers only further league win was recorded against Bathgate at Bayview on 22nd April. In the last match of the season, Leith Athletic were beaten 4-0 at Bayview in the Loftus Cup.

Considering the quality of the opposition, however, the season had been reasonably satisfactory, with the Fifers finishing fifth in the twelve-team Eastern League.

One other match worth mentioning during the 1915/16 season was a charity game at Bayview on 18th March 1916 played between an 'East Fife Select' and the 'Highland Cycle Battalion', arranged to raise funds for the 'Soldiers Comforts' and 'Red Cross' charities. On the day of the game, an East Fife official approached former Denbeath Celtic player Dom Currie as he stepped from the train at Methil station, the player having just returned on leave from active service. Dom was asked if he could play in the charity match and, despite having had little sleep on his long journey home, agreed to the request and pulled on an East Fife jersey for the first time. A thrilling match, played in atrocious weather conditions, finished 3-3, with Dom Currie scoring East Fife's third goal. This was not to be Currie's last appearance in the black and gold, as we shall see in the following chapter.

Season 1916/17 saw the Eastern League reduced to ten clubs following the withdrawal of Leith Athletic and Kirkcaldy United. The Methil Men started their league campaign in dazzling form and sat proudly at the top of the table after the first three games were won against Dunfermline Athletic, East Stirlingshire and Bathgate. Full points were also gained from their next two fixtures without even kicking a ball! On 16th September 1916, Broxburn couldn't get a train through to Methil and had to forfeit the points. The following week the same fate befell Lochgelly United, who couldn't raise a team for the league fixture at RecreationPark.

By mid-November, only one league match had been lost; a narrow defeat against St Bernard's at the Royal Gymnasium. From November 1916 to February 1917, however, there was very little football played due to travel restrictions and the player shortage brought about by the war. East Fife did manage to raise a side to beat Lochgelly United 2-0 in the first round of the Wemyss Cup at RecreationPark on 9th December, but no more fixtures were fulfilled until the points were shared with Cowdenbeath in an Eastern League fixture at Bayview on 3rd February 1917.

The player shortage brought about by the war was so serious that a meeting was called between the various football associations to discuss the crisis, with a view to allowing unregistered players to play for clubs left short of playing staff due to the conflict. The outcome was that the governing body, the Scottish Football Association, issued the following statement:

"During the duration of the war and until further notice, a professional in a recognised competition for a club other than that for which he was registered, who has written consent from his club to play, will be exonerated on written application".

In other words, what the SFA were saying was that any player registered with a senior professional club who wished to play as a guest for a club struggling to raise a team would be allowed to do so providing he had written permission from his parent club, and that the club he wished to play for informed the SFA in writing of the arrangement.

In their remaining Eastern League fixtures, East Fife continued with their winning form and finished the season in second place, four points behind winners Cowdenbeath. Indeed, the Methil Men would probably have won the tournament had it not been for the fact that they were unable to fulfil four fixtures.

In the local cup competitions, the finals of both the Fife Cup and the Wemyss Cup were reached, only for Cowdenbeath to emerge triumphant in both tournaments. The final of the Penman Cup was also reached, but the match had to be held over until the following season as the semi-final between Armadale and Cowdenbeath had still to be settled.

East Stirlingshire, Lochgelly United, Bathgate and Broxburn United were all forced to withdraw from the Eastern League before the start of the 1917/18 season. Raith Rovers and Dundee, who had been forced to leave the Scottish League due to wartime travel restrictions, then joined the six remaining clubs.

Just as the season was about to begin, St Bernard's announced that their Royal Gymnasium ground had been requisitioned by the army. Despite managing to find an alternative ground before the season started, the Edinburgh side were eventually forced to withdraw when it was discovered that there was no manpower available to build the new venue up to an acceptable standard.

Faced with the prospect of only having twelve league fixtures over the coming season, Cowdenbeath proposed that teams in the Eastern League should face each other twice at home and twice away, making a total of twenty four league fixtures for each club. The proposal was accepted and the season started on 18th August 1917 with a 1-0 home defeat at the hands of Raith Rovers.

The 1917/18 league season turned out to be extremely disappointing, with the Fife managing to fulfil all but two of their league fixtures, but managed only five wins. With four matches ending all square and thirteen games lost, the team finished the season in bottom place.

On a more successful note, the Penman Cup, held over from the previous season, was won at Central Park, Cowdenbeath on 2nd February 1918 with a single goal victory against Armadale. The Wemyss Cup also found its way into the Bayview trophy cabinet following a 2-0 victory over Raith Rovers in the last game of the season on 27th April.

Meanwhile, on the Western Front, the stalemate was about to be broken. Fearful that the U.S. Army, who had entered the war the previous year, were about to tip the balance in favour of the allies, the German Army decided to launch a big offensive before the Americans arrived.

Fortunately, the Germans' 'big push' was successfully thwarted and the Allies seized the opportunity to step up their offensive with the help of the US troops to finally end the conflict. On 11th November 1918, fighting ceased on the Western Front. Days later the German Navy surrendered, and the Great War was over.

With virtually all Britain's manpower involved in the war effort during the latter part of 1918, there was very little football played. East Fife's first match of the 1918/19 season came just four days before Christmas, when the 4th King's Own Scottish Borderers visited Bayview for a challenge match.

After the New Year was celebrated with a visit from Queen's Park Strollers on 2nd January, the rest of the season was played out with challenge matches against local rivals Raith Rovers, Cowdenbeath and St. Johnstone.

With the 'war to end all wars' now behind them, the local community could look forward to more peaceful times, of which the game of football was destined to play a huge part.

Chapter Six: The First Major Trophy

East Fife in 1920, pictured in front of the original pavilion on the north side of the ground. This pavilion was superseded by an old army hut erected on the opposite side of the park shortly after this photograph was taken. (Author's Collection)

Although the Eastern League was re-started for the 1919/20 season, East Fife elected to join the newly re-formed Central League along with Alloa Athletic, Armadale, Bathgate, Bo'ness, Broxburn United, Clackmannan, Dunfermline Athletic, East Stirlingshire, Falkirk Reserves, Hearts Reserves, King's Park, St Bernard's and Stenhousemuir.
Cowdenbeath and Lochgelly United decided to remain in the Eastern League, which now consisted mainly of Tayside and Angus clubs. Raith Rovers and Dundee were re-admitted to the Scottish League.
The 1919/20 season was a reasonably successful one for East Fife, with the first half of the league programme producing resounding wins against Bathgate and Clackmannan by 6-1 and 5-0 respectively as well as a single goal victory over Hearts' second eleven at Tynecastle. The third round of the Qualifying Cup was also reached following a 1-0 victory

against Dunfermline Athletic at East EndPark and a 6-0 home win against BrechinCity. Although Cowdenbeath emerged 3-1 victors from the third round tie at Bayview in front of a record 7,000 crowd on 18th October, the Methil club had already done enough to qualify for a third crack at the Scottish Cup. The fact that BayviewPark could hold a crowd of 7,000 in 1919 is quite remarkable considering how undeveloped the enclosure was at this time.

In an article which appeared in the *East Fife Mail* in May 1977, Earlsferry man David Spittal recalled:

"Bayview as I first remember it was enclosed by a tackety, rickety, wooden fence around seven and a half feet high with a few loose and missing planks. Consequently in those days there were a few non paying customers who squeezed in through the spaces, there being only one or maybe two policemen patrolling the ground. The pitch itself was practically grass-less, consisting of a strip of green along each wing with the rest hard, trodden, bare earth. There was no terracing and only a small wooden stand, which had seen better days, stood on the opposite side of the park from the present stand. That was BayviewPark in season 1919/20".

Recalling the players during this period, Mr Spittal continued:

"East Fife had Jock Neish in goal, 'Dirty Dick' Stewart at Right Back and Outside Right Willie Fisher. When Jock Neish was asked about a possible transfer south, he replied, "There's nae chance o' me gaun there, I'm following a serial in The Palace Cinema!""

On a raw and miserable Methil day on 24th January 1920, Arthurlie were beaten 4-0 in front of a 2,000 crowd as East Fife progressed to the second round of the Scottish Cup. They were rewarded for their efforts with a trip to Firhill to face Partick Thistle in round two, where a crowd of 15,000 saw the home side romp home 5-0.

Back on Central League business, favourable results in the remaining fixtures resulted in a final position of third, on equal points with runners-up Dunfermline Athletic and only two points behind champions Bo'ness.

Season 1920/21 saw the Central League increased to eighteen clubs following the admission of Eastern League sides Cowdenbeath, Dundee Hibs, Lochgelly United and St Johnstone. By this time the post-war success of the Central League was starting to worry the Scottish League. The clubs which constituted the Central League were mainly from the prosperous coal and shale mining communities of Fife and the Lothians, where healthy crowds meant that member clubs could pay their players good wages. Although the Scottish League remained adamant that a Second Division would not be re-introduced, general opinion was that the Central League clubs would be invited to join the Scottish League sooner rather than later, such was their status.

The Central League campaign started poorly with a disappointing defeat at Clackmannan, but a successful start was made in the Qualifying Cup with Lochgelly United eventually beaten at RecreationPark on 11th September following stalemate at Bayview. The second round of the competition saw the Fife make the short journey to Central Park, where Cowdenbeath were beaten 2-1 in front of a remarkable crowd of 12,000!

At the beginning of October, permission was granted to erect an 'old army hut' to form a Board room, a referee's room, new changing facilities for home and visiting players and 'a spray bathroom with lavatory'. The pavilion was positioned at the south-west corner of the ground and survived until being replaced by a new brick structure at the beginning of the 1970's!

The programme of Central League fixtures continued with a run of three straight wins against Lochgelly United, East Stirlingshire and King's Park before the next round of the Qualifying Cup was played on 16th October. The Fifers' next opponents in the competition were the un-fancied Blairgowrie

Amateurs, who were soundly beaten 5-1 at Bayview in front of a crowd of 4,000. Central League duties resumed on the following Saturday with a home match against Armadale, which the West Lothian side won 2-1 much to the vociferous disgust of the East Fife supporters. Despite the fact that this was the first home defeat of the season in any competition, letters poured into the *Leven Advertiser and Wemyss Gazette* demanding that the Board be sacked!

The following Saturday, 30th October 1920, the Methil Men made the long journey north to face Inverness Caledonian in the fifth round of the Qualifying Cup. A no-scoring draw was the outcome and the Highland League side travelled to Methil the following week for the replay, where the home side comfortably won 3-1. Qualifying Cup ties were considered to be far more important than league fixtures, which were put on the back burner, and a week later the Fifers lined up to face Alloa Athletic in the quarter-final at Recreation Park. A goal-less draw was the outcome, so it was back to Bayview on 20th November for the replay. Again there was no scoring and, in an effort to give more bite to the Fifers' attack, director James Stein travelled through to Edinburgh on the Wednesday following the match to sign Dom Currie, who had 'guested' for the Fife during the Great War, from Hearts. Currie's presence in the side had the desired effect and, in the second replay on 27th November, a crowd of 10,000 saw East Fife progress to the last four with a 2-1 win against Alloa at the neutral venue of Central Park, Cowdenbeath.

A new record home crowd of 8,000 paid to see the semi-final against Queen of the South at Bayview on Saturday 4th December. In ideal conditions, the home side had to weather early pressure from the 'Doonhamers', but eventually the Fife took control and goals from Dom Currie and Andy Moffat had the game as good as won by half-time.

The final of the Qualifying Cup was held at Central Park, Cowdenbeath, on Saturday 18th December 1920 against Bo'ness. As well as being current holders of the trophy, the West Lothian side were also current Central League champions and were still to be beaten in the current league competition. East Fife would have to be at their very best to win the trophy.

Cup fever hit Methil and its environs in the days leading up to the match. It seemed that the entire local population wanted to see the game and, as a result, a new Central Park ground record of 18,603 was set, although some sources put the figure at over 20,000!

There was a terrific atmosphere in the ground as Bo'ness won the toss and elected to play with the strong setting sun at their backs. Play was fairly evenly matched in the opening stages, but it was East Fife's Geordie Wilson who opened the scoring just before the half-hour mark when he headed home a Peter Neill cross.

By the time the second half started, a strong breeze had started to blow down the field and Bo'ness were faced with the prospect of having to play into the wind for the remainder of the game. Despite this disadvantage, however, Robb headed past Neish for the equaliser shortly after the re-start. East Fife rallied and, as well as taking control of the game, entertained their huge support with a dazzling display of skilful football. Most prominent of all the Fife forwards was Dom Currie, who time and again weaved his way through the Bo'ness defence as East Fife piled on the pressure. Currie's efforts finally paid of with fifteen minutes of the match to go when, following a goalmouth melee, he sent a powerful header into the net from the edge of the penalty area to regain the lead. In the final minute, Andrew Moffat scored a third goal to seal the victory and the Scottish Qualifying Cup was on its way to Methil!

Pictured with the Scottish Qualifying Cup in 1920 are (back row, from left): J.Robertson (Trainer), J.Ross, J.McGlashan, D.Wightman, J.Neish, A.Main, H.McBride, A.Stewart. Front row: P.Neil, D.Currie, A.Moffat, A.Burton, G.Wilson, A.Brown. (Author's Collection)

Having received a bye in the first round of the Scottish Cup, the Fifers travelled to Ayrshire on 5th February 1921 to face Stevenston United in the second round of the competition. A goal-less draw was the outcome, so the following Saturday the two teams locked horns again at Bayview, where the home side emerged 2-1 winners.

Huge crowds gathered at Methil station to welcome the team home, where some players were lifted shoulder high and carried along Methil High Street with the cup held aloft. It was, at the time, the greatest achievement in the history of East Fife Football Club.

After the euphoria of the cup success, the following series of league games proved disappointing, with only two games won from eight played. Defeats during this poor run of form included a 4-0 defeat by Dundee Hibs at Tannadice and a 3-0 reverse against St Johnstone in Perth.

East Fife could not have hoped for a better third round draw. When the names came out of the hat, the Methil Men found themselves paired with Celtic at Bayview, and immediately the club set about the task of improving facilities to enable the ground to hold the huge crowd anticipated for the cup-tie, scheduled to be played on Saturday 19th February 1921. Squads of workmen were employed raising an embankment on the north side of the ground, adjacent to the grandstand. A veranda was also added to the recently erected wooden pavilion on the opposite side of the park, for which tickets were sold at an increased price of three shillings (15 pence). Ground admission was raised to 1/6 (7½p), with a seat in the grandstand costing 2/- (10p).

Once the improvements were complete, it was expected that Bayview would be able to accommodate a crowd of 10,000 in comfort and safety. On the day of the match, however, 11,000 banner waving spectators turned out to witness the Fifers' first ever meeting with the Glasgow giants.

Few eyebrows were raised when the cup tie resulted in a 3-1 victory for the 'Hoops', with the home side's only goal coming from a McTavish penalty.

McInally scored a brace for Celtic, with their other goal coming from Gallagher.

With the cup fever behind them, East Fife were able to set about the task of fulfilling the huge backlog of league fixtures that had accumulated during their cup exploits.

Following the 3-2 home league win over Bathgate on the Saturday following the Celtic match, no fewer than nine games were played during March 1921.

If March had been a busy month, then April must have been hectic, as eleven Central League fixtures were played out during a four-week period, during which the club also found the time to lose 4-1 to Dunfermline Athletic in the Fife Cup semi-final on 27th April!

The East Fife team that faced Celtic at Bayview in the Scottish Cup on 19th February 1921. Missing from the photo is Dom Currie who, having just finished a shift down Wellesley Pit, was still in the process of getting himself ready for the match when the picture was taken! (Author's Collection)

A final league position of fifth was attained in the 18-team league, a commendable achievement considering 53 competitive matches had been played during the season. Season 1920/21 had undoubtedly been East Fife's most successful to date, with the club having managed to land their first major trophy, the Scottish Qualifying Cup. It would, however, be the last time the club would be eligible to enter that particular competition, as Scottish League membership was just around the corner!

Chapter Seven: Into the Scottish League!

As mentioned in the previous chapter, the football clubs that made up the Central League came mainly from the coal and shale mining communities of Fife and West Lothian. As the mining towns thrived with the growth of the mining industries and the associated influx of miners and their families, so did their local football clubs. This resulted in many of the Central League clubs managing to pay their players higher wages than they would have received playing in the Scottish League, and the knock-on effect that this situation had was that several Scottish League players migrated to the Central League. In order to stop the loss of its players to a rival competition, the Scottish League decided to admit the Central League clubs, with the exception of Hearts and Falkirk Reserves, to its membership. Sixteen Central League clubs along with Vale of Leven and Johnstone from the west and Forfar Athletic and Arbroath from the east became the Scottish Second Division at the start of season 1921/22. Several of the clubs which formed the new Second Division had tasted Scottish League football in the past, but at the start of season 1921/22 Alloa Athletic, Arbroath, Armadale, Bathgate, Bo'ness, Broxburn, Clackmannan, East Fife, Forfar Athletic, King's Park and Stenhousemuir all became Scottish League members for the first time.

In anticipation of their entry into the Scottish League, East Fife announced proposals for improvements to BayviewPark during the close season of 1921. The proposals appeared to be more than a little over ambitious, however, as is apparent from the following article that appeared in the *Fife Free Press* on 30th April:

"East Fife have embarked upon a scheme of extension, which aims at providing at BayviewPark for 35,000 spectators. Things certainly

have looked up for the Methil club ever since they won the Qualifying Cup and there is little doubt that to improve the enclosure will prove a sound financial speculation. A feu of the ground has been secured which guarantees fixity of tenure. The pitch will be carried westwards and levelled and the fact that the work is being undertaken just now ensures a fine growth and firm turf. A cinder track will enclose the new pitch and a new grandstand to seat 3,000 spectators is to be erected."

Of course, actual improvements to the spectator facilities at Bayview fell far short of these ambitious proposals before the new season got under way, but dramatic improvements were made to the playing surface. By the time Cowdenbeath visited Methil for a pre-season friendly on 15th August the pitch was in magnificent order and general opinion was that very few Scottish League clubs had turf of a similar quality.

On Saturday 20th August 1921, East Fife played their first ever Scottish League match against Bathgate at BayviewPark, where Neish scored the Fifers' first league goal from the penalty spot as the visitors won a disappointing match 2-1. The spectators made no allowance for first day nerves and the Editor of the *Leven Advertiser and Wemyss Gazette* was duly inundated with letters complaining about the standard of football served up by the home side!

Defeat at Stenhousemuir followed a week later, but on Saturday 3rd September East Fife recorded their first ever Scottish League win in the shape of a single goal triumph over near-neighbours Lochgelly United at Bayview. Further wins against Clackmannan and East Stirlingshire placed the Fifers in the top half of the table by mid-September and, by the turn of the year, eleven league matches had been won and six had been lost, with the points shared on three occasions.

There then came a disappointing run of five league games from which only one point was gained along with an early exit from the Scottish Cup at the hands of Motherwell.

The Fifers finished their first season in the Scottish League in tenth position, having played 38 matches of which 15 were won, 15 were lost and 8 were drawn.

The summer of 1922 was dominated by the construction of the new grandstand on the south side of BayviewPark, opposite the wooden structure erected in 1906. The club appealed for funds at the end of April in order to build a structure capable of seating 1,500 spectators at an expected cost of between £1,500 and £2,000, with the funds to be raised by the sale of public subscriptions of £50 each. For this investment the expected dividend would be 5% and all investors would be able to watch the match free from the grandstand for five years. Planning permission was granted at Buckhaven Dean of Guild Court at the beginning of July and the grandstand, which was fabricated in Glasgow and brought in sections to Methil by rail, was opened at the beginning of October. The actual capacity of the new facility fell far short of original proposals, however, boasting just 800 seats.

It was the second week in September before the Fifers recorded their first win of the season, a 4-0 home triumph over Stenhousemuir. After suffering defeat at the hands of Lochgelly United at RecreationPark in their following match, four straight league wins were recorded; the fourth win being a 2-1 victory at Central Park, Cowdenbeath on 14th October in front of a crowd of 7,000. Poor league form then ensued, and it was December before things started to pick up with wins against Arbroath, Vale of Leven, Armadale and East Stirlingshire.

Commenting on the 'poor crowd' of 2,500 who attended the Arbroath game, the *Leven Advertiser* reported that one disgruntled spectator had been heard to shout *"waken up, or ye'll get naebody here at a'!"*

In the first round of the Scottish Cup on 13th January 1923, non-league Berwick Rangers visited Methil and were thrashed

7-1 in front of 3,500. After a confidence boosting 4-1 league victory over Forfar Athletic, the Fifers travelled to Ayrshire to face Kilmarnock in the second round of the cup, where they held their more fancied First Division opponents to a 1-1 draw. In the replay, the Methil Men went one better and recorded their first ever win against a First Division side with a single goal victory. Their reward was a trip to Parkhead on 10th February to face Celtic in the third round where, in front of a 'disappointing' attendance of 12,000, East Fife went down 2-1 despite putting up a good performance. According to the *Leven Advertiser*, the Methil Men had 'gifted' Celtic their two goals and were unfortunate to lose the match!

Back on league business, full points were taken from just four more games over the remainder of the season, which all but ended any slim hopes the club might have had of winning promotion during their second year of Scottish League membership.

As well as the local cup competitions, three charity matches were played towards the end of season 1922/23. Revenge was gained over Scottish Cup opponents Celtic with a 2-0 victory at Bayview on Monday 19th April and in May two charity matches were played against Raith Rovers. After Raith had won the first game 2-0 at Stark's Park on May 5th, the two sides contested a 'fierce' game at Bayview the following week in which the Fifers' right back MacPherson suffered a broken thigh. Ironically, after having just raised money for local charities, the club then found themselves having to appeal for donations in order to compensate the player for his loss of earnings!

At the club's A.G.M. on 26th July 1923, Chairman Archibald Dryburgh expressed his disappointment that the supporters appeared to have deserted the club towards the end of the season. The new grandstand, on the other hand, had been well patronised throughout the year and had been full on two occasions. The Chairman was quick to point out that the revenue generated by the grandstand for just one match, if full, was enough to pay the interest on the club's overdraft for a whole season. Income from transfers was well down on the previous year as the club had resisted several approaches for players throughout the season.

Further ground improvements were carried out by a volunteer work force over the summer of 1923. The banking around the ground was terraced and it was anticipated that when the work was complete Bayview would be able to accommodate 20,000 spectators 'in comfort'.

On the playing side, junior club Methil Rovers were formed for the start of the 1923/24 season. The club were to be affiliated to East Fife and it was intended that they would eventually become a 'feeder club' to the senior team.

The forthcoming season was also to bring the threat of automatic relegation to the club for the first time with the formation of the Third Division, for which a further 16 clubs were admitted to the Scottish League. One of the newcomers, Dundee United, were admitted straight into the Second Division at the expense of East Stirlingshire, who were joined in the Third Division by Arthurlie, Beith, Brechin City, Clackmannan, Dumbarton Harp, Dykehead, Galston, Helensburgh, Mid-Annandale, Montrose, Nithsdale Wanderers, Peebles Rovers, Queen of the South, Royal Albert and Solway Star.

The 1923/24 season kicked off with defeat from Armadale at VolunteerPark followed by a narrow home win over Lochgelly United. Further disappointing results then followed, including an early exit from the Penman Cup at the hands of Cowdenbeath. The team's inability to find the net was the obvious reason for the poor early season form, with Phil Weir bagging the only three goals scored during the first six matches.

There wasn't much improvement in form over the remainder of the year with a total of only six league victories gained from the 21 games played before 31st December.

New Year's Day 1924 was celebrated with a 4-0 victory over Lochgelly United at RecreationPark and was followed with home wins over Armadale and Bo'ness, but once again the winning form could not be maintained and, in mid January, the team slumped to a 3-0 defeat at Central Park, Cowdenbeath.

A 3-1 win over Johnstone at NewfieldPark in the Scottish Cup on 26th January was rewarded with a second round tie against Falkirk at Brockville. Alas, any hopes of claiming another First Division scalp were dashed as the home side progressed to round three with a 2-0 win.

The remainder of the league season saw a further five matches won, including an 8-0 victory over Forfar Athletic and a 6-0 win over Stenhousemuir. A final position of twelfth in the twenty-team league was attained, well clear of relegation, with the record of having played 38, won 14, drawn 9 and lost 15, bringing a points total of 37. Not so fortunate were near neighbours Lochgelly United, who finished bottom and were relegated to the Third Division, never to return. At the other end of the table, local rivals Cowdenbeath finished in second place and were promoted to Division One, where they remained for a remarkable ten years as Fife's top football club! One pleasing statistic for the 1923/24 season was the club's financial status, which showed a 'favourable balance' of £14 at the end of the financial year. This amount may not seem much today, but back in the early 1920's, men could watch a whole season's football from the grandstand for just 25 shillings (£1-25). In those far off days before sexual equality, ladies could gain a season's admission to the stand for ten shillings and sixpence (52½p), with the price for schoolboys (and presumably schoolgirls!) set at 5 shillings (25p). A season's admission to the ground cost 10/6 (52½p) for men, 5/- (25p) for ladies and 2/6 (12½p) for boys and girls.

East Fife started the 1924/25 league campaign well. Heavy rain hampered the first match against Broxburn United at Bayview, which finished goal-less, but the following week a hat-trick from new signing Duncan helped defeat Dunfermline Athletic 4-0 at East EndPark.

The month of August was rounded off with a 2-1 victory against King's Park at Bayview that saw the Fife challenging at the top of the table and, by the end of October, East Fife were in pole position and looking good, with match reports in the local press raving about the team's skill and superiority. Unfortunately, a change of fortune lay just around the corner and a straight run of five league defeats followed the successful run. By the turn of the year, just eight of the 20 league games played had been won.

A 5-1 victory over Stenhousemuir on New Year's Day 1925 at Bayview was followed by defeat at Dumbarton two days later as form continued to blow hot and cold.

The disappointment of the league was forgotten in mid-January, however, when the Scottish Cup first round draw paired East Fife with Rangers in what was to be the first ever meeting between the sides, scheduled to be played on 24th January. As soon as the draw was announced, the East Fife directors set about improving facilities at Bayview in anticipation of the expected record crowd. The capacity of the ground was increased, for which four additional turnstiles were added at the main entrance and two temporary pay boxes erected in School Street. On the playing side, the team was strengthened when left-winger Dave Nairn was signed from Newburgh West End in the week prior to the match. The Fifers lost the game 3-1 in front of an official attendance of 9,500, but reliable sources put the crowd at nearer 12,000! Inside left Davie Wright scored East Fife's solitary counter.

It was back to league business the following Saturday with a 4-1 win over Bathgate at Bayview and over the remainder of the season the team's league form was reasonably good with convincing home victories recorded against Albion Rovers and Armadale by the respective scores of 5-0 and 4-1. The final league position of ninth was a fair reflection of the Fifers' form over the campaign, with 17 matches won out of the 38 games played along with five draws and 16 defeats. Preparations for season 1925/26 took place with an air of confidence at BayviewPark. A sound financial position coupled with a pool of 16 signed players of proven ability promised a successful future, at least in the short term. The men who would wear the black and gold over the coming season were goalkeeper Jock Neish; backs Willie Wood, Willie Gillespie and 'Tanny' Coyle; half-backs Matt Wilson, Paddy Cahill, Bobby Russell, Johnny Ross and John Moffat; with forwards Phil Weir, Mick Giblin, Andrew Bell, Dave Nairn, Duncan Lindsay, Davie Wright and Peter Barrett completing the pool.

One of the main factors in the Fifers' favour at this time was the good relationship that existed between all parties associated with the club, including its supporters. The following extract is taken from an article that appeared in the Leven Advertiser and Wemyss Gazette in August 1925:

"The Methil club is possessed of certain advantages which are denied to many clubs. A big factor towards success is the fact that relations between the Directors, players and supporters are, for the most part, harmonious. Under the guidance of Mr Archibald Dryburgh, the Bayview Company is a happy family"

The 'happy family' atmosphere must have suited Manager Dave McLean, as he turned down an offer to become manager of Cowdenbeath at the start of the season. The Central Park side had finished the previous campaign in fifth place in Division One, only two points behind Celtic, and saw the Methil boss as the man who could consolidate their position in the top league. Fortunately for the Methil club, McLean decided to stay put, leaving historians to speculate whether or not the popular Manager could have guided Cowdenbeath to the success he was destined to enjoy at the helm of East Fife! The high hopes of a good start to the campaign were dashed at the first hurdle when newly relegated Third Lanark romped home 4-0 at CathkinPark on 15th August then, a week later, another point was dropped at home to Stenhousemuir.

Saturday 29th August saw the Fifers travel to Arbroath to participate in the official opening of Greater Gayfield, where the match was kicked off by the Earl of Strathmore. The Fifers spoiled the 'Lichties' party by recording their first league win of the season in front of a crowd of 7,000.

After defeating Broxburn United at Bayview in the next league fixture, the Fifers hit another slump in form, with defeats following from Dunfermline Athletic, Albion Rovers and East Stirlingshire along with a share of the points in a second meeting with the 'Pars'.

The team's fortunes then turned around completely, and a run of six wins and two draws ensued, starting with victory against Queen of the South at Bayview on 3rd October 1925. During this eight-match unbeaten run, new signing Adam Mackie score a hat-trick on his debut as King's Park were beaten 4-3 at Bayview on 7th November.

The successful period was brought abruptly to a halt at DunterliePark, Barrhead, on 28th November, where home side Arthurlie won by the convincing score of 5-0.

On 19th December, severe snowstorms put the home fixture against Bathgate in doubt, but after cartloads of snow were removed from the pitch during the morning, Bayview was declared playable. The crowd of 2,000 who braved the wintry conditions were soon warmed by a sparkling display from the home side as four goals from midweek signing James Neish, single counters from Barrett and Weir and an own goal from Bathgate's Cairns saw the Fifers romp home 7-3.

After the points were shared with Stenhousemuir at Ochilview on New Year's Day 1926, the promotion challenge was maintained during early January with home wins against Third Lanark and Bo'ness. Later that same month, however, Bo'ness gained revenge by dumping the Fifers out of the Scottish Cup at the first hurdle.

The push for promotion was given a boost in mid-February when Centre Forward Jock Wood was signed from East Stirlingshire but, despite scoring twice on his debut against King's Park at Forthbank, the two games following Woods' arrival were both lost.

The challenge at the top of the table was maintained over the remainder of the season with a seven game unbeaten run that included wins over Clyde, Arbroath, Broxburn United, Armadale and Nithsdale Wanderers. With their promotion rivals displaying similar form, however, the Fifers finished in fourth spot, four points adrift of second placed Clyde.

Despite losing out on a promotion place, it had been the club's most promising league campaign so far. A total of 98 goals were scored in the 38 league games, a tally second only to Division Two Champions Dunfermline, who netted a remarkable 109. Top scorer at Bayview was Davie Wright with 23 goals, followed by Phil Weir and Dave Nairn with 16. Peter Barrett scored 9, Jock Wood scored 8 despite having only signed for the club in February and Adam Mackie found the net 7 times. Other players who scored on at least one occasion were James Neish, Matt Wilson, Duncan Lindsay, Willie Gillespie, Bobby Russell and Paddy Cahill.

Despite losing out on promotion, the season had been a pleasing one in many respects, with the club demonstrating that during their five seasons of Scottish League membership they had developed into an outfit that could eventually bring First Division football to Methil.

Chapter Eight: A Remarkable Achievement

The beginning of the 1926/27 football season was overshadowed locally by the national miners strike. The strike had started on 1st May in protest at the national reduction in coal-miners' wages following the Samuel Commission Report. Two days after the strike began, the TUC called a General Strike in support of the miners and Britain ground to a halt for nine days. Within 24 hours, there were no trains, trams or 'buses operating; the country's docks were idle, and most factories were temporarily closed down.

The effect the strike was having on the country was greatly reduced when thousands of volunteers from the professional, middle and upper classes stepped in to take on the role of factory workers, lorry drivers and public transport operators. Violent clashes ensued across the country and soldiers armed with machine guns were required to regain control of the nation's docks. On 12th May, the TUC realised it had no other option but to end the General Strike, but the miners were made of sterner stuff and decided not to return to work despite the major hardships most were suffering.

The fact that a large percentage of the local work force were employed in the mines meant that the local economy suffered greatly during the dispute. Obviously any money the miners may have had was used to feed their families, with the result that there was little money to spend on life's little pleasures, including Saturday afternoons at BayviewPark.

On 14th August the Fifers kicked off their league campaign with a 4-1 home victory over Alloa Athletic, witnessed by a 'disappointing' crowd of around 2,000, which was well down on the previous season's average. The following week, newly relegated Raith Rovers played host to East Fife in what was the first Scottish League encounter between the sides, and trounced their local rivals 4-1. League victories over Ayr United and Dumbarton were followed by a draw against East Stirlingshire and defeat at Forfar, before the first round of the Fife Cup brought a resounding 7-0 victory over St Andrews University on 23rd September. Unfortunately, the first round of the other local competition, the Wemyss Cup, told a much different story. At Central Park on 30th September, Cowdenbeath recorded their biggest ever win over East Fife with a 9-1 victory. Not surprisingly the report in the following edition of the *Leven Advertiser and Wemyss Gazette* contained only four lines!

During October, the Fife climbed to third place in the table following victories over Third Lanark, Bathgate and Clydebank, although a heavy defeat was suffered at Armadale during the middle of the month. Victory at Arbroath on 20th November would have resulted in a further climb up the table to second place, but instead a 2-0 defeat saw the team plummet to 7th position.

December started with a bang when 'Tiger' Russell returned to the side following a three-month absence. Although the influential left-half didn't find the net, he played a huge part in the 7-1 demolition of Arthurlie at Bayview, with the goals coming from a Jock Wood hat-trick, a Nairn brace and single counters from Barrett and Mackie.

On the first day of January 1927, Raith Rovers make the short journey to Methil for the first New Year's Day derby between the sides since 1904. A crowd of 7,000 turned out to witness the event, which the Rovers won 1-0 to inflict what was, despite their inconsistent form, East Fife's first home defeat of the season.

At the end of the month, the Fifers embarked on what was to become a truly remarkable Scottish Cup run. Due to travel to Dumfriesshire to face Thornhill in the first round, the non-league side offered to give up their home rights in return for a

£100 guarantee and the tie was switched to Bayview, to be played on 22nd January.

The Fife progressed to round two courtesy of an 8-1 victory, but not before surviving an early scare when the non-league minnows shocked the 2,500 spectators by opening the scoring in the first minute. Thornhill's joy was short lived, however, with Nairn equalising for the Fifers just two minutes later. After half-an-hour, Phil Weir put the Methil Men ahead and Jock Wood added a third before the interval. In a second half totally dominated by the home side, further goals from Nairn (2), Wood, Weir and Hope ensured a place in the second round and a home tie with Aberdeen.

On 5th February 1927 a crowd of 9,000 paid for admission to Bayview to witness the Scottish Cup tie with Aberdeen. This was the 'Dons' first ever visit to Methil, although their reserve side had previously played at Bayview in the Northern League. Jock Wood gave East Fife a shock early lead, but Cheyne equalised for the 'Dons' to take the tie to a replay at Pittodrie on the following Wednesday. Most of the 12,000 crowd who turned out for the second game expected the home side to chalk up a convincing win over their Second Division opponents, but the visitors were more than a match for the top-league side, and goals from Jock Wood and Phil Weir established a two-nil lead before Aberdeen's Bruce reduced the leeway. Against the odds, the Fifers held out until the final whistle, and recorded a famous victory to the delight of the loyal band of followers who had made the journey north by supporters' 'bus.

On 19th February, a new ground record crowd of 12,000 spectators paid to see East Fife take on Fife rivals Dunfermline Athletic in the third round of the cup at Bayview. The 'Pars', enjoying their first ever season in the First Division, were fairly confident of progressing to the quarter-final, but it was the home side who won through with goals from Jock Wood and Phil Weir to take another First Division 'scalp'.

Three Second Division sides, East Fife, Arthurlie and Bo'ness, went into the hat for the quarter-final draw. The Fifers managed to avoid all five First Division clubs; Rangers, Celtic, Partick Thistle, Falkirk and Dundee United; and were drawn

Pictured just before the 3-2 victory over Armadale on 26th February 1927 are (standing, from left): S.Robertson, J.Hope, P.Barrett, W.Wood, R.G.Peden, J.Bruce, J.Brown, W.Anderson, J.Barrie, and R.Robertson (Trainer). Seated (from left) are: J.Neish, P.Weir, J.Paterson, J.Wood(Capt.), A.Mackie, D.Nairn and H.McBride. (Photo: Courtesy of Ernie Mackie)

to play Arthurlie at DunterliePark.

Thousands of Black and Gold bedecked supporters made their way through to Barrhead on 5th March to see if their side could progress to the semi-final, but found that playing conditions were far from perfect. The following paragraph describes DunterliePark as seen through the eyes of a reporter from the *Leven Advertiser and Wemyss Gazette*:

"What a pitch! In the first place it was the smallest senior club field I have ever seen. There was no great distance from the penalty spot to the centre circle, while the corner flags were only three yards from the penalty areas. Strictly speaking the ground was unplayable as it was a perfect sea of mud. At the railway end, a patch of grass struggled for an existence, but at the pavilion end it was mud, mud

and more mud! When the long special train arrived from Methil there were only a few seats to be had in the 'band box' and what little terracing there was soon showed a predominance of the black and gold colours".

The Fifers adapted well to the conditions, however, and comfortably saw off their Second Division counterparts with goals from Edgar, Barrett and Russell, without reply.

Only Partick Thistle now stood between East Fife and the final of the country's top football tournament and, on 26th March, a crowd of 38,000 packed the neutral terraces of TynecastlePark in Edinburgh for the semi-final against the more fancied Glasgow side. At the end of the first half, the score was level at 1-1, with the Fifers' goal coming from 'Pasha' Paterson. Thistle's counter came from Grove. In the second half, East Fife captain Jock Wood netted what proved to be the winning goal and, when the final whistle sounded, scores of East Fife supporters dodged the lines of police, invaded the pitch and hugged their heroes. The Methil Men had achieved the remarkable feat of reaching the Scottish Cup final less than six years after being admitted to the Scottish League!

The final between East Fife and Celtic, played at HampdenPark on 16th April 1927, was the first Cup final to be broadcast live on the radio. Few who listened to the broadcast were prepared for the great start to the match when, after only two minutes, the 80,070 crowd were shocked when the Fifers took the lead through a header from Captain Jock Wood.

"Every Fifer went frantic and thousands of impartial spectators cheered to the echoes of the Second Leaguer's clever goal", reported the *Leven Advertiser and Wemyss Gazette.*

Unfortunately, the joy was short lived, as only a minute later, a misunderstanding between East Fife 'keeper Gilfillan and defender Robertson ended with the latter putting the ball into his own net to square the match. The score remained level until ten minutes before the interval, when McLean netted a Connelly cross from eight yards to put the 'hoops' ahead. The match was effectively won in 46 minutes when Connelly added a third. The dream was over, but it had been a marvellous cup run in which East Fife had become the first Second Division side to reach the Scottish Cup final during the 20th Century and only the fourth side to achieve the feat in the history of the competition.

Naturally, the challenge for promotion was put on the back burner as 'cup fever' enveloped Bayview. Following convincing wins against Forfar Athletic and Stenhousemuir just as the cup run was getting under way, four of the next seven league matches were lost, with 15 goals scored and 23 conceded in the process. The team rallied at the beginning of April with a convincing 4-1 win against Arbroath and an even more emphatic 8-2 demolition of Albion Rovers, during which the 100th league goal of the campaign was scored, but it was too little, too late. By this stage in the competition Bo'ness were already out of sight and the second promotion spot was as good as claimed by Raith Rovers. Although a narrow victory was recorded at home to Bo'ness on 23rd April, the two remaining fixtures against Arthurlie and St Bernard's were both lost and the team finished their league programme in sixth place.

Following their impressive showing in the Scottish Cup, the Fife were expected to do well over the following season and things certainly looked promising at the start of the 1927/28 league campaign. Albion Rovers were defeated 2-0 at Bayview on 13th August with goals from Phil Weir and Jock Wood, but the winning start could not be maintained. Only one of the next seven league matches was won, with home defeats suffered at the hands of Alloa Athletic and Bathgate along with a heavy 4-0 reverse at StationPark, Forfar.

At the beginning of October, the team bounced back in style with a 5-0 demolition of newly relegated Morton at Bayview. When the next two league matches against Queen of the South and Armadale were also won convincingly, the Fifers found themselves back in mid-table, having occupied fourth bottom place during their recent poor spell.

The winning form could not be maintained, however, and by the end of the year just two more league matches had been won, along with five defeats and two draws over the same period.

The first match of 1928, played on 2nd January, saw a complete turnaround in fortunes with a 5-1 home victory over Queen of the South. This was followed up with wins against Clydebank and Forfar and draws against Alloa Athletic and Morton before the end of a month which also saw Matthew Taylor replace Archibald Dryburgh as club Chairman.

The team's Scottish Cup form of the previous campaign could not be repeated when the tournament got under way on 21st January 1928, and Dundee United emerged victorious from the first round tie between the sides at Tannadice following stalemate at Bayview.

Winning league form returned following the cup exit, however, and seven of the following nine fixtures were won with the other two games ending all square. A 3-2 win against Dundee United on 24th March put the Fifers level on points with the Tannadice side and promotion was starting to look a distinct possibility. Indeed, the club had publicly stated earlier in the month that they were about to go 'all out for promotion' as it seemed likely that near neighbours Raith Rovers were about to be relegated and there was the distinct possibility that East Fife could become the district's top side.

The Fifers' hopes were dealt a severe blow in their next home match, however, when Stenhousemuir inflicted defeat by three goals to one. When Third Lanark emerged victors by the odd goal in five on 7th April in front of 8,000 at CathkinPark, the team slipped to fifth place in the table and the dream was all but over for another season.

As for Raith Rovers, the Kirkcaldy side staged a remarkable comeback over the final few games of the season and managed to escape relegation from Division One by finishing three points ahead of second bottom Bo'ness!

At East Fife's A.G.M. during the summer of 1928, it was reported that the club had never been in such a strong financial position. With funds available to freshen up the playing staff, the only players retained for the forthcoming campaign were goalkeeper Garth, defenders Duncan and McGachie and forwards Macbeth, Weir and Nairn.

Before the first pre-season trial match was held on 2nd August, right-half James Rarity was signed from Portobello Thistle and the services of inside-right Colin Brown were secured from Wallyford Bluebell. For the position of inside-left, David Kyle was signed from Law Scotia.

A further three players arrived at Bayview prior to the second trial match played on the following Thursday evening; centre-half Prentice from Beardmore Athletic, right-back Young from Cowdenbeath and forward Sharkey from St Ninians Thistle. Before the first competitive match of the season a further two players, Gabriel and Henderson, had joined the ranks.

Season 1928/29 kicked off at NewtonPark, Bo'ness, in dull and gloomy weather on a soft and treacherous pitch, where the performance of the new line-up almost matched the dreary conditions as the home side ran out 4-1 winners. A week later at Bayview the conditions were exactly the opposite, and the Fifers delighted the 3,000 crowd with a 4-2 win against Forfar Athletic in glorious weather.

As the season progressed, however, the leaky defence continued to give cause for concern and, by mid-October, no fewer than thirty league goals had been conceded.

The highest scoring match during this period was at Bayview on 15th September when Dundee United emerged victors by the odd goal in nine, but unfortunately the match hit the headlines for other reasons. Following the game, 250 Dundee United supporters rioted and fought with the police in Methil, and one policeman was struck with a bottle. Several visiting supporters were detained and appeared in Buckhaven Police Court on the following Monday morning.

In order to shore up the defence, Northern Ireland internationalist Joe Gowdy was signed from Falkirk at the beginning of October. Although the side still managed to concede five goals on Gowdy's debut against Leith Athletic at MarineGardens, a result which saw the Fifers slump to second bottom in the table, things started to look up with a 3-2 victory over Dunfermline at East EndPark on 13th October.

Following a 6-1 win against Queen of the South on Gowdy's home debut on 20th October and a 4-2 win at Alloa the following week it looked like the Fifers had finally put an end to their poor form.

Although there were further slip-ups before the end of the year, a league position of eighth was attained by mid-December.

There was a remarkable incident in the final match of the year, a home league fixture against Bo'ness on 29th December, which resulted in a 4-2 win for the home side. On a wet and greasy playing surface, on which both teams struggled to keep their feet, the visitors' centre-half Jock Fyffe was sent off following an 'unpleasant incident' when he 'deliberately turned McGachie upside down'.

What was notable about this incident? Unbelievably, it was the first time that any player had been sent off at Bayview during East Fife's entire twenty-five year existence! What made it all the more remarkable was that later in the match East Fife's Sharkey was also given his marching orders for retaliation after being fouled by Kelly.

The local press was quick to defend both culprits, saying that conditions had been very unpleasant both for the players and for the small crowd, which had 'put tempers on edge'.

On 19th January 1929, history was made when Partick Thistle visited Methil on competitive business for the first time. The occasion was the first round of the Scottish Cup at Bayview, where the First Division team proved to be too strong for the home side and progressed to the second round with a 2-1 victory in front of a 7,500 crowd.

Despite some impressive victories during the second half of the season, including a 6-2 demolition of Bathgate and a 5-1 trouncing of Dunfermline Athletic, the race for promotion was all but conceded with a disappointing run of three straight defeats during March. The *Leven Advertiser and Wemyss Gazette* carried an article towards the end of that month which, although expressing the opinion that the promotion challenge was over for another year, reported that things were looking promising for the future. The article went on to say that the players were gradually fitting together and playing more as a team, due mainly to the arrival of Joe Gowdy, whose presence was having a great steadying influence on the side.

"It is not too much to class East Fife as one of the three most attractive teams in the league to watch", the report went on. *" Their forte is attack rather than defence and the public, for whose entertainment they cater, clearly loves to see goals scored"*.

The report concluded that the nucleus of a real promotion side existed at Bayview and the club were fortunate to have at their disposal a set of enthusiastic players anxious to give their best. Another great servant during the 1928/29 season was Arthur McGachie, whose presence at the centre of the attack had resulted in hat tricks against both Clydebank and Bathgate and braces on a further eight occasions. Another prolific marksman was Phil Weir, who had scored doubles in five matches. Despite the attractive fare on offer, however, a loss of over £112 was reported for the season, due mainly to 'poor gates'. Incidentally, the 'poor gates' referred to averaged well over 2,000! What would the present East Fife board give to have their 2,000 seat Bayview Stadium filled to capacity every week?

At the Annual General Meeting on 24th June 1929, Chairman Taylor said that he would like to see more local talent developed to play for the club. *"During the playing season, one had only to see on Saturday morning, the number of young local players passing through Thornton Junction on their way to play for other clubs"*, stated the Chairman.

Ten players, Duncan, Gowdy, Rarity, McBeth, Gabriel, Weir, Brown, McGachie, Kyle and Nairn, were retained for season 1929/30 and former player Peter Barrett re-joined the club from Dundee to take up the position of inside-left. Added to that number were two new signings destined to make their mark on the Bayview turf in future seasons. Right-half Pat Casciani, who had 'learned the game on the coup in Dundee', was signed from Dundee North End, but the most notable signing, although not apparent at the time, was left winger Danny Liddle from Wallyford Bluebell. Within two years of signing, 'Dangerous Dan', as he was to become affectionately known, was to become East Fife's first full international cap, playing three times for Scotland in 1931.

The East Fife officials and supporters had every right to look forward to the 1929/30 season with optimism, and the Bayview grandstand was given a fresh lick of paint as the kick off approached. The interior of the dressing rooms was freshened up as well, with the drab army interior transformed to bright green by a team of volunteers.

The team was also to have a fresh set of strips for the new campaign, a luxury taken for granted in the modern game! Before the new season got under way, another new face was added to the playing staff with the addition of goalkeeper John Bernard from Kilmarnock. Described as 'a tall young man who combines brilliant anticipation with utter fearlessness', John was also the nephew of former Fife favourite Rab Bernard, who was influential in securing the player's signature.

The league campaign started well with a home win over Montrose and the good form continued as the season progressed. By mid-November only one league match had been lost, two had been drawn and no fewer than twelve had been won, including a 6-0 romp against Dunfermline Athletic at East EndPark and a 5-0 home win over Bo'ness.

On 23rd November 1929, table toppers Leith Athletic made the journey across the ForthBridge for a showdown with second placed East Fife. Football fever had by this time gripped Methil and a huge crowd of over 10,000 turned out for the match in which the league leaders scored three goals against a single counter from Phil Weir to take full points.

The Fifers bounced back from their disappointment in blistering fashion a week later with a 7-0 victory against Stenhousemuir at Bayview, where a crowd only one fifth the size of the previous week's attendance saw Arthur McGachie score four times, with the other goals coming from Nairn, Liddle and Weir.

The following two matches, both played away from home, were also eventful, but for entirely different reasons. On 7th December, throughout the match against Forfar Athletic at StationPark, the East Fife players had to contend with unsporting behaviour from the home crowd. The worst incident of the afternoon came when a spectator punched left-half Jimmy Gabriel in the face. The Fifers still managed to get the better of the home side, however, and won easily by four goals to one.

Unfortunately, a similar situation the following Saturday at VolunteerPark, Armadale, had an adverse effect on the outcome of the match. All through the first half, the home side entertained their supporters by kicking lumps out of the East Fife players. The crowd cheered every time one of the visiting players was fouled and, by half time, the game had degenerated into a farce.

During the second half the spectators decided that they, too, would like to get in on the action and a large number spilled on to the park behind Bernard's goal. The police were called to restore order and, when the dust finally settled at the end of the match, Fifers found themselves on the receiving end of a 3-2 defeat.

It would appear that the experience had a detrimental effect on the players' confidence. Over the following four weeks only two matches were won from six played, a sequence that included a home defeat from Raith Rovers in the New Year derby.

Another defeat sustained during this six-match spell was no less significant. On 11th January 1930, amidst speculation that star player Liddle was bound for Ibrox, fellow promotion contenders Albion Rovers emerged 3-0 victors in a crucial encounter at Cliftonhill.

Following a home defeat in the first round of the Scottish Cup at the hands of Queen of the South a week later, the promotion challenge was put back on track on 25th January with a 7-2 home win against Brechin City, but once again inconsistent form let the team down and lowly Dumbarton emerged victorious by the shock score of 6-3 in the following league fixture at Boghead. From that game until the end of the season, however, winning form returned. After taking full points from the next five matches against St Bernard's, Arbroath, Dunfermline Athletic, Bo'ness and King's Park, a league position of second was achieved, level on points with leaders Leith Athletic but with an inferior goal difference.

On 15th March 1930, a crowd of 5,000 turned out on a perfect spring afternoon for the league encounter against Third Lanark. Displaying the 'best exhibition of fighting spirit seen on their own ground this season', the match was won by two goals to nil, which opened up a four point gap over third placed Albion Rovers, who lost at home to Dunfermline on the same day. Enthusing about the performance, the local press claimed that promotion was now in sight.

Another bright and sunny day greeted the 3,500 spectators who attended the next league match against Queen of the

South at Bayview. Ground conditions were perfect as yet another convincing victory was recorded, during which Phil Weir equalled the club's record of 103 league goals in a season when he scored the fourth goal in the 4-1 win.

An aerial view of BayviewPark around 1930. The photo was certainly taken before the closure of the Wemyss and District Tramway in January 1932, as a tram can be seen passing in front of the Co-operative building in Wellesley Road, near to the junction with Fisher Street. Note that there are no 'penalty arcs' on the edge of the penalty areas, as these pitch markings not introduced until 1937. *(Author's collection)*

On Saturday 29th March the most crucial league match of the season was played at MarineGardens against Leith Athletic, where it was anticipated that the destination of the Second Division title could well be decided. Three special trains; two from Methil and one from Leven, helped to transport around 2,500 East Fife supporters to Edinburgh for the top of the table clash.

A crowd of 18,000, a record for a Second Division match, paid to see the showdown and few were disappointed, although the game finished goal-less.

"What a game it was at Marine Gardens!" enthused the *Leven Advertiser and Wemyss Gazette*, who went on to say that Joe Gowdy was the man of the match and had shown the form that had previously won him International honours with Northern Ireland. *"He was a superman"*, they claimed. Expecting yet another entertaining match, a special train to Larbert was laid on the following week for the encounter with Stenhousemuir at Ochilview. This time, however, the 300 travelling supporters were left bitterly disappointed following a 5-3 defeat.

Amazingly, the local press, who only the previous week had enthused about the performance in Leith, turned on the players. *"Are Joe Gowdy and his men going stale?"* they asked, adding that *"some of the players seemed tired and spiritless"*. Goalkeeper John Bernard was also singled out as one of the reasons for the promotion hopes being thrown into disarray, despite the fact that the custodian had performed heroics to keep a clean sheet against the league leaders just a week earlier. Little mention was given to the fact that the club's 1927 scoring record of 103 goals during a season had been broken during the same match!

All was forgiven on 12th April as Forfar Athletic were beaten 5-2 at Bayview in a match that also saw the Scottish League scoring record surpassed. The previous record of 109, set by Dunfermline Athletic in 1926, was equalled when Mitchell added a third in the second half following earlier strikes from Weir and Liddle. McGachie added a further brace to set the new record at 111 goals.

A home victory against Armadale at Bayview in the last league game of the season on 19th April 1930 would leave nearest challengers Albion Rovers having to win all three of their remaining matches to claim the second promotion place. Previewing the match, the *Leven Advertiser and Wemyss Gazette* commented not about the promotion winning aspect of the game, but referred to the previous unsavoury meeting between the sides:

"The heavier the revenge enacted by East Fife on Saturday the better will those who saw the match at Armadale be pleased. The conduct of the home players and spectators was a disgrace to Scottish Football".

Neither the local press or the spectators were disappointed as East Fife won promotion to the top flight for the first time in their history with a 3-0 win coupled with a 6-2 defeat for Albion Rovers at Stark's Park. Two goals from Tom Mitchell and a single from Joe Gowdy were the highlights in a match in which, according to press reports, East Fife appeared to be a well-balanced team in which every player pulled his weight. It seemed as though promotion had come at just the right time. The side had, since the influx of younger, fresher players two seasons previously, matured into a strong team capable of playing entertaining football and scoring goals.
Bearing in mind the fact that near neighbours Raith Rovers had failed to bounce straight back to the top flight and were about to start another season in Division Two, East Fife had never had a better chance to establish themselves as the district's top football club!

Chapter Nine: First Division Football Comes to Methil!

In preparation for the club's first season in the top flight, several important improvements were carried out at BayviewPark during the summer of 1930. As there was certain to be increased media interest over the forthcoming season, a press box was added to the front of the grandstand and telephones were installed at the east end of the pavilion to ensure match reports could be relayed to the various Saturday evening sports papers. In order to cope with the anticipated large crowds, additional turnstiles were installed at the west end of the ground.

The club were confident that, when all the improvements were in place, BayviewPark would have no problem in being passed fit for hosting First Division matches.

Interest amongst the supporters increased steadily over the close season. The first season tickets were ordered in late May and the club remained confident throughout the summer that at least a thousand would be sold before the start of the new campaign.

At the end of June the club held their Annual General Meeting in Bowling Green Hall, during which William Halley, John McArthur and Bailie Thomas Hogg were appointed to the Board. On the financial side, a healthy profit of £321 was declared for the season just finished.

Presiding over the meeting, Chairman William Moscrip stated:

"a provincial team such as ours is always at some disadvantage, but we are hopeful that we shall put on the field a team which will not disgrace Bayview".

By early July, Manager Walter Robertson reported that he had successfully negotiated terms with all of the previous season's team with the exception of Joe Gowdy and Arthur Mill. The

An undated crowd scene at Bayview, probably from the early 1930's. Note that almost every single man is wearing either a bunnet or hat, and also that it appears there are no women in the picture, unlike the present day, where females make up a fair percentage of the crowd! (Author's collection)

Directors were also reported to be negotiating at this time with Tom McInally, the former Celtic and SunderlandScotland internationalist, but the player eventually decided that his future lay elsewhere. Before the season got under way, both Gowdy and Mill had put pen to paper, which ensured that the promotion winning side was complete once more, with the addition of new signing Davie Moyes from Cowdenbeath. Interestingly, the Scottish Football League decided to schedule East Fife and Cowdenbeath's home fixtures for alternative Saturdays during season 1930/31. Being the County's top two teams, this arrangement was made in order to attract the best possible crowds to Bayview and Central Park and to avoid the problems associated with two first class football matches going ahead in Fife on the same afternoon. Raith Rovers and Dunfermline Athletic, both languishing in the Second Division, were considered to be much less of an attraction and just didn't fit into the equation!

East Fife's first match with the 'big boys' was played against Motherwell at Fir Park on 9th August 1930, where the home side recorded a comfortable 4-1 win in front of a 6,000 crowd. The Fife were 'beaten but not disgraced' according to the following edition of the *Leven Advertiser and Wemyss Gazette,* who went on to describe the Fifers' first goal in the top flight, when Joe Gowdy lobbed a loose ball down the middle of the park to Arthur McGachie, who collected and dashed between two defenders before firing an unstoppable shot into the corner of the net.

The following Saturday a crowd of 9,000 lined the Bayview terraces to witness the ground's First Division baptism against Dundee, where a Phil Weir strike was countered by 'two soft goals' for the visitors. The home side had been extremely unfortunate to lose, according to match reports.

Was victory just around the corner? Unfortunately not!

In the space of just a few weeks the Fifers were humiliated 6-1 by Hearts at Tynecastle, 6-2 at home to Celtic, 8-0 by Partick Thistle at Firhill and 5-1 against Airdrieonians at Bayview.

The seventh league match of the season, played in incessant rain at Central Park Cowdenbeath, on 20th September 1930, set a new club record of seven straight league defeats as the home side emerged victorious by two goals to one.

When victory finally arrived on the last Saturday in September, however, it arrived in style! Brown, McGachie, Gabriel and McCurley all found the net to send Ayr United packing with a 4-1 defeat at Bayview, but anyone expecting a turnaround in fortunes was to be sorely disappointed.

Although the losses became less severe as the end of the year approached, the club came to the decision that a new goalkeeper might help to keep the number of goals conceded down to a respectable level, and signed Steele from St Andrews Athletic in time for the following match against Kilmarnock at Rugby Park on 15th November.

The presence of Bernard's replacement certainly didn't help the situation. In actual fact the inclusion of the new signing in the team had exactly the opposite effect and, when the final whistle sounded at RugbyPark, Steele had had to pick the ball out of his own net five times. Believing that his debut had been too big an occasion, the club put Steele's inept performance down to first match nerves. For the trip to Hamilton the following week, the new signing was again entrusted with the goalkeeper's jersey, and this time the opposition found the net on just four occasions.

Determined to prove that they had not made a mistake in dropping Bernard, the same player made his first appearance at Bayview on 29th November where, despite a McGachie hat-trick and a single counter from Herbert, visitors Falkirk also scored four and the honours were shared.

Having lost no fewer than thirteen goals in three matches, Steele was dropped for the trip to Hampden to face Queen's Park at the beginning of December, and John Bernard was recalled.

The outcome was no better, however, as Bernard was asked to pick the ball out of the net five times as the 'Spiders' inflicted yet another heavy defeat!

After losing heavily to Rangers a week later, a point was won at Bayview on 20th December 1930 against Motherwell, but the match was marred by a serious injury to centre-forward Phil Weir. After having scored the Fifers' only goal of the afternoon, Weir was knocked out in a collision with Motherwell's Johnman. Unable to revive the player at the scene, the decision was taken to ferry Weir to hospital, where he remained in a coma on Saturday night.

The following day, however, the player made a remarkable recovery and, amazingly, volunteered to return to work on the Monday morning. They made them tougher in those days!

Another 1930s crowd scene at Bayview. Note the small boy peering through the barrier at the front, who has probably been passed to the front over the heads of the spectators behind him. (Author's collection)

The turn of the year brought a long overdue change in fortunes. On a bitterly cold New Year's Day on a sand covered Bayview pitch, the points were shared in a no scoring draw with Cowdenbeath. Three days later came the second league win of the season when Hearts visited Methil on competitive business for the first time and were beaten by a single goal. Predictably, the improvement in form didn't last and, following defeat at Ayr on 5th January 1931, the Fifers suffered a humiliating defeat from Celtic in Glasgow five days later. With the legendary Jimmy McGrory in dazzling form, the 'hoops' found the net no fewer than nine times before the final whistle sounded, with McGrory bagging five! It signalled a new record league defeat for East Fife and equalled the club's record defeat suffered at the hands of Cowdenbeath in the Wemyss Cup five years earlier.

The following Saturday presented the opportunity to avenge the humiliation when Celtic visited Methil for a Scottish Cup first round tie. The idea of the home side somehow managing to knock Celtic out of the cup only a week after their drubbing in Glasgow was perhaps a little ambitious, but at least some pride was regained as Celtic only narrowly managed to reach round two courtesy of a 2-1 victory. Indeed, had it not been for the heroics of the legendary John Thomson in the visitors' goal, the home side could well have forced a replay or even managed to win the tie!

After losing the next two games, the latter a 6-1 reverse against Leith Athletic, the decision was taken to drop Bernard once again and give Steele a second chance between the sticks. The result was a 3-2 home victory over St Mirren on 7th February, only the third league win of the season.

As the end of the season approached, form improved dramatically, and further wins were recorded against Hibernian, Kilmarnock, Hamilton and Airdrieonians. With three league matches remaining, the Fifers had managed to pull themselves back to just two points behind second bottom Ayr United and four points adrift of Hibernian.

Theoretically, it was still possible for East Fife to avoid the drop as they lined up against Falkirk at Brockville on 11th April but, with Hibs beating Hamilton Academical on the same day, a 1-0 defeat brought relegation with two games still to play.

A little of the gloom was lifted with victory over Queen's Park in the penultimate league match and, on the last day of the league season, Bayview had the honour of hosting the First Division Championship decider.

Rangers, with Celtic breathing down their necks three points behind and with a game in hand, went into the match on 25th April 1931 knowing that victory would bring the league flag to Ibrox. They were not to be disappointed as the match finished 4-0 to the light blues in front of a surprisingly small attendance of only 7,000.

Shortly after the curtain came down on the Fifers' venture into the First Division, the club received the honour of having a player selected to represent Scotland for the first time when Dan Liddle was picked to play for his country against Austria in Vienna on 16th May 1931. Unfortunately, the occasion was not as memorable as 'Dangerous Dan' would have wished as the home country pulled off a shock 5-0 win. Liddle kept his place in the side as Scotland travelled south to Rome to face Italy four days later, where again the touring side tasted defeat, this time by three goals without reply. The third and final match of the tour was played against Switzerland in Geneva on May 24th, where again Liddle pulled on the No.11 jersey. Some international pride was restored as the Scots won by the odd goal in five, but the East Fife forward failed to get his name on the score sheet with the goals credited to Easson, Boyd and Love.

Financially, the season in the top flight proved disastrous. Despite average home gates of around 5,500, the club reported an overall loss of £553, a huge amount considering the 'healthy profit' disclosed at the end of the previous campaign. The total takings at the Bayview turnstiles over the course of the season amounted to a disappointing £3,751. With guarantees paid to visiting clubs over the same period totalling £2,310, the situation arose more often than not that the hosts had gained far less in financial terms from games played in Methil than their opponents!

Preparing for the new season back in the Second Division, the club announced in July 1931 that they had successfully retained the services of Steele, Casciani, Duncan, McKee, Hamilton, Brown, Feeney, Weir, Lowry, McGachie, Herbert, Liddle and Mitchell. Before the new campaign got under way, the names of Hugh Shaw, Willie Gillespie and John Herbert had been added to the squad and John McCurley was signed on loan from Newcastle United. Out of favour, however, were Davie Moyes, Arthur Mill, John Bernard, Joe Gowdy, Colin Brown and John Bruce, who were all placed on the transfer list.

Despite having retained the nucleus of the side, the 1931/32 season proved to be largely uneventful.

A disappointing start to the league campaign was made, with only one point gained from the first three matches. Indeed, had it not been for a remarkable three goal second half comeback against Stenhousemuir at Bayview on 8th August, the opening three matches would have been lost.

There were, eventually, some notable wins over the course of the season, including a 7-0 triumph over EdinburghCity at MarineGardens and a 7-1 home victory over King's Park. Along with the emphatic victories, however, there were also some embarrassing defeats, not least the 6-1 hammering dished out by Forfar Athletic at StationPark on 9th January 1932. Due to the inconsistent form, the entire season passed without even the hint of a serious promotion challenge being mounted.

The Scottish Cup was also a disappointment, with Kilmarnock emerging 4-1 victors in the first round tie at RugbyPark on 16th January 1932.

The Fifers' finished in eighth place in the Second Division, three points behind seventh placed Hibernian and fourteen points adrift of Champions East Stirlingshire.

As the season drew to a close, some considerable enjoyment was created with the resounding 8-1 demolition of Dunfermline Athletic at Bayview in the semi-final of the Fife Cup on 20th April. The trophy found its way into the Bayview trophy cabinet ten days later when Cowdenbeath were beaten 3-1 in the final.

The summer of 1932 saw the inevitable departure of one of Bayview's most skilful players, when 'Dangerous Dan' Liddle signed for LeicesterCity. Signed at the beginning of the 1929/30 season, Liddle made 103 appearances during his three years with the club and, as mentioned earlier in this chapter, became the first player to be capped for Scotland whilst plying his trade with the Methil club.

The 1932/33 season proved to be just as disappointing as the previous campaign. New signings Marshall, Walker, Blair, Davies and Sharp made their debuts in glorious sunny conditions in the opening league match at Forfar on 13th August, but unfortunately the game was not as enjoyable as the weather conditions and the 'Loons' scored three without reply.

Although three of the following four league matches were won, indifferent form saw the club drop to sixteenth position in the table before climbing back into the top half of the league by the end of the year. There were, however, some high scoring wins during that same period. The biggest victory of the season came on 15th October 1932, when Armadale were trounced 8-1 at Bayview to warm the hearts of the 1,000 spectators who lined the terraces on a cold and gloomy afternoon. Two weeks later a slightly larger gathering witnessed the 6-1 demolition of Leith Athletic. On 12th November the Bayview faithful were treated to their third emphatic win in a row when Albion Rovers were on the receiving end of a 6-1 thrashing, with four of the Fifers goals scored by junior trialist Farren from St Andrews United. The score would actually have been much higher had it not been for the fact that the inexperienced youngster appeared not to fully understand the offside rule and was pulled up continually throughout the game!

Two league games in as many days heralded the beginning of 1933, with a 2-1 home win over Raith Rovers on 2nd January followed by a 5-3 defeat against Queen of the South in Dumfries. The heavy playing and travelling schedule was hardly the ideal preparation for the visit of eventual league winners Hibernian to Bayview the following Saturday, who scored five without reply to inflict the Fifers' biggest home defeat of the season.

With promotion now seeming unlikely to say the least, all attention was switched to the Scottish Cup and the first round fixture against St Johnstone in Perth on 21st January. Nobody gave the Second Division side much of a chance against a side that was still in the running for the First Division Championship but, on a snow covered MuirtonPark, the visitors produced their renowned cup fighting spirit to force a 2-2 draw. The replay was scheduled for Bayview on the following Wednesday afternoon with a 2:30 kick off and, with Methil and its environs once again gripped in cup fever, the Wemyss Coal Company generously allowed its employees time off work to see the game. Many of the other local employers followed suit, which resulted in a bumper crowd of 7,061 lining the terraces on a sunny but bitterly cold afternoon. Unfortunately for the majority of the crowd, however, the 'Saints' adapted to the icebound playing surface better than their hosts and progressed to round two with a narrow 2-1 victory.

Back on league business, three defeats in succession at Stark's Park, Boghead and East EndPark all but extinguished any faint glimmer of promotion and the club started to think about re-building the side for the following season. Consequently, several trialists were fielded in the remaining league fixtures as the club officials looked to the future.

A certain amount of apathy towards the league competition also started to creep in as the season drew to a close and, on 11th March, the club even took the liberty of including a number of reserves for the home league fixture with BrechinCity. It was certainly no co-incidence that a strong side was required to face Celtic in a Second XI Cup tie in Glasgow on the same afternoon!

The league season finished with the Fife in seventh place, twenty points behind champions Hibernian, but some consolation was gained when the Fife Cup was won for the third season in succession with a 2-1 final win against Raith Rovers.

During the summer of 1933, Chairman Moscrip and his Board of Directors decided that the time was right once again to clear out the 'dead wood', and duly announced that only six of the current playing staff would be offered terms for the coming season. The players in question, Alex Sharp, Pat Casciani, Phil Weir, Robert McCartney, John Herbert and William Walker, all accepted the terms on offer and put pen to paper. Added to that number was John McCurley, still on loan from Newcastle United, where he had been on the transfer list for several years.

Free transfers were handed to William Wilkie, Alex Duncan, James Hope, Arthur McGachie and William Marshall, with Tommy Boyce placed on the open to transfer list.

Presiding over the club's A.G.M. on June 8th 1933, Chairman Moscrip stated that the club felt it had not had value for money from certain players during season 1932/33, which was the reason that only seven players had been retained, adding that players' wages would, in future, be more in keeping with the rest of the Second Division.

Several new faces arrived at Bayview as season 1933/34 approached, including Archibald Pratt from Heart of Midlothian, James Morrison from Airdrieonians and Miller from Wellesley Juniors.

Of the players considered surplus to requirements, Arthur McGachie was quickly snapped up by Dunfermline Athletic, where he remained for only six months before being transferred to Cowdenbeath.

Uncomfortably hot weather greeted the players for the first pre-season trial match at Bayview on 5th August, watched by 1,500 spectators. Following the second trial held two days later, a new-look East Fife side was assembled for the opening league fixture against Dundee United at Tannadice.

Although all three goals in the 3-1 win were scored by players retained from the previous campaign, namely McCartney, Walker and Herbert, the side had a completely new look.

In goal was John Kelly, signed from Arbroath. Old favourite Pat Casciani along with new signing Archie Pratt occupied the full-back positions. At right and left-half, respectively, were Alex Sharp and newcomer Peter Ronan from CardiffCity. Recent signing James Morrison filled the position of centre-half.

The forward line consisted of four players retained from the previous season, Weir, McCartney, Herbert and Walker, with the addition of George Scott from Lochgelly Albert at inside-right.

Following the opening day victory, inconsistent form kept the Fifers anchored in a mid-table position, although good individual performances by one player in particular did not go unnoticed by the International League Selection Committee. At the end of September, William Walker was included as reserve outside-left for the Scottish League's match against the Irish League in Belfast, but in the event the player's services were not required and, instead of travelling to Northern Ireland, Walker played and scored for his club in the 6-3 league win against BrechinCity.

As the end of the year approached, performances on the field continued to blow hot and cold, with results totally unpredictable. Typical of this erratic form was the two defeats suffered in quick succession at the hands of mediocre East Stirlingshire and Arbroath, followed by a 4-1 victory at home to league leaders Stenhousemuir in their next fixture on 11th November!

Christmas seemed to have come early when Dundee United were thumped 5-1 at Bayview on 23rd December and hopes were high that a change in fortunes was on the cards at last, but yet again consistency eluded the side.

A point was dropped against the worst team in the league, EdinburghCity, at Powderhall on Christmas Day then, a week later, Raith Rovers handed out a 6-2 thrashing at Bayview in the New Year derby!

There was an interesting occurrence in the next home league match, against Dumbarton on 6th January. The advent of the neutral linesman was still a long way off in 1934, and officials were appointed from each side to 'run the line', a similar arrangement to modern-day amateur matches. East Fife Director William Halley was appointed linesman for the fixture with Dumbarton and, during the match, raised his flag to draw the attention of referee McCutcheon to an infringement. The referee came over and warned Halley that club officials were not allowed to try to influence the referee, to which Halley argued that he was only trying to attract the referee's attention to an incident.

The referee didn't take too kindly to the East Fife official talking back to him, and promptly sent Halley to the pavilion. Director John McArthur replaced Halley on the touchline and, no doubt, remained tight lipped for the remainder of the game!

As with the previous season, the Fifers looked to the Scottish Cup to take their minds off the poor league form and, once again, it was destination Perth to take on St Johnstone in the first round at Muirton. This time around, however, there was to be no holding the First Division side and the 7,400 crowd witnessed a comfortable 3-1 victory for the Perth team.

The remainder of the league fixtures were played out with the same inconsistent form that had, by now, become a trademark. When the final whistle sounded on the last day of the season, the Fifers found themselves occupying thirteenth place in the table, their worst final position since being admitted to the Scottish League thirteen years earlier.

As the curtain came down on season 1933/34, one of the club's most promising players, William Walker, was transferred to Falkirk for a small fee. The disappointment of losing a player of Walker's calibre didn't auger well for the future, but was compensated for with the signing of one Joe Cowan from near neighbours Raith Rovers.

Cowan had been a fans' favourite at Stark's Park and was rated highly by the Rovers who, not surprisingly, were reluctant to part with their star player.

Keen to sign for East Fife, however, the former Wellesley Juniors and Celtic player successfully took his case for a free transfer to the SFA and duly arrived at Bayview in time for the new season.

Confident that the arrival of Cowan would make the forthcoming campaign one to remember, a crowd of over 2,000 attended the pre-season trial match at Bayview on 4th August 1934.

The nucleus of the side which faced newly relegated Third Lanark at CathkinPark for the opening league match of season 1934/35 was largely the same as had finished the previous campaign, with the addition of Cowan at centre-forward, Crozier replacing McKinlay in goal and McLeish replacing Walker on the left wing.

Results for August proved disappointing, however, with the heavy league defeats suffered at the hands of Third Lanark and Alloa Athletic countered only by a single goal win against Morton.

The Methil Men also lost their grip on the Fife Cup during the same period, with a 5-2 first round defeat at Stark's Park.

The following month was an entirely different story!

Nine league points were gained from a possible ten during September, during which 19 goals were scored against 5 conceded. The most impressive performance during this successful spell came in the form of a 9-1 home win over Dumbarton, when Joe Cowan found the net a record seven times!

The impressive form continued until mid-November, by which time a further four victories, two narrow defeats and a draw had been added to the tally.

The side came down to earth with a huge bump on 24th November against St Bernard's at the Royal Gymnasium, where the home side inflicted a 6-1 defeat. As if the result wasn't bad enough to take, the team disgraced themselves by conceding three penalties and having two players sent off over the ninety minutes!

The heavy reverse seemed to dent the team's confidence in a big way, and a 5-1 defeat against King's Park in Stirling the following Saturday was followed by defeat at Stenhousemuir on 8th December. With the loss of Alex Sharp to Blackburn Rovers at the beginning of the month adding to the club's woes, something had to be done, and done quickly, to restore the flagging confidence.

Sharp was replaced at inside-left by John Steele, signed from Lesmahagow Juniors, and John Phillips, an outside-left, was signed from St Mirren.

The fresh faces brought an immediate turnaround in fortunes. Both players made their home debuts against Montrose on 15th December, and both found the net in a 4-2 victory.

In the two remaining matches before the end of the year, both Cowdenbeath and Leith Athletic were defeated, and a 3-0 win against Raith Rovers in the New Year derby put the icing on the cake.

However, the Fifers proved once again that pride comes before a fall and, in a disastrous series of league results that lasted from early January until mid-April, only five points were won from a possible twenty-two.

The sequence started with a 4-0 defeat from Dundee United at Tannadice on 5th January 1935, when regular 'keeper Crozier was ruled out with 'flu. His place between the posts was filled by Methven, on loan from Bowhill Rovers, who performed heroics to keep the home forwards at bay despite conceding four goals. The junior goalkeeper kept his place in the side to face Morton at Cappielow the following week, where the Greenock side truly rubbed his face in the mud by scoring eight to record their biggest ever win over the Fifers!

With the return of Crozier for the meeting with Edinburgh City at Bayview on 19th January, winning form returned and a 3-1 win was followed by a fine 5-0 victory against Forfar Athletic the following Saturday.

A share of the points with Cowdenbeath at Central Park in the next match was followed by a straight run of six defeats as the club dropped from promotion challengers to also-rans. By the time the penultimate home match of the season was played against BrechinCity on 6th April, apathy amongst the supporters had become so great that only 300 paid to see the match.

Once again the decision was taken to experiment with trialists as the 1934/35 season drew to a close, but despite a 6-1 win against Stenhousemuir in the final league match, the future looked anything but rosy in the eyes of the Bayview faithful. Time is a great healer, however, and before the end of the summer break, the optimists were once again looking forward to the new season.

"Hope springs eternal in the human breast", remarked the *Leven Advertiser and Wemyss Gazette* in their 1935/36 season preview, before going on to express the view that East Fife are capable of better things.

The report then described a certain new signing from Neilston Victoria as *"one of the most fancied juniors of last season"*. *"There is not much of him"*, the report went on, *"but what there is, is good"*. Little did the press realise that the player in question was to become a household name and club legend over the years to come. The new player was none other than future star Tommy Adams, destined to make his mark on the right wing over the next fourteen years.

Other new signings included former Partick Thistle, Alloa and KingsPark right-back John Young, left-back Early from Woodhall Thistle and provisional signing D. H. Cameron from Denbeath Star.

Following the pre-season trial match on 6th August 1935, the local press were even more enthusiastic about the prospects for the new season, stating: *"The defensive resources of the club inspire every confidence"*.

In reality, the defence was found to be sadly lacking, highlighted by the 6-1 thrashing handed out by newly relegated St Mirren on the opening day of the season at Bayview, which stands to this day as the Paisley side's record win against East Fife. The only positive thing about the match from the home side's point of view was the performance of Tommy Adams, who made a scoring debut.

Only one league win was recorded before the end of September from eight matches played as the club became firmly rooted in the lower echelons of the table.

The situation started to improve with a comfortable 3-1 home win against Raith Rovers on 5th October, followed by a 6-1 crushing of Montrose a week later, in which George Scott scored a hat-trick.

In the eleven league games played before the end of the year a further six wins were recorded, along with three draws and only two defeats.

A further three wins from four games during January 1936, including a 2-1 win at Stark's Park on New Year's Day, saw the Fifers back challenging for a promotion place once more. There was also the prospect of a bumper pay day, win or lose, in the Scottish Cup, as the draw presented East Fife with a trip to Ibrox in the first round. Inclement weather, however, forced the postponement of the tie on Saturday 25th January and the game was re-scheduled for the following Wednesday. Despite the fact that there was little improvement in ground conditions prior to the replay, the match went ahead on an ice covered park on a bitterly cold evening in direct competition to the attractive Third Lanark v Hearts cup-tie at CathkinPark. The result was a poor crowd of only 3,000 at Ibrox, an equally poor pay cheque of £50 less expenses to take back to Methil, and exit from the competition with a 3-1 defeat!

A youthful Tommy Adams sits on the extreme left of the front row in this team photograph taken during the 1935/36 season. Back row, from left: Pat Casciani, John Young, Joe Crozier, David Russell, John Snedden, Robert McCartney. Front row, from left: Tommy Adams, George Scott, Joe Cowan, John Steele, William Downie. (Author's Collection)

Back on league business, disappointing results followed the cup exit, with heavy defeats against both East Stirlingshire and Forfar Athletic effectively ending promotion prospects for another season. There was, however, an improvement in form as the league season drew to a close, which climaxed with the visit of King's Park to Methil on 14th March. In front of one of the lowest crowds of the season, centre-forward Joe Cowan was in dazzling form and found the net no fewer than six times in the 9-2 demolition of the Stirling club, despite fielding juniors Hutchison of Denbeath Star at left-half and Cord of Wellesley Juniors in goal.

Back to full strength the following Saturday, East Fife travelled over the Forth to play league leaders Falkirk at Brockville, where the smiles were well and truly wiped from their faces with an embarrassing 8-0 defeat! The win clinched promotion for the 'Bairns', who went on to win the Second Division Championship after only one season 'downstairs'.

A 3-1 win at Montrose in the last league game of the season secured a final position of sixth in the 18-team league, fourteen points short of a promotion place.

Some pride was restored with the 3-0 defeat of First Division Dunfermline Athletic in the final of the Wemyss Cup at East EndPark on 29th April, following wins against Cowdenbeath and Raith Rovers in the previous rounds.

The 1935/36 season concluded with an honorary social held to commemorate the contribution made to the club by long serving player Phil Weir. Signed from Edinburgh Emmet in 1922, Weir made 421 appearances during which he netted 225 goals, a club record which still stands.

During the summer of 1936, the *Leven Advertiser* once again abounded with enthusiasm for the forthcoming season, stating that the outlook at Bayview was the brightest for a long time. For once, it seemed as if the local press had got it right! Following the trial match on the first day of August, the Fife Cup ties which had been held over from the previous season were played off, which resulted in the Fife Cup joining the Wemyss Cup in the Bayview trophy cabinet following convincing wins against Burntisland Shipyard and Raith Rovers.

The league programme started with a goal-less draw at Brechin, but was quickly followed up with three straight wins against St Bernard's, Alloa Athletic and King's Park as the club moved up to second place in the table.

The next league match against league leaders Raith Rovers attracted a bumper crowd of 12,177 to Stark's Park, where the points were shared in a 2-2 draw.

With the following two games against Morton and Airdrieonians also ending all square, it was almost the end of September before the first defeat of the season arrived when Dumbarton took both league points with a 2-1 win at Bayview.

There then followed the inevitable slump, and the following two games were lost at Ayr and Cowdenbeath as the Fifers slipped down to mid-table.

Few held out much hope for an improvement when form side Alloa Athletic, unbeaten for seven weeks, arrived in Methil on 17th October for a league encounter. In their typically unpredictable style, however, the home side recorded their first win for seven weeks; both goals in the 2-0 victory coming from recent signing Willie Carver from Arbroath.

A slight improvement in form as the onslaught of winter approached saw the promotion challenge maintained and the return of Eddie McLeod to the team for the visit of BrechinCity a week before Christmas was, according to the local press, the reason behind an emphatic 7-0 win.

On New Year's Day 1937, a crowd of over 9,000 attended the derby with Raith Rovers at Bayview, where they were entertained by a thrilling encounter between the local rivals. The Kirkcaldy side, having dominated the match for the first hour, were 3-0 in front when the home side decided to roll their sleeves up. With thirty minutes remaining, Young pulled a goal back with a shot which hit both posts before crossing the line. McLeod then reduced the deficit to only one goal before Tommy Adams squared the match with only seven minutes remaining. Just when it seemed as if the points would be shared, Rovers' outside-right Glen scored his side's fourth in the final minute to take both points back to the 'Lang Toun'.

Despite losing to Dumbarton the following day, the promotion challenge was put back on track with three straight league wins against Airdrieonians, Leith Athletic and East Stirlingshire. The match against Leith at Bayview on 16th January 1937 was notable for a sporting incident that occurred when East Fife's Russell was knocked out by the ball, presenting the visitors' Meikleham with a clear run in on goal. Rather than take advantage of the situation, however, the Leith man elected to kick the ball out of play and assist the injured Fifer, a gesture which was much appreciated by the home supporters.

On 30th January, the East Fife team and officials set out for Forfar for a Scottish Cup first round tie at Station Park, but heavy snow forced the postponement of the match shortly after the party had arrived at the ground. On their return journey, the weather conditions deteriorated rapidly and the team 'bus became stranded along with other vehicles in five foot snowdrifts. The players tried unsuccessfully to dig the vehicles out, and eventually decided to set out on foot for the nearest town. After trudging for over a mile through snow which was never less than a foot deep, they arrived in Tealing, where they managed to board a service 'bus bound for Dundee.

The re-scheduled match was won 3-0 on the following Thursday at the same venue with goals from Adams, Downie and Scott.

Round two of the competition handed the Fifers a long trip to Inverness for a match with Highland League side Caledonian. The ever-considerate East Fife Board, mindful of the fact that the long journey north might dissuade many supporters from travelling, decided to lay on a special train for the occasion which would also accommodate the official party.

In addition, it was announced that the first 120 supporters who bought tickets for the journey would be able to travel at the special rate of 7/6 (37½p), with the club making up the overall shortfall of £20.

The generous offer was taken up and a most enjoyable day out in the Highlands was had by all, with the 6-1 victory over Caley the icing on the cake. The *Leven Advertiser and Wemyss Gazette* enthused over the occasion:

"The special, comprising of five up to date and very comfortable saloon coaches and a restaurant car, was probably the most modern conveyance to pass through the Methil and Buckhaven stations and without a doubt it contributed immensely to the pleasure and enjoyment of the trip. Another very pleasing feature was the fact that the passengers did not require to make a single change throughout the whole journey. When the party of 200, including the team and officials, departed at 8:30 the weather was dull and not too pleasant. Within an hour, the train pulled in at Perth, where two engines were coupled on for the long climb northwards. The journey resumed and only a few more miles were covered before the beautiful scenery which made it such a delightful trip was reached".

Back on home soil for the third round of the competition, Celtic were the visitors to Methil on 27th February 1937. Any hopes the home side had of pulling off a shock were dashed when Jimmy McGrory effectively ended the tie with two goals in the first quarter of an hour and the Glasgow side went on to enjoy a 3-0 win in front of a 12,069 crowd.

Having picked up only one league point from the two league matches played between the cup ties, the promotion challenge was once again wrecked with defeat in the two matches following the cup exit.

A 3-0 defeat from St Bernard's at Stockbridge Gymnasium on 6th March, the day after inside-right George Scott departed for Aberdeen for an undisclosed fee, was followed by a humiliating 4-0 home defeat at the hands of Cowdenbeath.

The reversal in form brought about a complete re-shuffle of the team for the visit of Forfar Athletic to Bayview on 27th

March, and the positional changes and replacements had the desired effect. Goals from Adams, Cowan and McCartney secured a 3-1 win for the home side as the Fifers' found the net for the first time in five matches.

The following Saturday a McCartney hat trick, a brace from McLeod and singles from Campbell, Adams and Cowan secured an 8-2 win against EdinburghCity at Powderhall. Further wins in the two remaining league games against Montrose and Ayr United secured fifth place in the final league table, the club's best finish since promotion was won in 1930.

Despite missing out on promotion yet again, there had certainly been signs of a steady improvement in recent seasons, and the East Fife faithful were certain that success lay just around the corner. Even the most die-hard follower would not have dared predict just how successful the club were destined to be over the season which was to follow!

Chapter Ten: Their Finest Hour

The 1937/38 season dawned with an air of pessimism, following a long illness endured by Dave McLean over the summer months. The Manager's lengthy absence from duty left the preparations for the new campaign in disarray, with new signings required following the departure of inside-forward George Scott to Aberdeen and goalkeeper Joe Crozier to Brentford. By early August the goalkeeping problem had been overcome with the signing of former Dundee United custodian James Milton as first choice 'keeper and Hector Simpson from Kennoway Amateurs as his understudy. The addition of centre-half Tom Gray from Ayr United helped strengthen the pool, but as the new season approached the club were still looking to fill Scott's inside-forward position and were still in need of an outside-left and a left-half.

All three new signings played well in the pre-season trial at Bayview on 7th August and, the following Saturday, it was a confident East Fife side that lined up to face Alloa Athletic at home in the first league match of the season, despite the aforementioned weakness on the left flank. Two goals from Eddie McLeod along with a Sneddon penalty proved enough to overcome the Clackmannanshire outfit on a dreary afternoon in front of a disappointing crowd of 2,000.

During the following midweek the club finally managed to secure the services of a left-half in the form of former Scottish internationalist Andy Herd from Hearts. Herd made his debut against King's Park at Forthbank two days later, where goals from McLeod and McCartney maintained the promising start to the campaign with a 2-0 win.

On Saturday 28th August however, following a 4-2 victory over Cowdenbeath in the Wemyss Cup final held over from the previous season, the Methil Men came back down to earth with a bump as Albion Rovers took both league points at Bayview with a 2-1 win. Lack of fitness amongst the playing staff was blamed for the poor run that followed, which included a 5-3 home defeat in the local derby against Raith Rovers in front of over 11,000 at Bayview on 11th September. Better days were just around the corner, however, and a 4-1 home win against Dumbarton on 9th October signalled the start of a ten match unbeaten league run during which only one point was dropped, against Airdrieonians at Broomfield on 20th November.

Two very influential players were added to the side during this period. Inside-forward Larry Millar played his first match for the Fifers against Dumbarton on 9th October 1937 and, just a week later, Willie Laird started his long and distinguished association with East Fife in the home fixture against Airdrieonians.

The final victory in the winning sequence came on 11th December 1937 at Bayview, where visitors EdinburghCity were trounced by the Fifers' all-time record score of 13-2 in atrocious weather conditions. What a shame there were only 1,500 spectators present to witness the feat!

The match kicked off in driving snow and, after surviving early pressure from the visitors, East Fife took the lead through Joe Cowan before adding a further two goals through Henderson and McLeod. The visitors hit back and Carruthers scored twice to reduce the leeway to just one goal at half time. The second forty-five minutes belonged entirely to the home side, however, and a hat-trick from Tommy Adams, braces from McLeod, Sneddon and McCartney along with an own goal made the tally thirteen by the time the final whistle sounded.

Not only does this score still stand as East Fife's record win, it also turned out to be the biggest Second Division score-line of the Twentieth Century!

The win saw the Fifers climb up to second place in the league table, three points behind leaders Raith Rovers, but having played a game more.

Despite losing the next league match by the odd goal in five at Dumbarton, a 4-0 home win against King's Park on Christmas Day had the supporters eagerly awaiting the mouth-watering clash with Raith Rovers at Stark's Park on New Year's Day 1938.

A special train was run from Anstruther to Kirkcaldy via Leven and CameronBridge and another from Methil, Buckhaven and Wemyss, such was the interest in the match. The result was a Second Division record attendance of 19,700, but the actual number of spectators who witnessed the match will never be known as a gate was forced before kick-off and several hundred saw the game for free!

Goals from McLeod and Cowan either side of half-time gave East Fife a commanding 2-0 lead before the Rovers pulled a goal back through Whitelaw. The Kirkcaldy side's hopes of staging a comeback were dashed with only a minute remaining when an own goal sealed victory for the Methil Men. Indeed, the visitors would actually have added a fourth before the final whistle but for a penalty save from Raith custodian McKay!

The challenge at the top of the table was maintained two days later with a 6-2 home win against Montrose, but defeat at Stenhousemuir on 8th January, followed by a share of the points at home to St Bernard's, severely dented the Fife's promotion hopes.

At this point, however, we shall take a break from the rigours of the league to concentrate on the epic tale of the Fifers' 1938 Scottish Cup success.

The story began at BroomfieldPark, Airdrie, on 22nd January, where the home side entertained East Fife in what was considered to be one of the less attractive fixtures of the first round. Nevertheless, several hundred Fifers considered the tie alluring enough to travel through by special train and a crowd of 5,000 was assembled inside the ground when both teams took to the field. After a goal-less first half, it looked like the home side were destined for the second round when they took the lead midway through the second period. The visitors had other ideas, however, and two goals from Robert McCartney during the final quarter-of-an-hour were enough to book the Fifers a place in round two.

A home tie against Dundee United was the prize, and the match against the team that had humbled Hearts in the opening round was played at Bayview on 12th February. There was to be no repeat of the dazzling form that saw United pull off a sensational 3-1 win against the mighty Edinburgh side, however, and 11,000 spectators watched Adams, McLeod, McCartney, Millar and Henderson all score without reply to record a comfortable 5-0 victory.

Few gave East Fife much hope of progressing further in the competition when they were paired with Aberdeen in round three, despite the tie being scheduled for Methil. The home side confounded their critics, however, and a record crowd of 17,000 were treated to an entertaining match on 5th March. After the 'Dons' had taken the lead in seventeen minutes, the Fifers came more into the game and Joe Cowan scored a deserved equaliser on the stroke of half time. Despite some near things at both ends of the park during the second half, there was no further scoring and the two sides had it all to do again in the replay at Pittodrie.

Even the most optimistic 'Methilite' would have thought that their side's chance to overcome the First Division high fliers had gone, but this didn't deter several hundred making the journey north by special train for the deciding game four days after the stalemate at Bayview. Once again Aberdeen took the lead, and once again the Fifers equalised on the stroke of half time, this time through an Andy Herd penalty. Just after the re-start, the visitors belied their Second Division status by taking the lead through Larry Millar, who headed home from a Tommy Adams free kick. Despite having to endure intense Aberdeen pressure for the remainder of the match, there was no further scoring and the victorious East Fife team received a heroes welcome when they disembarked from the train on their return to Methil.

Near neighbours Raith Rovers were also having a successful cup run, and they too managed to pull off a shock against higher league opposition in the third round in the shape of Partick Thistle. When the draw for the quarter-finals pitched the two local rivals against each other at Bayview on 19th March, cup fever took hold in the east of the county!

Both clubs agreed that, in light of the keen interest in the tie, admission would be raised to 2/- (10p) for entry to the ground, 3/- (15p) for the small enclosure in front of the grandstand, 5/- (25p) for a seat in the centre of the grandstand and 4/- (20p) for the wings. In addition, it was agreed that the match would be all-ticket, with the crowd limit set at 17,000.

Tickets went on sale at Bayview on Monday 14th March, and all were sold within an hour!

Not wishing to pass up the opportunity to rake in a few extra pounds, the club decided to print a further 2,000 tickets, which resulted in a new ground record of 18,642 packing the Bayview terraces for the big match.

In the event the game turned out to be a tense and nervous affair, but there was no lack of excitement with both sides managing to create several scoring opportunities. As half-time approached, the Methil Men piled pressure on the Rovers goal, but just couldn't break down their stubborn defence. Two goals inside the first fifteen minutes of the second period through Larry Millar and Eddie McLeod, however, had East Fife cruising. Indeed, the lead could well have been stretched even further before Rovers pulled a goal back against the run of play through Joyner. Just when it looked as though the home side had booked their place in the semi-final, Whitelaw equalised from the penalty spot in the dying minutes to force a replay.

An even larger crowd of 25,500, again a record attendance, packed into Stark's Park on the afternoon of Wednesday 23rd March for the second game. With the draw for the semi-finals already made, an encounter with fellow Second Division side St Bernard's at Tynecastle awaited the winners. Raith were the better side during the opening exchanges and created good chances through Whitelaw and Haywood before the latter opened the scoring in seven minutes. The home side's lead was short lived, however. After both McLeod and McCartney had forced good saves from Raith custodian Watson, McCartney equalised following a neat interchange with Millar after quarter-of-an-hour's play.

The remainder of the first half was played out with East Fife the better side, but the score remained level when the teams retired for their half-time cup of tea.

Determined not to waste their home advantage, Raith piled on the pressure after the interval, but the visitors came back strongly and were awarded a penalty in 57 minutes when Rovers' Cabrelli handled the ball when attempting to clear. Andy Herd made no mistake from the spot to put the Methil Men ahead.

In 72 minutes the home side were level once again when the ball deflected off Bobby Tait and spun over the head of Milton and into the net.

Just as the crowd were preparing for a further half hour of extra time, the tie was decided in controversial fashion. A McCartney drive appeared to be heading into the net when Rovers' centre-half Morrison scooped the ball off the line with his hand. The East Fife players surrounded the referee, complaining that the ball had actually crossed the line before the Raith man got to it, but a penalty kick was the verdict.

A small section of the record 18,642 crowd who paid to watch the Scottish Cup Quarter-Final between East Fife and Raith Rovers at Bayview on 19th March 1938 (Author's Collection)

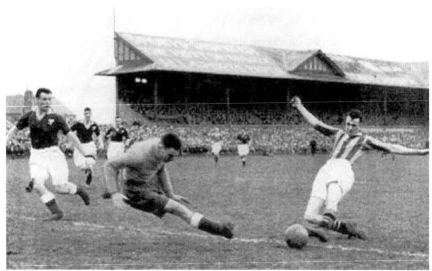
Action from the Raith v East Fife Scottish Cup fourth round replay at Stark's Park on Wednesday 23rd March 1938. (Author's collection)

Justice was done when Andy Herd stepped up to blast the ball home and East Fife were through!

A crowd of 34,200 lined the terraces at TynecastlePark for the semi-final against St Bernard's on Saturday 2nd April. The Fifers had the advantage of a slight wind for the duration of the opening forty-five minutes, but it was the Edinburgh side that took the lead after twenty minutes' play through Johnston. St Bernard's enjoyed their advantage for just two minutes. Exactly midway through the first half, a Russell cross was helped on by McCartney and landed at the feet of Herd, who made no mistake.

After the interval, tired legs caused play to deteriorate somewhat and it was no surprise when the match finished all square at a goal apiece.

Four days later the two sides lined up once again at the same venue, where a slightly smaller attendance of 30,185 saw St Bernard's dominate the first half. When the referee's whistle sounded to signal the end of a the opening forty-five minutes, however, all the Edinburgh side had to show for their efforts was a Dawson shot which came back off the cross-bar. The

Fifers came more into the game after the interval but, despite increased goal-mouth action during which two goals for East Fife and one for St Bernard's were disallowed, the match remained goal-less at the end of the regulation 90 minutes. Nine minutes into extra time the Fifers took the lead through McLeod, who scored from close range following good work from Adams and Millar. Just when it looked like the teams would change ends with East Fife in the driving seat, St Bernard's equalised when a header from centre-forward Flucker was deflected into the net. With no side finding the net during the final fifteen minutes, the tie was forced into a second replay.

The thirty minutes of extra time had far reaching implications on the other side of the Forth. Desperate to know the outcome of the match before departing for the fishing grounds, several steam drifters belonging to the Anstruther fishing fleet delayed their departure to wait for the score to come through by telegraph, few fishing vessels having radio equipment in 1938. When the outcome of the match did eventually reach the local telegraph office before being relayed by word of mouth down the pier to the boats, the receding tide was so low that the vessels were in danger of becoming grounded at the harbour mouth!

Despite the Fifers' attempts to have the third match switched to Stark's Park, Tynecastle was once again declared as the preferred venue and, on Wednesday 13th April, an attendance of 35,264 paid a total of £1,244 to see the action.

Once again, St Bernard's were the better side during the first half, but couldn't find the net and half time arrived with the score-sheet blank.

The Fifers started the second half in a more determined style and, after both McLeod and Herd had come close to breaking the deadlock, Millar gave Saints' 'keeper Smith no chance with a header. The Fife were in the ascendancy now and piled on the pressure, but the next goal game from the Edinburgh side when future Dundee United Manager Jerry Kerr scored from the penalty spot despite valiant efforts from 'keeper Milton. The Fifers were not to be denied and, with only six minutes of the match remaining, Tommy Adams crossed the ball into the goal-mouth from the right wing where Danny McKerrell, signed on loan from Falkirk only two days earlier, was on hand to head home the winning goal.

When the final whistle sounded, dozens of black and gold bedecked supporters invaded the pitch and hugged their heroes, just as they had done at the same venue eleven years earlier!

Cup fever gripped Methil and the east of Fife as the final against Kilmarnock, to be played at Hampden on 23rd April, approached. With the club's allocation of tickets almost sold out, no fewer than six special trains were scheduled to depart from Methil and Leven stations alone, not to mention the hordes who intended to travel from all over the east of the County by alternative means.

In order to escape the pre-match tension, the players escaped to St Andrews for a few days relaxation.

The day of the eagerly awaited match duly arrived and, by all accounts, the black and gold colours of the Methil side were more prominent than their more fancied First Division opponents both in Glasgow city centre and at HampdenPark itself.

The 79,000 assembled spectators were treated to an enthusiastic opening period from the Fifers, with Killie 'keeper Hunter called into action to save from McLeod during the early stages. Kilmarnock slowly began to take control of the match, however, and before long outside-left McGrogan was causing all sorts of problems for the East Fife defence. The Second Division side weathered the storm and, after quarter-of-an-hour, the Kilmarnock supporters were shocked into silence when the underdogs took the lead. Eddie McLeod pounced on a mistake by Killie left-back Milloy and sent in a strong effort which came back off 'keeper Hunter. The East Fife inside-right was not to be denied and hit the rebound into the net to send the black and gold bunnets high in the air. Kilmarnock were stung into action and equalised eight minutes later through unmarked inside-left McAvoy. Both teams stepped up a gear, and several chances were created at both ends of the park during the remainder of the first half, but the referee's whistle sounded for the interval with the honours even at a goal apiece.

In an action packed second half, there were goalmouth incidents aplenty, but neither side managed to find the net although East Fife thought that they had scored the winner in the dying minutes. Danny McKerrell shoulder-charged Hunter after he had caught a McCartney header (a perfectly acceptable practice in those days!) and the Kilmarnock goalkeeper sat down behind the goal line still clutching the ball. As the Fifers jumped for joy, the Killie custodian stood up and claimed that the ball had not crossed the line, a view shared by referee Watson. Minutes later the whistler signalled the end of the match.

For many Fifers, the cost of making the long journey back west for the replay on Wednesday 27th April was well beyond their means. Several supporters, determined not to miss the second game, went to extraordinary lengths to secure the necessary cash. One 'die-hard' even sold his canary's cage to raise money, deciding to give the bird the freedom of his bedroom in future. Another obtained a large amount of groceries from his local shop on credit before proceeding to sell the items for cash!

The Scottish Football Association, fully aware of the difficulties faced by both sets of supporters in travelling to Glasgow for a midweek game, decided to reduce admission charges for the replay in order to boost the attendance by attracting neutral spectators from the local environs. The Glasgow public responded well to the gesture and, although the terraces were slow to fill, the attendance eventually swelled to 91,710.

There was one change to the side, with Manager Dave McLean having successfully negotiated with Hearts for the loan of left-back John Harvey on the eve of the replay to replace the injured Andy Herd.

Kilmarnock won the toss and elected to play with the slight wind at their backs, and allowed the Fifers to kick off. The First Division side soon had their second league counterparts under pressure, but the East Fife defence held firm during the opening exchanges.

The men in black and gold responded well to the Killie onslaught and forced the ball up the field despite hefty challenges from their opponents. In sixteen minutes, sheer determination from the underdogs paid off when a throw in found McCartney, who helped the ball on its way across the field to Millar. The inside-left shrugged off the challenge of Robertson and threaded the ball through to Danny McKerrell, who unleashed a fierce shot on the run which gave Kilmarnock 'keeper Hunter no chance. The Methil Men were ahead!

The cheers from the black and gold bedecked spectators were soon drowned out as Kilmarnock re-started the game amidst a deafening roar of encouragement from their supporters. The Ayrshire side surged towards goal and, within six minutes, managed to turn the match around. Sneddon was adjudged to have been too physical in his attempt to thwart Kilmarnock outside-right Thomson in the penalty area and the same player almost burst the net with the resulting spot-kick.

The favourites were buzzing now and, only two minutes after levelling the score, took the lead when McGrogan burst in from the left wing, beat Laird and forced the ball home despite the frantic efforts of goalkeeper Milton.

There was no further scoring during the remainder of the first half, despite further goalmouth action at both ends of the park and a dazzling run from Tommy Adams that had the crowd roaring with anticipation.

The half-time talk in the Kilmarnock camp seemed to give the blue and whites fresh impetus, and straight from the kick off the East Fife goal was under siege. Two minutes after the re-start the Ayrshire side missed a golden opportunity to increase their advantage when Collins was sent clean through, but the centre-forward lifted the ball over the bar from only ten yards. After surviving further anxious moments as the First Division side piled on the pressure, East Fife squared the match once again just before the hour-mark, when a speculative header from Miller found McLeod, who beat the advancing Hunter with an overhead kick.

The equaliser instilled fresh confidence in the Fifers and, for the remainder of the regulation ninety minutes, the Second Division side belied their status as they threw everything at their opponents. When the final whistle sounded, however, the score was still level at two goals apiece, which meant that once again extra time would be necessary to decide the outcome. Anyone who believed that the superior fitness of the First Division side would now come to the fore was now about to be proved wrong.

After Kilmarnock started the thirty minutes of extra time with their tails up, the Fifers regained control and, using their wings to great advantage, soon had their opponents' goal under severe pressure. Sensing that the underdogs were about to have their day, the crowd roared encouragement and, five minutes into the second period of additional time, Millar intercepted a clearance from Killie 'keeper Hunter and shot home to send the black and gold bunnets high in the air once again. It was all East Fife now and, with the light fading, Danny McKerrell sealed a famous victory when he fired home his second goal of the match. When the referee signalled the end of the game, the joy felt by the victorious Second Division side was almost matched by the relief of their opponents. The difference between the teams had become so great as the game drew to a close that the winning margin would have been far greater if the contest had continued for much longer! Thousands swarmed on to the Hampden pitch to congratulate the players, despite the efforts of the Glasgow police. One Methil man, fearful that the match ball might end up in the wrong hands, concealed it under his jacket and brought it home!

The victorious Fifers proudly show off Scottish Football's greatest prize, the Scottish Cup. Back row, from left: David Russell, Willie Laird, Robert Tait, James Milton, John Harvey and Andy Herd. Front row, from left: Tommy Adams, Larry Millar, Robert McCartney, John Snedden, Eddie McLeod and Danny McKerrell. (Photo: Courtesy of John Ross)

News of the Fifers' shock victory was relayed back to Fife and, outside Leven's Troxy Cinema, there were jubilant scenes when the cinema manager announced that the cup was on its way to Methil.

Cheering crowds and excitement the likes of which had never been seen before greeted the victorious team when they arrived home at midnight. The team 'bus embarked on a tour of the local area, with Captain John Snedden and Andy Herd sitting on the roof holding the cup aloft to the loud cheers of the crowds lining the streets.

Two days later, the team and officials attended a celebration dinner at the White Swan Hotel, where Provost Smart, in toasting the club's success, admitted that the local council were rather unprepared for the event as nobody actually thought the Scottish Cup would be brought home to Bayview! The cup was put on display in several shop windows in the local area and one Methil shop proprietor's wife was rumoured to have slept with the cup in her arms at night for safe keeping!

The winning of the Scottish Cup was a truly remarkable event that brought great joy to the residents of the east of Fife; an event that would surely be remembered by all who witnessed it for the rest of their lives.

Meanwhile, the euphoria of the cup run had caused the serious business of the league championship to take second place. Most of the league fixtures were slotted into the busy schedule, but some had to be held over until the outcome of the cup adventure had been decided.

Sandwiched in between the first two cup games, the Fife suffered defeat against Leith Athletic at MarineGardens before recording a home win against BrechinCity. A further three points were gained from the next two fixtures against Albion Rovers and Stenhousemuir but, following the third round cup success over Aberdeen, league form slumped. Defeats at both Alloa and Cowdenbeath effectively ended promotion prospects, before a single point was picked up against Dunfermline Athletic in a match squeezed in between the first and second semi-final replays against St Bernard's.

The next league fixture was played on the Monday evening following the first cup final match with Kilmarnock, and resulted in a 2-1 defeat at FirsPark against East Stirlingshire. Indeed, the Fifers were forced to play an incredible five competitive matches during cup final week. Two days after the East Stirlingshire game came the Wednesday cup final replay, which was followed on Thursday evening by the outstanding league fixture against Forfar Athletic at Bayview, where a crowd of over 5,000 turned out to greet their heroes. Just 24 hours later, the final league match of the season was played against Dundee United at the same venue. As if the hectic schedule wasn't bad enough, the Scottish League even had the audacity to fine the club for fielding an under strength team against East Stirlingshire!

Jubilant crowds lined the streets of Methil and Leven to welcome the victorious Scottish Cup winning team home. (Author's collection)

A final league position of fifth was attained, only five points behind second placed Albion Rovers, but sixteen behind champions Raith Rovers, who won a place in the record books that year by scoring an incredible 142 goals from 34 matches as they secured the title.

It is interesting to note that no fewer than four Second Division clubs broke the 100-goal barrier in season 1937/38. As well as the Rovers' 142, Cowdenbeath scored 115 league goals, East Fife netted 104 times and Airdrieonians just got into three figures with 100.

Everyone associated with East Fife Football Club looked forward to season 1938/39 with enthusiasm, sure that the cup success would breed sufficient confidence in the side to claim a promotion place, if not the Second Division championship, over the forthcoming campaign. The club had never been in such a healthy financial position. The revenue gained from the 373,000 spectators who paid to watch the eleven cup matches meant that the club could afford to have a large pool of players on their books. Apart from Danny McKerrell and John Harvey, who had returned to their respective clubs, the only member of the cup winning team to leave Bayview during the summer of 1938 was Davie Russell, who joined Sheffield Wednesday for a reported fee of £2,000.

A crowd of over 6,000 paid to see the first league match of the season against Morton at Bayview, and few went home disappointed after East Fife won a thrilling match by the incredible score of 6-5.

After the points were shared with Stenhousemuir at Ochilview the following week, full points were taken at home to East Stirlingshire with another astonishing final score of 7-5. It seemed that caution in defence was being thrown to the wind in favour of an attacking formation!

The winning form continued until the end of October, when Cowdenbeath inflicted the first defeat of the season with a 1-0 win in front of over 10,000 at Bayview. The win put the visitors at the top of the table and pushed the home side down to third place.

There was, during the early part of the season, a change of leadership at the club with the resignation of Chairman Bailie James Gray on 6th September 1938, who relinquished his post after the club were fined £25 for presenting gold watches to their players in recognition of their Scottish Cup win at a public ceremony.

Mr Gray was so disgusted at this action by the Scottish Football Association that he severed all links with football as a result. John McArthur, who had served the club as a Director for nine years, was appointed as the new Chairman.

The challenge for promotion was maintained as the season progressed and, by the time Montrose were beaten 4-0 on a frozen Bayview pitch on Hogmanay, fourteen of the 21 league matches played had been won, along with four draws and three defeats.

Two days later Dundee United were defeated 5-2 in front of a 10,000 crowd at Tannadice, before both points were taken from Forfar Athletic at Bayview on 3rd January 1939.

Towards the end of January, the Fifers lined up against lowly Montrose at Bayview as the defence of the Scottish Cup began. A disappointing crowd of only 4,200 turned out to witness the event, but it has to be said that there was, on the same day, the counter attractions of four other Scottish Cup ties in Fife. At Central Park, Cowdenbeath were playing host to Partick Thistle and, only a few miles along the road, Dunfermline Athletic were entertaining Morton.

The big local attraction was, however, the visit of both halves of the 'Old Firm' to the area. At Stark's Park, Raith Rovers faced Rangers and, only five miles along the coast, non-league amateurs Burntisland Shipyard were playing host to Celtic! Unfortunately the attendance at Bayview was not the only disappointment of the afternoon. Montrose, struggling in the lower half of the Second Division, won a poor match by two goals to one and progressed to the second round and a lucrative home fixture against Celtic.

The early cup exit signalled a turnaround in fortunes and, with confidence at a low ebb, two successive league defeats followed against Dumbarton and Dunfermline Athletic, the latter a 7-3 thumping at Bayview on 11th February.

Despite the recent failure to achieve good results on the field of play, the club were still confident that they were on the verge of a return to the First Division and set about investigating ways of increasing the capacity of BayviewPark during the early part of 1939. One ambitious scheme proposed at the time actually hoped to take advantage of the current unrest in Europe caused by Adolf Hitler! With the ever-increasing possibility that another major military conflict was just around the corner, a cunning plan was hatched which, it was hoped, would benefit both the club and the local community. In order to increase capacity at the east end of the ground, the club approached both Fife Education Committee and the A.R.P. (Air Raid Patrol) to explore the possibility of extending the east terracing into the Aberhill Primary School playground. The proposed extension was to form the roof of a new air raid shelter, which would be for the use of both the school and the general public. Not surprisingly, when Fife Education Committee and the A.R.P. were advised that the club expected them to meet all costs, the idea was thrown out! East Fife did, however, decide to press ahead with improvements to the grandstand and to the north terracing, and this work was put out to tender.

Despite a 6-0 home win over BrechinCity on 25th February, further home defeats at the hands of Dundee and St Bernard's severely dented the promotion challenge as the end of the season loomed.

A 3-1 home win against fellow promotion hopefuls Airdrieonians on the first day of April was followed by a tough trip to play already-crowned Champions Cowdenbeath at Central Park the following Saturday. A 2-2 draw was the outcome, which meant that the final game of the season against Alloa Athletic would have to be won in order to leapfrog the second placed Clackmannanshire side and claim the second promotion place.

Goals from McCartney, McKerrell, Carroll and Bolan secured a 4-1 victory for the Fifers at RecreationPark on 15th April, but there remained one major snag. Alloa still had one fixture remaining at home to BrechinCity and a far superior goal difference.

On 29th April, the 'Wasps' regained second place with a tense 1-1 draw, which was good enough to win promotion on goal average and push the Fifers back to third place.

Little consolation was gained from the Penman Cup victory against St Bernard's at Bayview on the same afternoon. East Fife had, by the narrowest of margins, failed to achieve First Division status once again.

As the season drew to a close, matches were arranged against Lothian and Borders non-league clubs in order to keep the club's huge pool of players in prime condition. Three such games, two against DunbarTown and one against Penicuik Athletic, were played simultaneously with the first team's fixtures against East Stirlingshire, Cowdenbeath and Alloa. This first venture at running a reserve side was short lived, however, as the decision was taken during the summer of 1939 to free nine players and retain only fourteen for the forthcoming season.

The reason for cutting the playing staff is unclear, but it certainly wasn't for lack of funds. Profits for the financial year just ended stated that the club had made a profit of £6,066, an enormous amount for a Second Division outfit considering Glasgow giants Rangers made £7,082 over the same period. No wonder the East Fife Board of Directors anticipated a rosy future as far as the financial well-being of the club was concerned!

Chapter Eleven: War and Peace

The decision to cut the playing staff seemed to have had no adverse effect at the beginning of the 1939/40 season, with the opening game of the campaign resulting in a 3-0 league win over Morton at Bayview. The next two matches produced a draw at Dumbarton and a convincing home win over St Bernard's. From then on, however, things went rapidly downhill.

On 1st September 1939 Hitler invaded Poland and, the following day, East Fife lost 2-1 to Airdrieonians at Broomfield in what proved to be the last Scottish League match for almost six years. Six days later the Scottish Football Association suspended all football as the nation prepared to go to war with Germany.

A ban on junior football was also imposed, but didn't last for long much to the relief of local clubs Wellesley and Denbeath Star.

At a meeting of the officials of East Fife Football Club, Chairman John McArthur stated that he could make no definite arrangements for the future. All the club's players were currently engaged in their various occupations and would be available to play if the ban on senior football was lifted by the S.F.A., in which case it was proposed to form a 12 club league involving teams from Fife and Angus.

It soon became apparent that the total closure of all football grounds was a panic reaction and, fearful that a lack of Saturday afternoon entertainment might have a detrimental effect on the morale of the population, the Government intervened to allow the game to resume. The S.F.A. announced that they would be happy for clubs to play out a series of friendly matches for the duration of the hostilities (remember that the war was only expected to last months, not years!), but the Scottish League objected, saying that if there was no league football then there would be no point in playing at all. The outcome was an agreement to form two

151

Regional Leagues, East and West, each containing sixteen clubs. Prior to the outbreak of hostilities there had been 38 clubs in the Scottish League, which meant that six clubs would not be invited to take part in the new competition. As a result BrechinCity, Montrose, Forfar Athletic, EdinburghCity, Leith Athletic and East Stirlingshire were forced to close down.

East Fife became members of the Regional League (East), along with Aberdeen, Alloa Athletic, Arbroath, Cowdenbeath, Falkirk, Hearts, Hibernian, St. Johnstone, Dundee, Dundee United, Dunfermline Athletic, Raith Rovers, King's Park, St. Bernard's and Stenhousemuir.

With the league not scheduled to begin until the end of October, East Fife and Raith Rovers arranged to play off the two legs of their Penman Cup tie during the intervening period. The first game produced a convincing 3-0 victory for an under strength East Fife at Bayview on the last day of September, which caused one spectator to remark on leaving the ground: "what would the score have been if East Fife had been at full strength?" The supporter only had to wait seven days for the answer, when full strength East Fife were thumped 5-0 by Raith Rovers at Stark's Park in the return leg! Another heavy defeat followed in the first Regional League match as the Methil Men went down 8-1 to Dunfermline Athletic at East EndPark. Such was the unpredictability of wartime football, however, that the Fifers could boast a 5-2 win over Hibernian at Easter Road and a 9-3 home victory over Stenhousemuir before the end of the year.

New Year's Day 1940 saw the Methil Men gain revenge for their Penman Cup exit by beating Raith Rovers 5-2 at Stark's Park, only to suffer a 6-3 reverse at the hands of Dundee United the following day.

There being no Scottish Cup competition during season 1939/40, the 'Wartime Emergency Scottish Cup' was inaugurated, with the first round ties to be played over two legs. The Fifers were drawn against Clyde, who were asked if the first game could be switched to Bayview as Celtic were to play Raith at home on the same day in the same competition. This would have been in both clubs' favour, as both matches would have had no competition for spectators if the dates were switched. Clyde refused to change, however, claiming that the first Saturday of the competition was sure to attract a larger crowd than the second week. East Fife lost the first leg 3-1 at Shawfield on 25th February and, despite winning the return match, exited the competition 3-2 on aggregate.

Despite the withdrawal of Cowdenbeath from the league at the beginning of February and the withdrawal of Arbroath at the end of the season, football in the east of Scotland was expected to continue during season 1940/41 in the form of a Midland League. Although the Fifers had suffered a severe financial loss over season 1939/40 of £2,317, they were persuaded to join the new combination along with Dundee United, Dunfermline, Dundee, Raith Rovers, King's Park, Stenhousemuir and St Bernard's. During the summer of 1940, however, there was a dramatic escalation in hostilities. By the end of June the Germans had invaded Denmark and Norway, forced the surrender of Holland and Belgium by invading the low countries, and marched into Paris. The following month saw the Luftwaffe start its bombing campaign on London and the Royal Air Force retaliated by launching bombing raids on Germany.

The fact that Britain was now well and truly at war with Germany, coupled with a lack of enthusiasm from most of the league's proposed members, forced the plans for the Midland League to be shelved. As a result, East Fife Football Club closed down for season 1940/41.

The following summer, competitive football returned to the east of Scotland in the form of the North-Eastern League. One major factor behind the formation of the competition was the agreement to include a Rangers XI, which would undoubtedly boost crowd figures and make the eight-team league financially viable. The seven clubs who were to join Rangers

in the new competition were Aberdeen, Dundee United, East
Fife, Dunfermline Athletic, Leith Athletic, Raith Rovers, and
St. Bernard's.

*"After one season without senior football, we are to get as nearly
back to normal as conditions will permit from next week"*,
commented the *Leven Mail* at the end of July 1941.

The 'nearly back to normal conditions', however, did not
include Manager Dave McLean, who left to become Manager
of Hearts, and Tommy Adams, whose loan period with
Hibernian was set to continue for the time being.

Indeed, East Fife found it impossible to field a regular side
due to the fact that most players were regularly on active
service. Despite having to field makeshift teams, however,
impressive home victories were recorded over Dunfermline
Athletic (8-0) and Raith Rovers (5-1), although it has to be said
that all clubs at the time were suffering from the unavailability
of regular players. Having said that, even with their entire
front line unavailable, the Methil Men scored four goals
against a weak St Bernard's on 6th September! The first half of
the North Eastern League competition, played between
August and November, finished with the Fife in second place,
just one point behind Rangers.

In November and December the North Eastern League Cup
was played for and, after beating Raith Rovers 9-2 on
aggregate in the first round, the Methil Men lost 4-3 on
aggregate to Dundee United in the semi-final.

During the second half of the league competition, played from
January to May 1942, the Fife struggled to put out a decent
side, and on occasion fielded just six 'regulars'. Despite the
player shortage, a final league position of fourth place was
attained, which earned the right to face Aberdeen in the semi-
final of the second North-Eastern League Cup competition. In
a hard fought encounter over two legs, the 'Dons' won
through to the final 2-1 on aggregate.

The 1942/43 season saw a change in membership of the
North-Eastern League. St. Bernard's and Leith Athletic were

154

not invited to renew their membership and the reserve sides of Hearts and Hibs, who were regarded as bigger crowd pullers, filled the vacant places. Sadly, this decision led to the demise of St Bernard's and the famous old Edinburgh club was wound up the following year. Leith Athletic did re-appear after the war and played in the 'C' Division until 1953, but there can be no doubt that the decision to expel the club from wartime football was a contributory factor in Leith's eventual demise.

The player shortage brought about by the war saw several well-known names turn out as 'guests' for the Fifers during the following season. At the pre-season trial match at the beginning of August, guest players included BirminghamCity's Welsh international Charlie Jones and future England international Harry Johnston, who was later to captain Blackpool to victory in the 1953 F.A. Cup final. Later that month the legendary Bill Shankly joined the Fifers for a five game spell whilst stationed at Arbroath and, in September, Liverpool's Methil born star Jim Harley arrived at Bayview under a similar agreement.

Again, the North Eastern League was competed for in two parts during season 1942/43. During the first competition, from August to November, the Fifers finished in third place behind Aberdeen and Dunfermline Athletic. In the second phase of the competition, during which Hibernian were defeated 7-1 at Bayview and 6-3 at Easter Road, a final position of second place was achieved once again. In the Mitchell Cup, Rangers were beaten over two legs before progress was halted by Raith Rovers in the semi-final. The Kirkcaldy side also proved too strong over both legs of the first round of the North Eastern League Cup, winning 4-1 at Bayview and 2-1 at Stark's Park.

During the summer of 1943, the war was beginning to turn in favour of the allies. The German Army was defeated in Tunisia; the RAF stepped up bombing raids on Germany and American troops gained control of Sicily. Not long after season 1943/44 was under way, Italy's unconditional surrender was followed by the announcement that the Italians had declared war on Germany.

The allies' advance into Europe meant that there was no let-up in the number of players unavailable due to active service. On the other hand, there were again several servicemen stationed locally who were able to turn out as 'guests' for the Fifers. Their number included Wilcox (DerbyCounty), Collins (YorkCity) and George Maxwell (Blackpool). Also making their first appearances in black and gold jerseys at this time were two East Fife stars of the future, George Aitken and Davie Duncan.

The first half of season 1943/44 was disappointing, with the Fifers only managing to win four North Eastern League matches out of fourteen. The Mitchell Cup campaign was also disappointing, with Rangers winning 2-0 at Bayview in the second leg of the first round after a 2-2 draw at Ibrox.

A benefit match for John Snedden, Captain of the 1938 cup winning side, was played on Christmas Day 1943 at Bayview against Raith Rovers, the Kirkcaldy side winning 3-1. Revenge was gained on New Year's Day 1944 when East Fife beat their near neighbours 4-0 at Stark's Park in the first game of the second series of North Eastern League matches. The second half of the 1943/44 league campaign saw the Fifers improve on their showing in the first half of the competition, finishing in third place behind Aberdeen and Rangers.

In the second Mitchell Cup competition of the season, Dundee United were defeated over two legs before the Fifers bowed out of the competition on aggregate to Rangers in the semi-final despite winning their home leg 3-1.

Meanwhile, the war had continued to progress in favour of the Allies and, following the D-Day invasion of Normandy on 6th June 1944, the British and American troops continued to advance into Europe. Just as the 1944/45 season got under way, the Allies took control of Paris and Brussels and the

Americans marched into Germany. The end of the war in Europe was in sight.

On the football front, future Scotland star Allan Brown made his East Fife debut against Dundee United in a 2-1 North Eastern League defeat at Tannadice on 12th August. Brown's home debut followed on Saturday 19th August with a 5-1 defeat at the hands of Rangers. The Fifers' performances in the league, which now included Arbroath and Dundee, continued to disappoint and the first series of matches ended with only six victories from eighteen games and a vastly inferior goal difference. The second series of matches showed a marked improvement, and a final league position of third was achieved, one point behind Rangers and only three points behind winners Aberdeen.

In the Mitchell Cup, the Methil Men were unfortunate to be eliminated in the semi-final by Aberdeen on corner kicks after the tie had finished all square on aggregate at 4-4.

The summer of 1945 finally brought an end to the Second World War.

A week after the death of Adolf Hitler in Berlin, Germany surrendered unconditionally on 7th May. The atomic bombs dropped on the Japanese cities of Hiroshima and Nagasaki by the US Air Force at the beginning of August put and end to the conflict which, when it began six years earlier, was only expected to last a few months.

Victory in the Japan came too late to stop a further season of 'wartime competition', however. The North Eastern League was disbanded and its member clubs, with the exception of Aberdeen, became part of the Southern League 'B' Division along with Airdrieonians, Albion Rovers, Alloa Athletic, Ayr United, Cowdenbeath, Dumbarton, St Johnstone and Stenhousemuir. Aberdeen were admitted to the 'A' Division of the Southern League, which contained most of the teams who had competed in the Southern Wartime League throughout the conflict.

Just before the 1945/46 season got under way, old favourite Tommy Adams returned to Methil much to the delight of the Bayview faithful, after having spent most of the war on loan to Hibernian. Although the Fifers started their league campaign with a 2-1 defeat from Dundee at DensPark followed by a no scoring draw with Dunfermline Athletic at Bayview, a run of five straight wins saw the team sitting in second place by mid-September. Defeats at Albion Rovers and Dumbarton either side of a home win over Airdrieonians were offset by an impressive 8-0 victory against Arbroath at Bayview on 20th October 1945.

Largely inconsistent form then ensued until the end of the year. A 7-2 win over Stenhousemuir at Bayview was followed by a 4-1 reverse at the hands of league leaders Dundee and further defeats from Dundee United, Cowdenbeath and Airdrieonians.

A 4-0 New Year's Day win over Raith Rovers at Bayview sparked a revival in form and the Fife remained undefeated until the end of the league season, recording 6-2 wins over both Dumbarton and Arbroath in the process. Incidentally, the match against Raith on New Year's Day 1946 also saw the introduction of the first 'tannoy' loudspeaker system at BayviewPark, a 'much appreciated innovation' according to the *Leven Mail*.

A final league position of second was attained but, as the Southern League was considered to be part of the wartime league set-up, it had been agreed at the beginning of the season that there would be no promotion and relegation when the competition reached a conclusion. East Fife, along with Southern League 'B' Division Champions Dundee, were destined to remain in the bottom league for at least one more season.

As the 'B' Division contained only fourteen members, each playing a total of 26 league matches, a 'B' Division League Cup competition was played for throughout February 1946.

After overcoming Dunfermline Athletic over two legs in the first round, East Fife recorded their first ever victory at Somerset Park to knock Ayr United out of the competition in round two. A home defeat by Dumbarton in front of a 5,000 crowd on 16th February ended the Fife's interest in the tournament.

During March and April 1946, all clubs competing in the 'A' and 'B' Divisions of the Southern League participated in the Southern League Cup, which was the forerunner of the present day Scottish League Cup. In the first round, played on a sectional 'mini-league' basis, East Fife were drawn to play Alloa Athletic, Cowdenbeath and Raith Rovers. The Fife suffered defeat only once during the series of sectional matches, a 3-2 reverse at Stark's Park against Raith Rovers, and recorded 7-1 (home) and 7-3 (away) wins over Cowdenbeath in the process of winning their group. A crowd of 32,500 turned out at the neutral venue of Easter Road on 6th April 1946 to see the Methil Men go down 3-0 to Hearts in the quarter-final.

The final tournament to be played during season 1945/46 was the Victory Cup. A crowd of 8,000 witnessed an East Fife side, containing five of the 1938 cup winning team, record an impressive 2-0 win over Kilmarnock at Bayview on 20th April. In the second leg of the first round a week later, however, the Ayrshire side successfully turned the tie around with a 3-0 win at RugbyPark.

The season had been a good one for East Fife both on the park and financially, with a profit in the region of £1,000 reported. With the war over and the level of unemployment expected to drop dramatically as the country picked itself up and dusted itself down, football clubs across the country rightly anticipated a marked rise in football match attendances.

Two players who were to become household names in the east of Fife and beyond signed up at Bayview during the summer of 1946. Firstly Henry Morris, described as a 'sharp shooting centre-forward', was signed from junior side Dundee Violet at the beginning of June. Days after Morris put pen to paper he was joined by one of his Violet team-mates, inside-forward Dougie Davidson. Before the season got under way, right-half Jimmy Philp, another player destined to become a household name, had arrived in Methil.

On 10th August 1946 a crowd of 8,000 paid to see the Fifers play their first league match of the season at Bayview, where they suffered defeat at the hands of reigning Division 'B' Champions, Dundee. A little pride was salvaged four days later with a 2-1 victory over visitors Albion Rovers in the first round of the 'B' Division Supplementary Cup.

The league campaign was kick-started in Perth with a 4-1 victory against St Johnstone on Saturday 17th August and, a week later, eight goals were shared in a league encounter with near neighbours Raith Rovers in front of a 10,000 crowd at Bayview.

The following midweek, revenge was gained against Dundee with a 4-2 home win in the second round of the Supplementary Cup, during which Henry Morris scored his first hat-trick for the club.

A crowd of 15,000 turned out at Tannadice to see the Fifers overcome Dundee United 4-2 in the semi-final of the competition on Wednesday 4th September and, over the following two Wednesdays, Raith Rovers were beaten over both legs of the final by an aggregate score of 7-3 to place the 'B' Division Supplementary Cup in the Bayview trophy cabinet.

Back on league business, full points were taken from both Dunfermline Athletic and Stenhousemuir, the latter thanks to a resounding 7-1 win, before defeat was tasted for the second time with defeat at Ayr.

The final week of September and the whole of October 1946 was totally taken up with the first round (sectional) matches of the first official League Cup. East Fife came out of the hat in the same section as Dunfermline Athletic, who were beaten 7-0 (home) and 2-0 (away); Alloa Athletic, who were defeated 6-0 (home) and 2-0 (away) and St Johnstone, beaten 3-0 (home) and 2-0 (away). After this incredible series of first round results, the Methil Men qualified for the quarter-final of the competition having won all six games and having scored a total of 22 goals with none conceded in the process! The quarter-final tie, in which the Fifers had been drawn to play Hearts, was held over until the following March.

In November the league programme resumed with a 4-1 win against Albion Rovers at Cliftonhill. Top scorers for the club at this time were their two close season signings from Dundee Violet, Henry Morris and Dougie Davidson. Between them the pair had netted 38 goals up to and including the 4-1 win over Albion Rovers, a feat that had the Scottish International Selection Committee closely monitoring the situation.

One notable arrival at Bayview at this time was Danny McLennan who, despite being only a teenager, had already been on the books of Rangers, Stirling Albion and Falkirk. Although McLennan was destined to make his name with the Fifers, it was to be a further four years before the young left-half managed to win a regular place in the side.

January 1947 saw the club embark on a reasonably successful Scottish Cup run. After a 6-2 thrashing was handed out to near neighbours Dunfermline Athletic at Bayview on 25th January (when 'cup fever' caused the postponement of the entire East Fife Amateur League programme!), the Fifers recorded fine wins against East Stirlingshire and Queen's Park before going down 2-0 to Motherwell in the fourth round.

Both legs of the long awaited League Cup quarter-final were played out during March 1947. In the first meeting at Tynecastle on 1st March, a crowd of 19,806 saw Tommy Adams score the only goal of the game to give the Fife a shock victory, but four days later hopes of a semi-final place were dashed when the 'maroons' won the return match 5-2 in front of a 15,000 Bayview crowd.

Back on league business, inconsistent form ensued until the competition reached its conclusion, during which time the Methil Men were defeated by league favourites Dundee at DensPark but managed to record impressive home wins against Cowdenbeath and Ayr United. A final league placing of third was not enough to secure a promotion place, and Champions Dundee were promoted along with second placed Airdrieonians.

On the local cup scene, season 1946/47 saw the re-introduction of the Fife Cup, which had been suspended for the duration of the war. The Fife Association decided that both the 1945/46 and 1946/47 tournaments should be played simultaneously and East Fife duly won the previous season's Fife Cup by beating Raith 7-1 in the semi-final and Cowdenbeath 3-0 in the final. Although Raith were beaten in the semi-final of the 1946/47 competition, there was no time to play the final, which was held over until the following season.

Despite failing to win promotion, morale and confidence was still high at BayviewPark both on and off the field at the end of the 1946/47 campaign. The fact that the club had remained operational for most of the war had proved to be a key factor in the Fifers ability to maintain a challenge near the top of the league table and compete well in the national cup competitions. The ambitious Board of Directors, sensing that the club had on its books the nucleus of a successful side, set about the task of finding the right man to take over at the helm and steer the team to success.

Chapter Twelve: Halcyon Days

The League Cup winning side of 1947. Back row, left to right: Jimmy Philp, Willie Finlay, George Aitken, John Niven, Willie Laird, Sammy Stewart. Front row, from left: Tommy Adams, Dougie Davidson, Henry Morris, Jake Davidson, DavieDuncan. (Author's Collection)

Despite failing to win promotion during the previous league campaign, East Fife supporters had every reason to expect a rosy future when former Rangers and Scotland internationalist Scot Symon was appointed full-time Manager in June 1947.

Only a week after the appointment was made, Mr Symon started to build a team capable of achieving top league status by signing two players who were destined to become household names during their time with the Methil club; 18 year old Jimmy Bonthrone from Kinglassie Colliery and 19 year old Charlie Fleming from Blairhall. He also persuaded all the previous season's squad to sign new terms, with the exception of George Aitken, who was in dispute with the club. As well as on the park, things were looking promising off the field of play. At the Methil Highland Games in July 1947,

Provost Slater announced that it was the Town Council's intention to build a 42,000 capacity sports stadium on a site adjacent to the Highland Games field in Kirkland Walk. It was widely anticipated that East Fife would eventually move into the proposed stadium, if and when it was built.

An attendance of 3,500 turned out at Bayview on 2nd August 1947 for the pre-season trial match to catch a glimpse of Mr Symon's first signings and to view the trialists on display. Not one of the assembled crowd would have dared predict just how immediate the new Manager's success would be.

Seven days after the trial match, a crowd of over 7,000 witnessed a winning start to the League Cup campaign with a 3-2 win over league newcomers Stirling Albion. Following further favourable results against Albion and the two other teams in their group, Kilmarnock and Ayr United, the Fifers completed the series of first round matches sitting proudly at the top of their League Cup section.

In a repeat of the previous season's quarter-final, Hearts were defeated at Tynecastle on 27th September, only this time by the odd goal in seven. The match was, according to William Phenix in his 1948 publication *Through the Years with East Fife F.C.* "the most memorable of memorable ties". Unlike the previous year, this tie was played over only one leg, and goals from Dougie Davidson and Davie Duncan during the regulation 90 minutes forced the game into extra time. Two further goals from Tommy Adams won a place in the semi-final and a meeting with Aberdeen at DensPark, Dundee.

In a tense match against the 'Dons', the score-sheet remained blank until ten minutes from time, when Henry Morris scored to claim the scalp of yet another 'A' Division club and win a place in the League Cup Final.

With Falkirk recording a surprise victory against Rangers in the other semi-final, there was a real chance that the League Cup would soon adorn the Bayview trophy cabinet, as it was reckoned that the Methil Men were more than capable of beating the 'Bairns', who had finished the previous season battling to avoid relegation from the 'A' Division.

Thousands of East Fife fans travelled through to Hampden for the final on Saturday 25th October 1947, which was watched by a crowd of 52,781. Although there were goalmouth incidents aplenty, the goalkeepers of both sides were in terrific form and, at the end of 120 minutes' play, neither team had found the net. The Fifers certainly created the greater number of chances during the match, forcing twenty-two corners compared to Falkirk's seven, and were unfortunate not to score through a Dougie Davidson 'pile-driver' which Falkirk 'keeper Jerry Dawson did well to save.

The replay took place at the same venue the following week, witnessed by a disappointing crowd of 30,664. The supporters who stayed away missed a goal feast, with East Fife scoring after only eight minutes through Tommy Adams, ironically following a goalkeeping error from Dawson. Only sixteen minutes were on the clock when Davie Duncan scored a second, again following a mistake by the Falkirk 'keeper. The Division 'A' side were stung into action and, on the half-hour mark, pulled a goal back through Aikman before taking control of the game and piling the pressure on the East Fife goal.

The Fife defence held firm, however, and Davie Duncan increased their advantage when he collected the ball near the corner flag, turned and floated a speculative lob towards the Falkirk goal that crept in at the far post.

With only two minutes left, the destination of the League Cup was put beyond doubt. Henry Morris almost knocked Jerry Dawson on his back with a screaming shot which the Falkirk 'keeper failed to hold and the ball broke to Davie Duncan, who fired home to complete his hat trick. Moments later, the final whistle sounded with the score 4-1 in favour of East Fife.

In winning the League Cup, East Fife had repeated their remarkable feat of 1938 by landing a major trophy whilst still a Second Division side.

For Scot Symon, pulling off such an astonishing feat after only four months in the hot seat was a dream start to his managerial career.

The five league matches played during the cup run also produced pleasing results, with Leith Athletic and Raith Rovers defeated on their own soil, St Johnstone beaten at Bayview and the points shared at both Dunfermline and Hamilton.

Once the League Cup had been safely deposited in the Bayview trophy cabinet, the successful run of league games continued and, amazingly, lasted until January of the following year when Dundee United inflicted the first league defeat of the season at Tannadice by the odd goal in five.

Even with just under half of their league fixtures remaining, it looked like the Fifers were destined for a return to the top flight!

In the Scottish Cup, a promising run was ended at the quarter-final stage against Rangers at Ibrox on 6th March 1948 with a 1-0 defeat in front of over 90,000 spectators.

The first and second rounds of the competition had seen both Kilmarnock and St Johnstone beaten at Bayview in front of all-ticket sell out crowds of 14,000. In the first match, goals from Davie Duncan and Dougie Davidson were enough to see off the Ayrshire side and, in the following round, a Henry Morris brace along with goals from Tommy Adams, Jackie Davidson and Davie Duncan were more than enough to record the club's first ever Scottish Cup win against the 'Saints'.

In round three, Dumbarton were narrowly beaten at Boghead with a Jackie Davidson strike, before interest in the competition was ended at Ibrox.

Just days after the Scottish Cup exit, Davie Duncan made the first of his many international appearances when he was

166

picked to play for the Scottish League against the English League in Newcastle. According to press reports, Duncan had a fine game.

Following the league reversal at Tannadice in January, only one further match was lost during the entire league campaign, against Kilmarnock at Bayview on 28th February. When Cowdenbeath were beaten 3-0 at Central Park at the beginning of April, the team were in the enviable position of needing, at the most, just four more points to win the championship.

Still sitting in second place going into their home fixture against Stenhousemuir on 7th April 1948, the Fifers knew that victory would secure promotion with five games still to play. A 4-0 win, in which Charlie Fleming commemorated his league debut with a brace, proved to be more than enough to secure a place back amongst Scottish football's elite.

League leaders Albion Rovers, just a point ahead and with only one fixture remaining, knew that it was only a matter of time before they relinquished pole position, and the Fifers knocked the Coatbridge side off their perch just three days later.

In a remarkable match against Stirling Albion at Bayview on 10th April, the 'B' Division League Championship was secured with a 6-4 victory. Incredibly, although Henry Morris opened the scoring during the first half, the visitors replied with four goals before the interval. It was a more determined East Fife side that took to the field after the break and, by the time the second period was half-way through, the match was tied at four goals apiece thanks to a Davie Duncan hat-trick. Late goals from George Aitken and Henry Morris during the last ten minutes were enough to secure victory and win the title.

Signing off with a 4-1 win against runners-up Albion Rovers at Cliftonhill on 24th April, the season was completed with an eleven-point cushion separating the champions from the Coatbridge club.

As the season drew to a close, the club were represented at full international level for the first time in seventeen years when Davie Duncan made a scoring debut for Scotland in their 2-0 win against Belgium at Hampden on 28th April. Over the following month, Duncan won a further two caps for his country against Switzerland in Berne and France in Paris. Before the curtain finally came down on season 1947/48, a third trophy was added to the haul in the shape of the 'B' Division Supplementary Cup. In the first round, Arbroath were soundly beaten 6-0 at home following stalemate at Gayfield, before Albion Rovers were thrashed 13-2 on aggregate in the semi-final.

The final paired the Fifers with Stirling Albion, who were beaten 2-1 at Annfield and 7-0 at Bayview as the trophy found its way into the Bayview trophy cabinet for the second year in succession. It had been a remarkable season for the club and a great start to Scot Symon's managerial career. In winning the 'B' Division Championship, 25 matches had been won, three were drawn and only two lost, with 103 league goals scored and 36 conceded. In winning the League Cup, 28 goals were scored in the ten matches played and eight goals were scored in the Scottish Cup run.

In the Supplementary Cup, the net was found a remarkable 28 times in only six games! Top scorer for the club was Henry Morris with 62 goals, followed by Davie Duncan with 39. Could the momentum be maintained during the following season? The calibre of the reserve team players certainly looked promising. Young Charlie Fleming, who until now had made only a couple of first team appearances, had scored prolifically for the reserves all season and managed to rattle up the amazing total of 53 goals, including four in the 9-0 Fife Cup victory against Burntisland Shipyard on 9th April when the full reserve side was fielded instead of the recognised first eleven. Mindful of the fact that on two occasions during the season Bayview had been filled to capacity, the club

Jimmy Philp, part of the famous half-back line of Philp, Finlay and Aitken, was signed on a free transfer from Hearts in 1946. During his six seasons as a player with the club, Jimmy made 191 appearances and scored five goals. Jimmy continued to be associated with East Fife after his playing days were over and assisted the club in a number of roles. (Author's Collection)

announced towards the end of the 1947/48 campaign that ground improvements would be carried out prior to the much awaited return to the top flight. Land to the north of BayviewPark was purchased from Wemyss Estate, which allowed the main terracing to be re-constructed and extended. The additional land also allowed the playing surface to be widened by a yard.

Permission was also granted during the summer of 1948 for the east terrace to be extended into the AberhillSchool playground. In addition to the terracing extensions, the grandstand was upgraded and the stand enclosure terracing concreted.

With the help of supporters and others associated with the club, the improvements were complete in time for the beginning of season 1948/49, when BayviewPark boasted a new capacity well in excess of 20,000.

The 1948/49 season kicked off on 14th August with a trip to Edinburgh to face Hibernian at Easter Road. Despite scoring twice through Tommy Adams and Henry Morris, the Methil Men were well beaten by the home side, who ran out comfortable winners by five goals to two. The following Wednesday evening, Motherwell were the first visitors to the new look Bayview, but hopes of a home win were dashed as the 'Steel Men' scored the only goal of the game to secure both league points.

The Bayview faithful, however, didn't have long to wait for success. Falkirk were beaten 2-1 at Brockville on Saturday 21st August with goals from Davie Duncan and Dougie Davidson and, the following week, a record league crowd of 15,700 paid to see St.Mirren defeated 3-1 at Bayview thanks to goals from Tommy Adams, Davie Duncan and Charlie Fleming. This match also marked the beginning of Charlie Fleming's days as a first team regular and, the following week, the young 'Cannonball' scored a hat trick at Dens Park as Dundee were demolished 5-2.

At home again during the following midweek, Partick Thistle were put to the sword with goals from Tommy Adams and, once again, Charlie Fleming.

Would the new goal-scoring sensation manage to maintain his scoring prowess? You bet!

The competitive matches which followed were the six first round League Cup ties, in which Charlie scored eleven of his side's twenty goals as they overcame Hearts, Partick Thistle and Queen of the South to win the section.

In the quarter-final of the competition, however, Fleming failed to find the net as Raith Rovers gained sweet revenge for their 1938 Scottish Cup defeat by beating their local rivals 5-3 at Stark's Park. An all-ticket crowd of 24,000 saw the home side race to a 3-0 half time lead through goals from Maule, Joyner and Brady in a match which was, by all accounts, one of the finest ever played between the sides. In the second half, a Henry Morris hat trick was countered by home goals from Penman and Joiner, as the Rovers progressed to the semi-final and a meeting with fellow 'B' Division side Hamilton Academical. For the record, the Kirkcaldy side went on to reach the final, where they were beaten by Rangers at Hampden.

Out of the League Cup, East Fife turned their attention to the 'A' Division programme, and recorded three successive victories to go top of the league. The run culminated with the club's first ever win against Celtic, a 1-0 victory at Parkhead on 13th November courtesy of a Davie Duncan strike.

Pride comes before a fall, however, and the following Saturday Aberdeen took full points at Pittodrie with a 3-1 win. A new record crowd of 22,500 packed into Bayview on Saturday 27th November for the visit of Rangers, who inflicted the home side's second successive defeat with a 2-1 win. Inconsistent form then prevailed until the turn of the year, with victories over Morton and Motherwell countered by defeats from Hearts and Clyde.

With the other three Fife clubs plying their trade in the 'B' Division, there could be no New Year's Day derby in 1949 and Falkirk make the relatively short journey over the Forth to Methil, where a Henry Morris goal secured a point in a 1-1 draw.

The next three matches saw the Fife slip down the table following defeats from St.Mirren and Hibernian and a no scoring draw against Partick Thistle.

The first round of the Scottish Cup brought a welcome break from league duties and, on their second visit to Methil in under a month, Falkirk were beaten 2-1 on 22nd January.

The win seemed to inject fresh confidence into the side, and a week later full league points were taken from Dundee with a 3-0 win at Bayview.

The second round of the Scottish Cup paired East Fife with local rivals Cowdenbeath at Central Park, where victory was secured thanks to goals from Henry Morris and Charlie Fleming in front of a new Central Park record attendance of 23,500.

There then followed a three game unbeaten sequence of league matches which ended with another win against Celtic, who were beaten 3-2 at Bayview on 26th February as the home side recorded their second win of the season against the Glasgow side.

The victory over the 'Hoops' set the Fifers up nicely for their Scottish Cup quarter-final tie against Hibernian at Easter Road the following week, which was won 2-0 thanks to goals from Jackie Davidson and Charlie Fleming.

Alas, the Scottish Cup dream ended at the semi-final stage when Rangers comfortably progressed to the final with a 3-0 win in front of an attendance of 103,458 at Hampden on 26th March; the first six-figure crowd to watch East Fife in action.

In the six league fixtures that remained following the cup exit, convincing wins were recorded against Clyde, Queen of the

South, Albion Rovers and Hearts, who were beaten 5-1 at Bayview on the last day of the league season.

Rangers, who were engaged in a fascinating battle for the league title with Dundee towards the end of the campaign, emerged 3-1 winners from their midweek fixture with the Fifers at Ibrox on 13th April.

It has to be said, however, that for the Rangers game East Fife were without the influential figure of George Aitken, who had played superbly on his debut for Scotland in their 3-1 victory over England at Wembley just four days earlier. Described by *British Pathe News* as *"the biggest upset since Bannockburn"*, England were swept aside by a Scottish team made up almost entirely of players from Scottish League clubs, in which Rangers' Willie Waddell was outstanding.

Aitken played a part in Scotland's opener, when his throw-in from the left touch-line found Billy Steel, the only 'Anglo' in the side. The DerbyCounty man threaded the ball forward to Hibs' Lawrie Reilly, who squared for Third Lanark's Jimmy Mason to flick the ball into the net. With household names such as as Stanley Matthews, Jackie Millburn, Stan Mortensen, Tom Finney and Billy Wright in the England side that afternoon, it speaks volumes for George Aitken's reputation that he should feature so prominently in Scotland's victory. At the end of April, Aitken won his second cap in a 2-0 win against France at Hampden.

A final position of fourth was attained in the 'A' Division table, no mean feat for a team promoted only twelve months earlier.

May 1949 saw a new chapter in the history of the club opened as they embarked on their first ever trip abroad. A twenty strong party, consisting of fourteen players, four Directors, Manager Scot Symon and Trainer JohnnyGear, departed from Kirkcaldy Railway Station on 18th May bound for Harwich, where they boarded a ship for Denmark.

When the team disembarked in Esjberg, they were greeted on the quayside by former player Davie Russell, who was at the time employed as coach of a Danish club.

The first match of the tour was played in Sweden on 23rd May against a Stockholm select side, who were beaten 5-1 with goals from Duncan (2), Fleming, Morris and Davidson. Returning south to Denmark three days later, Ballklub 1909 provided stiffer opposition in Odense and were beaten by a single goal in front of a crowd of 6,000.

The final match of the tour was played against Odense Ballklub on 29th May and, following a 4-2 victory, the players were each presented with an ashtray emblazoned with a picture of Hans Kristian Andersen as a souvenir of their visit! Chairman John McArthur was presented with a silver plate. On their return to Harwich, the team took in the Woodcock v Mills fight in London before catching the train home.

Weeks later, Odense coach Davie Russell said that he was hoping to bring a Danish Select team over to tour Scotland in the coming season, "to restore some of the prestige which the Methil Men robbed them of during their recent tour". Unfortunately, the visit failed to materialise.

Over the summer of 1949 further improvements were carried out at Bayview. The concrete anti-tank blocks which had been placed strategically on Leven beach during the Second World War were transported to Methil and used to heighten the terracing at the west end of the ground. The blocks were so heavy that the bridge over the Scoonie Burn had to be strengthened to take the weight! It was expected that once the work was complete, the ground's capacity could be increased by around 3,000.

Season 1949/50 kicked off with six League Cup sectional matches against Hearts, Raith Rovers and Stirling Albion. The first match against Raith on 13th August tested the newly heightened terracing with a bumper crowd of over 20,000,

Dougie Davidson, star of the late 1940's. Signed from Dundee Violet in June 1946, Doug made his debut along with Henry Morris and Jimmy Philp against Dundee on 10th August 1946 in a 'B' Division fixture. Although never capped for Scotland, the inside-right did attract the attentions of the international selectors during his early days at Bayview after he and centre-forward Morris netted 38 goals between them in the space of just three months. (Author's Collection)

who were treated to a 3-0 win against their newly promoted local rivals. The League Cup section was won with ease and only one point was dropped in the process, against Hearts at Tynecastle.

The quarter-final paired the Fifers with Forfar Athletic, who included in their ranks a certain Tommy Adams, recently signed up by the 'B' Division side on a free transfer. On 17th September 1949 the first leg was played at StationPark, where the Fifers won 3-1 thanks to goals from Morris (2) and Black. The visiting spectators, however, kept their biggest cheer of the afternoon for Tommy Adams, who scored the 'Loons' only goal. The second leg was played at Bayview on the following Wednesday, where the home side hardly broke sweat as they romped home 5-1.

The semi-final against Rangers at Hampden on 8th October was a memorable occasion, although one mixed with joy and sadness. East Fife went ahead in the first half through a Brown header, and managed to hold on to their slender lead until six minutes before the end of normal time, when Rangers levelled.

In the second period of extra time, with tension filling the air, the sequence of events that East Fife supporters would speak about for years to come started to unfold. Charlie Fleming gathered the ball on the half way line and slowly headed towards goal. Then, with a sudden burst of speed, he swerved past Cox, Woodburn and Shaw. Fifteen yards from goal, 'Cannonball' unleashed a shot that hit the back of the net with such velocity that Rangers 'keeper Bobby Brown didn't even see the ball whiz past him!

The black and gold bedecked supporters in the 75,000 strong crowd danced with delight, then slowly became aware of a commotion in the main stand.

The excitement had been too much for East Fife Chairman John McArthur. When Fleming scored, Mr McArthur stood up as if to cheer, but uttered no sound. Instead, he collapsed on the lap of fellow Director Tom Anderson and, after being carried into the pavilion, died a few minutes later. Ironically, John McArthur had been advised by his doctor only days earlier that the excitement of attending football matches was endangering his health. Choosing to attend the League Cup semi-final had cost the Chairman his life, but he died watching his beloved football club achieve the one thing that had so far eluded them; victory over the great Glasgow Rangers.

Three weeks later, on 29th October 1949, the League Cup Final at HampdenPark had a 'derby' flavour, as East Fife took on second-leaguers Dunfermline Athletic.

In the week prior to the match, the team had to wear special training suits to keep dry and warm as torrential rain swept over Bayview Park, but conditions improved dramatically before the big day arrived. Unfortunately, the improved conditions did nothing to swell the crowd and the event was witnessed by a disappointing attendance of just 38,897. Speaking prior to the game, Manager Scot Symon modestly declared: *"It's a football game and that means anything can happen, but I reckon our chances are 50/50 and, of course, we are decidedly optimistic".*

Mr Symon's apprehension was proved to be unfounded when, in only the second minute of the game, Davie Duncan raced down the right wing and crossed into the goalmouth; Dunfermline 'keeper Johnstone failed to grasp the ball, and Charlie Fleming was on hand to fire home from just four yards.

The Methil Men continued to apply relentless pressure to their opponents' goal, and before long their tally was doubled through Davie Duncan, who fired home a left footer from an acute angle. Midway through the half the contest was all over bar the shouting when Henry Morris capitalised on slackness in the Pars defence to knock home number three.

Apart from an effort on the stroke of half time that hit the woodwork and rolled along the goal line before being cleared, Dunfermline just never looked like scoring throughout the entire ninety minutes.

In footballing terms, the game hadn't been a classic by any means, but the winning smile on the face of Captain Willie Laird when he accepted the trophy said it all. In winning the League Cup for the second time, East Fife had brought their tally of major trophy wins to three. Incredibly, this was the first time they had done so as a top league club!

Some 'die-hards' waited outside Hampden to congratulate the team and several players were slapped on the back amidst cries of "It'll be the Scottish Cup next!"

Around 500 supporters braved the chilly October evening outside BayviewPark awaiting the return of the victorious team. When the coach eventually pulled up outside the ground, Jimmy Philp and Bobby Black could be seen perched on the roof holding the trophy aloft.

The assembled crowd pleaded for Willie Laird to say a few words but, being the 'strong silent type', the team Captain let Chairman William Halley do the talking. Assisted by Director Tom Anderson, Halley climbed on top of the main turnstile block to address the supporters, where he stated: *"We have set a high standard of football in the County and, with your continued support, we shall maintain it"*.

Meanwhile, just as the club were embarking on their successful cup run, the league programme started well with a superb single goal win in the opening fixture against Hearts at Tynecastle on 10th September. Two weeks later it looked like the winning start was to be maintained as the Methil Men romped to a 4-1 half time lead against Raith at Stark's Park.

Arguably the most entertaining winger ever to grace the Bayview turf, Tommy Adams drew loud cheers from the East Fife supporters when he scored Forfar Athletic's late consolation goal against his old club in September 1949. "There is not much of him, but what there is is good", claimed the local press when Tommy first arrived at the club from Neilston Victoria in 1935. During his time with East Fife, the Outside Right made 239 appearances and scored 75 goals. (Author's Collection)

Three goals in a great second half fight-back by the Kirkcaldy side, however, resulted in a share of the points! Winning form then returned with a convincing 4-1 home victory against Queen of the South, but the win had to be achieved without the help of Henry Morris and George Aitken, who were both on international duty for Scotland against Northern Ireland in a World Cup qualifier in Belfast. East Fife's loss was certainly Scotland's gain, as Morris scored a debut hat trick in his country's 8-2 victory. One little known statistic concerning this game is that when Henry opened the scoring, he became the first British player to score in a World Cup match!

A sequence of results then ensued which were, in the eyes of the local press, regarded as extremely disappointing. Wins against Motherwell, Clyde and Third Lanark were countered by a disappointing defeat at the hands of 'A' Division newcomers Stirling Albion and fruitless trips to Easter Road and DensPark. Such was East Fife's status in Scottish Football at this time that a run of six league matches in the top flight which produced only three wins was considered by some to be unacceptable. Changed days indeed!

Unrest in the home dressing room during this spell was largely responsible for the inconsistent form. Henry Morris, who missed out on a second cap for Scotland after being injured in the home league game against Motherwell on 5th November, stormed out of a press conference just over a week later, stating that he was unhappy at Bayview and wanted a transfer.

Henry's outburst followed a statement at the press conference by Manager Scot Symon, who said that he had written to all clubs interested in East Fife players advising them that none were available. A week later fellow Scotland internationalist George Aitken, only days after winning his fourth Scotland cap against Wales at Hampden, also claimed that he would be happier plying his trade elsewhere.

The rift between club and players was soon patched up and, a week before Christmas, the supporters were treated to a fantastic 5-1 trouncing of Celtic at Bayview, where a Henry Morris brace along with single strikes from Duncan, Black and Fleming gave the Fifers their biggest ever win against the Parkhead side.

Following a narrow defeat against Hearts at Tynecastle in the next match, the year was rounded off with a 2-1 win against Aberdeen at Pittodrie.

The 22,515 crowd that saw Ian Gardiner make his debut in the 3-0 victory over Raith Rovers in the 1950 New Year Derby is recorded as the largest ever assembled at Bayview. This, however, is debatable.

Not only did the *Leven Mail* give the attendance as 21,715, they stated that the 22,500 who paid to see the match against Rangers in November 1948 was still the record.

What seems likely is that the spectators seated in the 800 seat grandstand were not included in the 21,715 quoted in the Leven Mail for the Rovers match and, when these two figures are added together, the 'record attendance' of 22,515 is the result. Does this mean that the crowd figures quoted in the press at this time did not include those seated in the stand? If this is the case, then the attendance at the Rangers game could actually have been 23,300! Unfortunately, no official records exist at the club, so we may never know!

No fewer than six league matches were played during January 1950, with the only defeat suffered during the month inflicted by Rangers, who won 2-0 at Bayview on Jimmy Bonthrone's debut a week after the Raith match.

The 1950 Scottish Cup campaign got under way on the last Saturday in January when Highland League side Fraserburgh visited Methil. Although the north-east outfit put up a good fight, they were no match for the Fifers, who won comfortably with goals from Morris (2), Gardiner and Fleming without reply.

In what turned out to be Jackie Davidson's last match before being transferred to Kilmarnock for £1,500, Henry Morris bagged another brace in the following round against Falkirk at Brockville as the visitors won by the odd goal in five, with Charlie Fleming netting the other counter.

The favourable form was maintained in the three league fixtures played between the two cup ties, with full points gained from Clyde and Partick Thistle either side of a home draw against Hibernian on 25th March which attracted a crowd of 20,000 to Bayview.

The quarter-final of the Scottish Cup saw the Fifers paired with the 'Warriors' of Stenhousemuir at Ochilview, which was safely negotiated with a 3-0 win. Again, Henry Morris found the mark on two occasions, with the other goal coming from Black.

In the two league games preceding the semi-final, Dundee were beaten by a single goal at Bayview before Celtic exacted revenge for their Methil humiliation by winning 4-1 at Parkhead on 25th March.

The semi-final of the Scottish Cup was played against Partick Thistle at Ibrox on the first day of April, where goals from Charlie Fleming and Henry Morris were enough to win the game 2-1 and put East Fife into the Scottish Cup Final for the third time in their history.

Unfortunately, events leading up to the final against Rangers on 22nd April 1950 left the Fifers without first and second choice goalkeepers Niven and McGarrity, so third choice 'keeper Gordon Easson was forced to make his first team debut in what was one of the biggest games in the club's history, watched by 118,262 spectators; the biggest crowd ever to watch an East Fife match.

The worst fears of the Fife supporters were realised only 45 seconds into the game, when Willie Finlay scored with a diving header to give Rangers the lead. Slowly, however, the Fifers defence and midfield gained confidence and pushed forward, but there was no further scoring before half-time. The early stages of the second half saw East Fife again surge forward, but the Rangers' defence, in which George Young was outstanding, soaked up any chances created. Having weathered the storm, Rangers started to push forward once more and young Gordon Easson was forced to dive full length to save a fierce Sammy Cox free kick from the edge of the penalty area. The light-blues just couldn't be kept at bay, however, and Willie Thornton scored his side's second and third goals with close range headers to end the contest.

Just four days after the cup final, two East Fife players represented Scotland in a 3-1 victory against Switzerland at Hampden. As George Aitken made his fifth and final appearance for Scotland as an East Fife player, Allan Brown became the third East Fife man to score on his International debut. Aitken's five caps won whilst playing for East Fife is a club record which is unlikely to be surpassed.

Brown went on to represent his country on a further two occasions during the following month against Portugal in Lisbon and France in Paris, and scored in both games.

The league programme concluded with defeat against Third Lanark at Cathkin and victory against Falkirk at Brockville, to finish in fourth place for the second season in a row. Although there was a gap of thirteen points between East Fife and champions Rangers, the club could still be proud of their final placing and, taking the winning of the League Cup into account along with their Scottish Cup final appearance, it could be argued that season 1949/50 was the best in the history of the club. What couldn't be denied was that East Fife had by now become one of the most respected clubs in Scottish Football.

Following the euphoria of the 1949/50 campaign, however, the 1950/51 season turned out to be a huge disappointment. The League Cup was surrendered at the first hurdle, with the club completing their series of first round sectional games in third place.

After the promise shown over the previous two seasons, it was expected that a serious challenge could once again be made at landing the league title, but results fell far short of expectations over the first half of the campaign, with heavy defeats suffered at Tynecastle, CelticPark and Ibrox. The poor form was due in no small way to the unease and uncertainty which existed off the field of play. Throughout the first half of the season, certain key players complained that they were unhappy at Bayview and the club were forced into a legal battle in order to retain international stars Allan Brown and George Aitken.

Neither player had pulled on a black and gold jersey since the end of the previous season and, eventually, in December 1950, Brown was sold to Blackpool for a reported fee of £27,000, followed in early 1951 by the departure of Aitken for Third Lanark. Having already won three caps during his time at Bayview, Brown went on to be capped a further eleven times during his days at Bloomfield Road, bringing his tally to fourteen. Similarly, George Aitken went on to play for Scotland a further three times whilst playing for Sunderland to add to the five caps won during his time with East Fife.

Not surprisingly, the unrest behind the scenes and the departure of key players continued to have an adverse affect, and it came as no surprise when Raith Rovers won the New Year Derby at Stark's Park with ease.

Hopes of a good run in the Scottish Cup were also brought to an early halt, with Celtic emerging 4-2 winners in the first round replayed match at Parkhead on 31st January 1951 following a 2-2 draw at Bayview.

There was even the threat of relegation hanging over the club in the latter stages of the season, but survival in the top league was eventually secured with an unbeaten run of seven league matches, which included a 3-0 home win against Celtic, as the season drew to a close.

A final league position of tenth was achieved, twenty points behind champions Hibernian and just five points clear of relegated Clyde. Although the team had rallied towards the end of the campaign, it was clear that a difficult task lay ahead for Manager Scot Symon during the 1951 close-season as he attempted to raise morale and freshen up the side.

A tough series of first round League Cup matches awaited the club at the beginning of the 1951/52 season. With both Rangers and Aberdeen in the Fifers' section along with Queen of the South, qualification for the second round was always going to be difficult and, not surprisingly, Rangers emerged as group winners. One significant event during the series of League Cup matches was the first team debut of Andy Matthew, a product of the club's youth set up, against Aberdeen on 8th August.

Results from the opening series of league fixtures told a different story from the disappointing League Cup results. After the opening game was lost against Hearts at Tynecastle on 8th September, during which Jimmy Philp bid a sad farewell, a ten match unbeaten run ensued which was eventually brought to a halt against Hibernian at Easter Road in mid-November as the Fifers mounted a serious challenge amongst the clubs vying for the championship.

At the beginning of December, the club once again had the honour of having a player selected for international duty, but this time from an unusual source! On 5th December 1951, in a match arranged to commemorate the 75th anniversary of the Welsh Football Association, Charlie Fleming played for the 'Rest of the UK' against Wales at NinianPark in Cardiff. After going three goals down to the home nation early in the second half, Charlie scored with a long range effort to spark off a spirited fight-back by 'The Rest', but Wales held on to win by the odd goal in five.

Pole position was finally achieved at Dens Park on 8th December when Dundee were defeated by the odd goal in seven, a position that was consolidated by beating Celtic 3-1 at Bayview a week later.

The winning form could not be maintained however and, with the next four fixtures all ending in defeat, the lead was surrendered to Hibernian.

The team that opened the league season against Hearts at Tynecastle on 8th September 1951 in what turned out to be Jimmy Philp's last appearance in the black and gold. Back row, from left: Archie Smith, Sammy Stewart, Johnny Curran, Jimmy Philp, Peter Aird, Danny McLennan. Front row, from left: Jacky Stewart, Charlie Fleming, Ian Gardiner, Jimmy Bonthrone, Andy Matthew. (Photo: Courtesy of John Ross)

Just when an air of despondency was descending on the club and its supporters, the visit of Rangers to Methil on 5th January 1952 went a long way to lift the spirits of the Bayview faithful. East Fife took the lead through Jackie Stewart in only six minutes, the ball finding its way into the net off Rangers' left-back George Young. The home side's lead didn't last long, however, and six minutes later Willie Thornton had the visitors back on level terms. Early in the second half, Jimmy

Bonthrone sent the black and gold bunnets high in the air when he scored the goal that gave the Fifers their first-ever home win against Rangers in a competitive match during peacetime.

Although the next match was lost against Motherwell at FirPark, the following three games were won convincingly against St.Mirren, Queen of the South and, most importantly, against fellow championship contenders Hibernian.

On a sadder note, Henry Morris' first appearance of the season in the victory against Queen of the South on 2nd February also turned out to be his last in a first team jersey. With Henry continuing to play for the reserves until the end of season 1952/53, the fact that a player of his calibre appeared only once in the first eleven during the course of two seasons demonstrates the quality and depth of the East Fife player pool during the early 1950's. Morris, who to this day shares with Jock Wood the club record for scoring the most league goals in a season (41), was eventually handed a free transfer in April 1953.

Taking a break from the league programme, the first round of the Scottish Cup was safely negotiated with a 4-0 victory at Eyemouth, but hopes of a good cup run were ended with a 2-1 defeat against Airdrieonians at Broomfield in round two. Defeat against Partick Thistle at Firhill on the first day of March signalled the start of a faltering finish to the league programme and, of the four matches remaining, two were won and two were lost. The final league match of the season on 26th April saw Motherwell defeated 6-1, which ensured a best-ever final position of third in the table, eight points behind Champions Hibernian and just four adrift of runners-up Rangers.

It was a case of 'so near, and yet so far'. Of the ten matches lost during the league campaign, eight had come during the second half of the programme and many of these defeats were against teams from the lower half of the table. Season 1951/52 proved that the team could beat the very best in the land, although they repeatedly failed to perform against the less fancied clubs. In theory, winning the Scottish League title was well within the capabilities of East Fife Football Club, but would the championship flag ever fly over Bayview? Perhaps the following campaign would produce the kind of consistent form expected from a title-winning side!

The early summer of 1952 should have seen the Fifers embark on their second trip abroad, with the team due to sail south for a tour of Spain, Portugal and Gibraltar on 21st May. Surprisingly, despite their obvious attraction as one of Scotland's top teams, the club found difficulty in arranging matches against Spanish and Portuguese sides. When it became apparent that there was not going to be enough games played to cover the expense of the trip, the tour was cancelled.

Season 1952/53 began with yet another first round exit from the League Cup, with the Fifers finishing second to Third Lanark in a section that also contained Falkirk and Queen of the South.

The league programme, however, started in blistering style with a 7-1 home win against Clyde which saw the club top the league on the first day of the campaign.

The points were shared in the following match against Motherwell at FirPark, but the next five matches were all won to maintain pole position. The winning sequence culminated on 18th October with a 3-2 win against Rangers in front of 20,000 at Bayview, thanks to a Jimmy Bonthrone brace and a single counter from Davie Duncan.

Despite two defeats over the next four league games, including a 6-3 reverse against Aberdeen at Pittodrie, first place in the league was maintained until 22nd November, when home defeat against nearest challengers Hibernian saw the two clubs exchange places. A 3-1 home win against Third Lanark, however, was enough to regain first place, a position which was maintained until the middle of January 1953.

A first round Scottish Cup tie against Vale of Leithen at Bayview on 24th January brought a welcome break from league fixtures and a barrowload of goals for the disappointing crowd of 5,338 as the Fifers romped home 7-1, but once again hopes of a good cup run were dashed at Airdrie in the second round.

Back on league business, pole position was surrendered on the last day of January at Ibrox, where the home side recorded a convincing 4-1 win. Despite victory against Aberdeen in their next fixture, the Fifers couldn't regain their place at the top of the table. It was at this point that a decision was made which would, in the eyes of many, have a far-reaching effect on the eventual outcome of the season, when the club decided to accept invitations from several English clubs to embark on a series of energy-sapping midweek friendly matches south of the border.

The reason for these matches being played was that the host clubs had recently installed floodlights, and were keen to arrange midweek 'glamour' fixtures against the top teams in the country. The novelty of floodlit games against attractive opposition would obviously produce large crowds, which would in turn swell the coffers. East Fife, challenging for the Scottish League Championship, were considered to be very attractive opponents.

The midweek matches came in for a fair amount of criticism from the Bayview faithful, however, who rightly claimed that such games were an unnecessary drain on the players' energy and injuries could also be incurred. Despite the vociferous protests from the supporters, the matches went ahead and, on 16th February 1953, six goals were scored without reply at non-league GloucesterCity. The following evening, Worcester were beaten 7-2.

The following Saturday, a crowd of 23,000 saw the points shared with Dundee at Dens Park and a week later the fans' fears appeared to be justified when Partick Thistle took both points from a tired East Fife side at Bayview.

The beginning of March saw the club off on their travels again, this time to Sunderland, where the home side were beaten 3-1 at RokerPark in front of an astonishing crowd of 37,565!

Up north again three days later, the critics were silenced as Airdrieonians were beaten 3-1 to keep the league title within reach.

Two midweek friendlies were then played in the space of two days. On 10th March, a sell out crowd of 26,560 witnessed a 2-0 win against BristolCity at Ashton Gate and, the following evening, SwindonTown were beaten 3-2 on their own soil.

The Fifers then had the luxury of a blank week as the quarter-finals of the Scottish Cup were played out, which gave the team plenty of time to prepare for the visit of Celtic the following Saturday, 21st March 1953. A 4-1 home victory was the result in a match that saw Celtic's Charlie Tully carried off after colliding with the touchline barrier. The game also marked the last first team appearance of Davie Duncan at Bayview, although he remained with the club until being transferred to Raith Rovers in January 1954.

After drawing 2-2 with Carlisle United at BruntonPark on the following Tuesday, Third Lanark were beaten 3-0 at CathkinPark on the last Saturday in March.

When St.Mirren were beaten 7-0 at Bayview at the beginning of April, it looked like there was a real chance of the league title coming to Methil. There was now a firm belief that manager Scot Symon, who had only just announced his departure from Bayview at the end of the season, would soon deposit the only major Scottish honour yet to be won by the club safely in the Bayview trophy cabinet.

Before any further league matches could be played, however, there was yet another trip south to consider. On Thursday 9th April, Notts County were soundly beaten 5-2 at Meadow Lane and, after a brief return home to catch breath, the Fifers were beaten 4-1 by Newcastle United at St James' Park on the following Wednesday evening.

There were now only three league matches remaining.

Going into the match against Celtic in Glasgow on 18th April, East Fife were level on points with league leaders Rangers. A share of the points in a 1-1 draw at CelticPark was enough to regain first place, although the Ibrox club had a game in hand. Two days later a bumper 47,000 crowd lined the terraces at Easter Road for the crucial league match against Hibernian, the third club in the league championship equation, where the Fifers' championship dream was as good as ended with a 2-1 win for the home side. On the same evening Rangers regained first place with a 3-0 win at Motherwell and, the following Saturday, Hibs maintained their challenge for the title by beating Third Lanark 7-1.

During the following midweek, salt was rubbed in the Fifers' wounds when they lost 4-2 at Tynecastle, but by then the challenge for the league title was a lost cause.

Although Hibernian managed to keep up the momentum and successfully negotiate their remaining league fixture, the championship went to Ibrox on goal average after Rangers gained three points from their remaining two fixtures against Dundee and Queen of the South.

Once again, it had been a case of 'so near and yet so far'. Was it nerves that told in the end? Or was it, as some maintained, the energy-sapping schedule of midweek friendlies at distant venues that cost the Methil Men the Scottish League Championship?

It was the closest that East Fife had ever come to winning the title and, with Scot Symon departing for Preston North End, it was widely believed that the club would never again have such a golden opportunity to land the one prize that had so far eluded them. Symon lasted just one season at Deepdale before taking over at the helm of Glasgow Rangers in June 1954 where, not surprisingly, he went on to become one of the greatest managers in the history of the Ibrox club.

Chapter Thirteen: The Dawson Years

Following the departure of Scot Symon to Preston North End, former Falkirk, Rangers and Scotland goalkeeper Jerry Dawson took over as Manager of East Fife before the start of the 1953/54 season. The club expected the success they had enjoyed in the years since the war to continue unabated and, for the first season at least, all seemed well with Dawson at the helm. Despite losing his first game in charge with a 4-1 reverse at Broomfield against Airdrieonians in the first of the League Cup sectional matches on 8th August 1953, the previous season's form soon returned. After a late Charlie Fleming equaliser secured a share of the points with Celtic at Bayview during the following midweek, home victories against both Airdrieonians and Aberdeen put the League Cup campaign firmly back on the rails. After moving back to the top of their section with a single goal victory over Celtic at Parkhead on Wednesday 26th August, a quarter-final clash with near neighbours Dunfermline Athletic was secured with a thrilling 4-3 win against Aberdeen at Pittodrie three days later.

The Methil Men effectively killed off Dunfermline's challenge for the trophy in the first leg of the tie on 12th September with a 6-2 victory in which Charlie Fleming notched an unbelievable five goals. The second leg was played out at East EndPark on the following Wednesday evening, where a Fleming hat-trick secured a 3-2 win and a semi-final tie with Hibernian. Amazingly, over both legs of the tie, 'Cannonball' Fleming had notched all but one of his side's nine goals!

Not surprisingly, Charlie's goal scoring feats attracted the attentions of the international selectors, and the player was duly picked to represent his country against Northern Ireland in Belfast on 3rd October 1953. Despite scoring twice in Scotland's 3-1 victory, Charlie, like Henry Morris before him, never won another cap!

This would, perhaps, be an appropriate time to reflect on the international honours won by the club's players over the 22 years since Dan Liddle first pulled on a Scotland jersey back in 1931. During this time no fewer than six East Fife players, Davie Duncan, George Aitken, Henry Morris, Allan Brown and Charlie Fleming, as well as the aforementioned Liddle, represented Scotland at full international level a total of sixteen times. Amazingly, four of that number, Duncan, Morris, Brown and Fleming, all scored on their debut!

In addition to their full international caps, it should be remembered that Davie Duncan and Allan Brown also represented the Scottish League against their English counterparts in 1948 and 1950 respectively. Jackie Stewart did likewise against the Irish League in 1953, followed by Ian Gardiner, also against the Irish League, a year later.

The League Cup semi-final against Hibernian was played before a 38,000 crowd at Tynecastle on 10th October, where two goals from right-back Don Emery and a single counter from Jimmy Bonthrone proved just enough to overcome the Edinburgh side 3-2 and put the Fifers into their third League Cup final. It was a remarkable achievement considering the competition was only in its eighth season!

A crowd of 88,529 paid for entry into HampdenPark for the final on 24th October 1953 against Partick Thistle, conquerors of Rangers in the other semi-final. Ian Gardiner and Charlie Fleming gave East Fife a two-goal lead at half-time, but Thistle pulled up their socks for the second period and eventually squared the match at 2-2 with goals from Walker and McKenzie. Partick played the better football for most of the second half but, as the match drew to a close, the Fifers started to come back into the game and pressurised the Thistle goal. With only two minutes left on the clock, Frank Christie notched the all-important third East Fife goal and the League Cup was on its way to Methil for the third time.

The team's form during the first half of the league programme was reasonably satisfactory. After sharing four goals with Hearts in the opening game, the Fifers secured a draw in the local derby at Stark's Park before beating Falkirk 4-1 at Bayview on 26th September. The first league defeats of the season came on the Saturdays either side of the League Cup final; a 3-1 reverse against Clyde at Shawfield on 3rd October followed by a 2-0 defeat at Ibrox two weeks later. Back at Bayview for only the second home league match of the season, St.Mirren were beaten 2-0 in Methil on the last Saturday in October then, on 7th November, a trip to Annfield proved pointless when Stirling Albion won by the odd goal in five. On Saturday 14th November, Celtic were the visitors to Bayview, where Jimmy Bonthrone opened the scoring before a Charlie Fleming a hat-trick completed the home side's tally as the visitors were defeated 4-1, the exact same score by which the Glasgow side had been beaten during the previous season. Wins over Airdrieonians and Partick Thistle, draws with Dundee and Hearts and a narrow defeat from Hibs were to follow before the long journey south to Dumfries was made on Boxing Day 1953 to face Queen of the South. It may have been the long journey south which was to blame, or it may have been down to over indulgence in Christmas cake the previous day, but when the final whistle blew all the festive cheer was with the home side. By winning 5-0, Queen of the South recorded their biggest ever win over East Fife, a score line which was repeated in November 1960 and has never since been bettered.

January 1954 started reasonably well, with a 1-1 draw against Raith Rovers at Bayview in the New Year Derby followed by a 3-3 draw at Brockville against Falkirk the following day. Victories over Clyde and Hamilton Academical were to follow before Rangers were beaten 2-1 at Bayview on 23rd January to record the Fifers' third home league victory in succession over the Glasgow giants.

A week later Queen of the South were the visitors to Methil for a Scottish Cup first round tie, and the Fifers were confident they could exact revenge for their embarrassing defeat from the Dumfries club just a month earlier. Yet again the Methil Men were left red-faced, however, as Queen of the South inflicted another drubbing on the home side – this time by three goals to nil. Exit from the Scottish Cup under such circumstances seemed to knock all the confidence out of the team and, from the five league matches that followed, the only point gained was from the encounter with St.Mirren in Paisley. Then came a complete reversal of form, with the last six league fixtures of the season producing wins against Partick Thistle, Stirling Albion, Aberdeen, Hamilton and Queen of the South along with a share of the points with Dundee. The revenge 4-0 victory over Queen of the South on the last day of the league campaign saw Charlie Fleming score yet another hat-trick to finish the season as top scorer with 36 goals.

A final league position of sixth was achieved, on equal points with fourth-placed Rangers and fifth-placed Hibernian, but nine adrift of league champions Celtic. Had it not been for the disappointing series of results during the early part of the year, the Fifers could well have challenged the 'Hoops' for the league title during the run in to the end of the season.

The 1954/55 season started with East Fife winning their League Cup section once again, but it certainly wasn't all plain sailing! Victories were recorded both home and away against Hibs and Queen of the South, but a 3-0 defeat from Aberdeen at Bayview followed by a 5-1 reverse at Pittodrie should really have knocked the Fifers out of the competition. Fortunately, a quarter-final place was secured thanks to the 'Dons' dismal showing in their fixtures with both Hibs and Queen of the South. The League Cup quarter-final against Morton was contested over two games. After a 2-2 draw in the first leg at

Cappielow on Wednesday 22nd September, a 2-0 home win in the second leg with goals from Bonthrone and Fleming saw the Fifers progress to the semi-finals.

The following Saturday, 2nd October, turned out to be one of the most depressing afternoons in East Fife's history. With a League Cup semi-final against Motherwell to look forward to, a confident East Fife side welcomed Rangers to Methil for the third league fixture of the season, having beaten Raith and drawn with Kilmarnock in their first two matches.

Winning 2-1 at half time with goals from Fleming and Christie, it looked as if the Fifers were capable of pulling off their fourth home victory in a row over the Glasgow side, but it was not to be. In a disastrous second half, the home defence collapsed and Rangers scored six goals without reply to win the match 7-2, their biggest-ever win over East Fife.

The drubbing from Rangers was hardly the ideal preparation for the semi-final against Motherwell at Hampden on Saturday 9th October where, despite playing reasonably well on the day, the Fifers exited the competition to the 'Steel Men', who won the right to face Hearts in the final with a 2-1 victory. Ian Gardiner, who had been capped for the Scottish League against the Irish League just three weeks earlier, scored the Fifers' only goal.

League form dipped following the League Cup exit, but revenge over Motherwell was gained with a 5-3 league victory at FirPark on 20th November.

One innovation worth mentioning at this time was the installation of a 'land-line' from Bayview to nearby Wemyss Memorial Hospital at a cost of £150 and an annual rental of £13 payable to GPO Telephones, for the purpose of broadcasting live East Fife matches to patients on Saturday afternoons. The network was eventually extended to CameronHospital in Windygates, Victoria Hospital in Kirkcaldy and Kirkcaldy GeneralHospital, an arrangement that also allowed for the transmission of Raith Rovers matches in the opposite direction!

Considering the poor league form that had plagued the team during the early part of the season, it came as a welcome surprise when two goals from Charlie Fleming secured a 2-2 draw with Celtic in Glasgow on 4th December. When the same player bagged another brace in the 5-0 win against Stirling Albion a week later, it looked like the team had turned the corner, but a dismal run of nine league games without a win then ensued that lasted until the following March! Only two points were gained from draws with Aberdeen and Dundee during this disappointing spell and, as if league form wasn't bad enough, the Fifers bowed out of the Scottish Cup at the first hurdle to Kilmarnock on 5th February 1955.

One major factor that undoubtedly contributed to the poor form was the transfer of Charlie Fleming to Sunderland in early January. Although East Fife received cash plus Tommy Wright in exchange for 'Cannonball', the Scottish international forward took time to settle and failed to find the net regularly during his early days at Bayview.

There was also the suggestion that the poor form was down to the fact that team had once again been exhausted by the series of midweek friendlies which were played during this period. Energy-sapping trips to Accrington and Reading were made in the weeks prior to Leeds United's visit to Methil on 7th March 1955 for the official opening of the Bayview floodlights. The Yorkshire men won 2-1 on the night with a star-studded side that included the legendary Welsh wizard John Charles at centre-half.

The floodlights should actually have been officially switched on with a match against Sunderland on 28th February as part of the Charlie Fleming transfer deal, but the RokerPark side pulled out due to their involvement in the latter stages of the F.A. Cup.

The Fife were now deep in the relegation mire, but there arrived a faint glimmer of hope in the form of new signing Angus Plumb from Falkirk in early March. Plumb was immediately drafted in to the side to lead the attack in place of Wright and scored a brace on his debut as Motherwell were overcome 4-2 at Bayview on 12th March.

Next came a no scoring draw with Hibs at Easter Road before Celtic came to Methil on 30th March and, despite losing by the odd goal in seven, the Fifers were starting to look like an improved side.

The battle to avoid relegation was put firmly on the rails with a run of four straight wins in April starting with an impressive 4-0 victory over Stirling Albion at Annfield and followed by convincing wins against St.Mirren, Hearts and Falkirk.

A 2-2 draw in the return fixture with Falkirk at Brockville on 23rd April 1955 finally saved East Fife from relegation and, according to Manager Jerry Dawson, it was all down to the signing of Angus Plumb. Since joining the ranks at Bayview the influential striker had managed to score eleven goals in eight games as the Fifers rose from second bottom to a more respectable final position in the middle of the league table.

During the summer of 1955, several 'A' Division clubs intimated that they would not be entering their reserve sides into the 'C' Division for the forthcoming campaign, which meant that the competition would be unable to operate successfully. The Scottish League had no option but to allow the five non-reserve members of the 'C' Division, namely Dumbarton, East Stirlingshire, Montrose, Berwick Rangers and Stranraer, entry into the 'B' Division. The knock-on effect was that the 'A' Division was increased in size eighteen members, which in turn meant that the two clubs just relegated from the top league, Motherwell and Clyde, were handed a last minute reprieve!

East Fife started season 1955/56 with the same team that had finished the previous campaign. At first it seemed that the decision to stand by the previous season's eleven was the correct one when Raith Rovers were beaten 4-2 at StarksPark in the first of the League Cup sectional matches. The winning feeling was not to last, however, as four of their remaining five fixtures were lost resulting in exit from the competition at the first hurdle.

Tommy Wright finally found his scoring boots with a brace in the opening league match against Motherwell on 10th September, but his two goals were in vain as the 'Steel Men' romped home 5-2 in front of a 10,000 FirPark crowd.

A 2-1 home victory over Kilmarnock in the next match raised the Fifers' hopes, but they were quickly dashed the following week with a 4-0 reverse against Raith in Kirkcaldy.

The poor form continued and, by the end of the year, only four league games had been won from seventeen fixtures, with eight matches lost and the points shared in five. Included in the aforementioned results, however, was an impressive 8-1 home win against Airdrieonians and a share of the spoils with Celtic in Glasgow.

Taking a break from the rigours of league football, two very impressive results were recorded in floodlit friendlies at Bayview during the first half of the season. Sunderland, with former Fifers Charlie Fleming and George Aitken in their ranks, were beaten 1-0 under the Bayview lights on 10th October, before Nottingham Forest were put to the sword by the odd goal in five on 22nd November.

A crowd of 13,000 saw Raith beaten 3-0 in the New Year Derby at Bayview, but again the joy was short lived as the next four league matches produced just one win and three defeats.

As if their league form wasn't bad enough, the Fifers made an embarrassing exit from the Scottish Cup at the hands of Stenhousemuir at Bayview on 8th February. The match was the first game in the history of the Scottish Cup competition to be played under floodlights; the kick off time having been brought forward by fifteen minutes in order to beat the Hibs v Raith Rovers tie at Easter Road! Unfortunately, the occasion turned out to be more memorable for the visitors than the home side as the 'Warriors' ran out 3-1 winners in front of a 6,000 crowd.

The twelve remaining league fixtures produced seven wins and five defeats, enough to secure top league status for another year albeit by just a few points. One pleasing aspect about results during this series of matches, however, was that both Celtic and Rangers were beaten at Bayview by the scores of 3-0 and 2-1 respectively.

Despite having won the battle against relegation, general feeling amongst the East Fife supporters during the summer of 1956 was that the forthcoming season would produce yet another fight to maintain the club's top league status. The main reason behind the despondency was that once again the club decided to retain the same players that had worn the black and gold jerseys during the previous campaign.

"They're not getting any younger", remarked one supporter in a letter to the *Leven Mail,* who went on to predict that if there were no new faces at Bayview then East Fife would do no better than they had in the season just past. New faces or not, it seemed extremely unlikely that the club would proceed beyond the first round of the League Cup, having been drawn in the same section as Rangers, Celtic and Aberdeen.

In the first sectional match Rangers proved too strong for the ageing Fifers and easily won 3-0. Although Aberdeen were defeated 2-1 at Bayview in the next game, the remaining four matches were all lost, resulting in a final placing of bottom. The first league match played during the 1956/57 competition produced a 3-1 win over Queen of the South, with the goals coming from Leishman, Bonthrone and McLennan. After drawing with Motherwell at FirPark in the second game, Raith Rovers took both points at Bayview on 22nd September with a 3-2 victory. It was October before the second league win was recorded, a thrilling 4-3 win over Aberdeen at Bayview, with Leishman, Plumb and Wallace all getting their names on the score sheet along with an own goal from the visitors. The following week the Fifers went one better and won their first away match of the season; a very impressive 5-2 victory over Hearts at Tynecastle in front of a 22,000 crowd. Again, the Methil Men had one of their opposite number to thank, with Hearts' Glidden putting the ball into his own net for the Fifers' fourth; the other goals coming from Bonthrone, Leishman and a brace from Plumb.

After the points were shared against Falkirk in the next match, the now familiar series of 'floodlit friendlies' kicked off with a journey south to face both Reading and Brentford in the midweek before their league fixture against Dunfermline Athletic at Bayview on Saturday 27th October. The 'Pars' took full points with a 4-3 victory, a result which many supporters once again blamed, with no little justification, on the exhaustion resulting from the two matches played in the space of as many days in the south of England.

Worse was to follow. Newly promoted Queen's Park dumped the Fifers 3-0 at Hampden in the next game before Celtic ran out 4-0 winners in Glasgow a week later. Although a home win against Airdrieonians was to follow, heavy defeats from Hibs and Rangers saw the team slip down the table as the end of the year approached.

Following a disappointing 4-1 defeat against Raith Rovers in the New Year Derby at Stark's Park, there was no let up in the slump and only one point was won from the following six league matches. The dismal run was finally halted with a 4-1 victory over Dunfermline Athletic at East End Park on 23rd February 1957; the first league win since Dundee had been beaten 2-0 at Bayview on the Saturday before Christmas! During the bad run of league results, progress was made in the Scottish Cup with a 4-0 home win against St.Johnstone. After holding Kilmarnock to a no scoring draw at Bayview in the next round, however, interest in the competition was ended with a 2-0 defeat at RugbyPark in the replay.

Still in serious relegation trouble, the Fifers played host to Queen's Park on 2nd March and lost to the First Division newcomers for the second time in the season. Then, in typically unpredictable fashion, Celtic visited Methil a week later and were beaten 2-0 with goals from Gillon and Matthew! Anyone thinking that the club had turned the corner with this result, however, was soon to have their hopes dashed as only one point was won from the next five games, leaving the Fifers second bottom of the league with only two matches remaining. A Jimmy Bonthrone goal in the penultimate league match against Dundee at DensPark on 20th April resulted in a much needed win and a slight glimmer of hope going into the last game. The Fifers were now on equal points with Dunfermline and Queen of the South, but unfortunately both had a game in hand.

The Fifers' fate was finally decided in the last league match of the season when Jimmy Bonthrone almost single-handedly rescued the club by scoring all five goals as St.Mirren were swept aside 5-2 at Bayview. With Dunfermline and Queen of the South both losing, this result meant that the latter would have to beat Celtic by twenty clear goals in their last game to finish above East Fife! In the event, the 'Doonhamers' only managed to draw with Celtic and the Dumfries club joined the 'Pars' on their way back down to Division Two.

During the years that had passed since the last major trophy had been won, namely the winning of the League Cup in 1953, lack of success on the park gradually left its mark on the club's finances. After having considered the situation for some time, the decision was taken during the summer of 1957 to revert to part-time status in order to cut costs.

As well as the financial troubles behind the scenes, matters on the field of play were far from perfect and, to say that the 1957/58 season started poorly, is an understatement.

In the pre-season trial match, played at Bayview on 3rd August 1957, the first team lost 3-1 to the reserves. *"We'll just have to wait and see"*, commented the *Leven Mail*, before adding: *"the mere fact that the first eleven should lose to the reserves is bound to disturb the calmest of minds"*.

The fears of the local press reporter were to prove correct. In the first competitive match of the season, a League Cup sectional fixture on 10th August 1957, the part-time Fifers were dumped 4-0 by Hibernian in Edinburgh. Meanwhile, at Bayview, the reserves were soundly thrashed 8-1 by the Easter Road side's second eleven. The following midweek saw Celtic visit Methil in the same competition, where a 12,000 attendance saw the 'hoops' deepen the gloom with a resounding 4-1 win.

Things then went from bad to worse as the Fifers suffered another home defeat at the hands of Airdrieonians before being thumped 6-1 by Celtic in Glasgow.

In an attempt to stop the team losing so many goals, Manager Jerry Dawson decided to implement a new game plan for the match against Airdrieonians at Broomfield, in which no East Fife half-back was allowed to enter their opponents half. East Fife lost 9-1, a defeat which equalled the club's previous record defeat from Celtic over 26 years earlier!

Sandwiched in between these acutely embarrassing results was a home draw against Hibernian, which meant that the series of League Cup first round fixtures was completed with the team at the bottom their section having gained just one point.

On 7th September the Fifers played their first league match of the season and suffered defeat yet again, this time from Clyde at Shawfield. A greatly improved performance the following week saw the points shared in a 2-2 draw with Partick Thistle at Bayview, which prompted the *Leven Mail* to comment with renewed optimism: *"we'll stick out our necks and prophesy that East Fife won't go down this season"*.

The following Saturday, 21st September, it seemed as though the local press had got it right as near neighbours Raith Rovers were beaten 2-0 at Stark's Park in front of a 13,000 crowd. A week later Queen's Park were beaten 4-0 at Bayview and everything in the garden seemed rosy once more!

Then, on Saturday 5th October 1957, disaster struck at TynecastlePark, Edinburgh.

Undaunted by the failure of his game plan against Airdrieonians, manager Dawson decided to employ the same tactics for the league match against Hearts. The end result was that the East Fife players, according to the local press report, *"could only stand and stare and offer what little resistance they could"* as Hearts ripped them apart by nine goals to nil. It was, and still is, the biggest defeat in the history of East Fife Football Club.

The shell-shocked Fifers went on to concede a further eight defeats before the end of the year, during which time they managed to win only three games. They did, however, manage a creditable 3-3 draw with Rangers at Ibrox on 30th November and were considered unfortunate not to have won the match, having led 3-1 at half time through goals from Matthew, Mochan and Ingram.

A share of the points in the New Year Derby with Raith Rovers at Bayview was followed by further defeats from Aberdeen and Clyde before full points were taken from Queen's Park at Hampden on 11th January 1958. Then came a run of five league defeats during which only one goal was scored against nineteen conceded before Third Lanark were beaten 2-1 at Cathkin Park on 19th March.

The Fifers also suffered a 2-1 home defeat from Hearts in the first round of the Scottish Cup in front of a 13,500 Bayview crowd during this poor sequence of results.

Meanwhile, Jimmy Bonthrone, who had found the transition from full-time to part-time football hard to take, was transferred to Dundee in exchange for former Under-23 international player Felix Reilly at the beginning of March. On the same day that Bonthrone left for DensPark, the Fifers attempted to bring Charlie Fleming back from Sunderland along with Joe McDonald in exchange for Andy Matthew, without success.

Home defeats from Rangers and St.Mirren following the league win against Third Lanark made relegation almost certain by the end of March, and Manager Jerry Dawson left Bayview 'by mutual agreement' following the St.Mirren game.

Defeat at Motherwell on 12th April seemed to all but seal the Fifers' fate, before an incredible run of three wins in the space of six days brought a faint glimmer of hope to the club.

On 16th April Falkirk were beaten 2-1 with goals from Cox and Duchart at Bayview, before a Duchart goal proved enough to record a single goal victory over Hibernian at Easter Road two days later. When Aberdeen were beaten 3-2 at Bayview on 21st April with goals from Duchart, Mochan and Reilly, it seemed as though there was real hope of avoiding the drop.

A win against Dundee at DensPark in the final game of the season on 30th April would have secured the Fifers' First Division status, but it was not to be. A 2-0 win for the home side sent East Fife down to the Second Division after ten years in the top flight. It was, as the *Leven Mail* reflected, a bitter pill to swallow.

Chapter Fourteen: From Bad to Worse

Just before the start of the 1958/59 season, Charlie McCaig took over at the helm of the club following the departure of Jerry Dawson. Other new arrivals at this time were Alan Boyd, an outside-right signed from Aberdeen, Alex Will, a half-back from Dundee United and outside-left Arthur McIvor, who had previously seen service with Dundee and Stirling Albion.

Missing from the squad, however, was Andy Matthew, who had been transferred to Rangers in July for £5,000 after eight years with the Fifers. During his time at Bayview, Matthew scored 32 goals in 194 appearances and won an 'unofficial' Scotland cap against the British Army in season 1953/54.

One unwelcome headache at this time was the controversy surrounding inside-left Felix Reilly. The player had arrived at Bayview as part of the deal that took Jimmy Bonthrone to Dundee, but walked out on the club after playing just nine matches and emigrated to Canada. The club were, at the beginning of the season, unsuccessfully attempting to claim what compensation they could from the player.

Determined to bounce straight back up to the First Division, a large playing staff was retained for the 1958/59 season. It was decided to keep a reserve side, which was entered into the East of Scotland League, a senior competition containing such sides as Gala Fairydean, Hawick Royal Albert and Ferranti Thistle. Ferranti were the same club who later entered the Scottish League as Meadowbank Thistle before changing their name to Livingston and moving to the West Lothian new town.

The season kicked off on 9th August with a 3-1 home defeat against Dunfermline Athletic in the League Cup. Despite winning their second sectional match 3-0 against BrechinCity at GlebePark and recording convincing home wins over Brechin and Stirling Albion by 5-1 and 5-2 respectively, the

Fifers exited the competition at the first hurdle by losing their away fixtures at Dunfermline and Stirling.

Meanwhile, the reserves made an impressive start to their East of Scotland league campaign with 6-1 home wins over both Murrayfield Amateurs and Gala Fairydean.

The first team travelled to Coatbridge for their first league match of the campaign, where the points were shared in a 1-1 draw with Albion Rovers.

It seemed as if the Fifers' stay in the Second Division would, indeed, be short, as the next three league matches were won against Berwick, Cowdenbeath and Alloa, a run which saw twelve goals scored and only one conceded.

Only two points were picked up over the following four games, however, before the push for a quick return to the top flight was put back on track with a 5-1 home win over Dundee United at the beginning of October.

There then followed a period of inconsistent form, during which the Fifers were soundly thrashed 5-1 by Hamilton Accies at Douglas Park before beating St. Johnstone 6-2 at Bayview in the very next game!

In the run up to Christmas, three consecutive home defeats saw the promotion hopes severely dented.

First came defeat at the hands of league leaders Ayr United, who maintained pole position with a 3-1 victory on 29th November. The following Saturday, Brechin City were the visitors to Methil, where they won by the incredible score of 7-2, a record win for the Glebe Park side over East Fife which still stands. Incredibly, the Fifers played host to Dumbarton a week later and were thrashed 6-2, the biggest win ever recorded by the 'Sons' in Methil!

It was left to the reserve side to put the smiles back on the supporters' faces and the second string hit the net nine times without reply against Ferranti Thistle in their East of Scotland League fixture at Bayview seven days later.

The first eleven managed to get back to winning ways at Montrose with a 2-1 win on the Saturday before Christmas and made it two wins in a row with a 5-1 win over Albion Rovers at Bayview on 27th December.

During December, Felix Reilly decided that he was unhappy in Canada and, cap in hand, wrote to East Fife to ask if they would loan him money to pay his airfare home. Realising that any further attempt to get compensation from the player would prove fruitless, the club agreed to Reilly's request and he resumed his playing career at Bayview in January 1959.

Defeat at the hands of Cowdenbeath at Central Park on New Year's Day was followed by a four game unbeaten league run during which victories were recorded against Stranraer, Forfar and Stenhousemuir and the points shared with Arbroath. Despite losing 2-1 to Aberdeen in the Scottish Cup on the last day of January, the Fifers gained a good deal of respectability from the manner in which their First Division opponents were made to fight all the way to the final whistle in order to secure a place in the following round.

Heavy defeats from Dumbarton and St. Johnstone as the season approached its conclusion all but ended hopes of a quick return to the First Division, although just two matches were lost over the remaining eight fixtures. The end of the 1958/59 season arrived with the club occupying eighth position in the league table, 22 points behind champions Ayr United and 13 behind second placed Arbroath.

The reserves, on the other hand, had an extremely successful season in the East of Scotland League, where they ran up some heavy scoring. Their most convincing performance was against Civil Service Strollers on 14 January, who were beaten at Bayview by fourteen goals without reply!

Despite the success of the second eleven, the unhealthy financial state of the club dictated that costs should be cut even further during the close season of 1959. Twelve players were freed, which meant that there would be no reserve football during the forthcoming campaign.

The rapid decline in the club's fortunes also put paid to their ambitious plans to re-locate to a new stadium at Kirkland, originally proposed in the late 1940's. Work on the new ground was started shortly after the proposal was first mooted, with a large embankment built around the proposed playing surface. The site became an eyesore during the intervening years, however, and in 1959 the local council decided that the land should be restored to its original state.

As season 1959/60 approached, it became apparent that a major boardroom battle had been raging at Bayview during the close season, which resulted in the resignation of a number of Directors. In addition, it was intimated that the club was in debt to the tune of £10,000, a fortune in the late 1950's!

Indeed, the general situation at Bayview was so bad that the Fifers were in real danger of extinction.

Realising that the club needed the help of the local community to survive, the *Leven Mail* appealed for the supporters to rally round, commenting that:

"Team doesn't mean the 11 players who wear the Fife colours on Saturdays. It means everyone; Directors, Manager, players, trainers, coaches, groundsmen and YOU, the supporters".

Responding to the appeal, the newly formed Leven branch of the East Fife Supporters Club announced the formation of a £2,000 'Save East Fife' fund.

A public meeting of the supporters club was then held in a packed centre stand at Bayview, where Vice Chairman William Murray faced a 'barrage of questions from all directions'.

Despite the lack of funds, Manager McCaig still managed to bring Ian Gardiner back from Raith Rovers prior to the start of the season for £1,500, in addition to signing former Tottenham Hotspur winger Archie Campbell from Lochee Harp.

The *Leven Mail* was full of hope as the League Cup sectional matches got under way, saying that it looked like being a pretty successful season. *"Hush, whisper it, could this be East Fife's year?"* they remarked following convincing wins against Forfar and Queen of the South.

At first it seemed as though the optimism of the press was justified, as the League Cup section was won with ease to set up a quarter-final meeting with lowly Cowdenbeath.

Against the odds, however, the Central Park side won both home and away to progress to the semi-final 5-2 on aggregate, but the smiles were well and truly wiped from their faces with a 9-3 drubbing from Hearts at Easter Road.

To add to the misery at Bayview, goalkeeper Ron McCluskey broke a finger during the second half of the first leg at Central Park. Former custodian Bert Allan, who had only recently been freed by the club, was asked to return for the second leg and was subsequently re-instated as first choice 'keeper for the remainder of the season.

The start of the league programme was not so successful and Dundee United took full points from the opening fixture at Bayview with a 3-1 win. Although only one further defeat was suffered during the next seven games, only two were won, which could hardly be considered promotion-winning form. In mid-October, form dipped even lower, with both Stenhousemuir and Falkirk inflicting heavy defeats to the tune of 4-0 and 5-0 respectively.

By the end of the year only three more victories had been recorded and six games had been lost, although one of the wins was a 7-1 trouncing of Stranraer on 19th December. New Year's Day 1960 did at least bring the smiles back to the faces of the Bayview faithful, as revenge was gained over Cowdenbeath with a 4-1 win in Methil. The following day the restored faith was well and truly undone with a 5-1 defeat in

Dumfries against Queen of the South, during which goalkeeper Ron McCluskey made a brief return to the side. Despite beating Albion Rovers 4-1 the following week, the rest of the season was nothing short of disastrous. A first round exit from the Scottish Cup at home to Partick Thistle was followed by a truly miserable run in to the end of the season. From the remaining fourteen league fixtures, not a single match was won; only two points were gained from draws against Falkirk and Montrose, and an incredible twelve games were lost. When the curtain came down on the league programme East Fife found themselves second bottom of the table, with the wooden spoon going to none other than Cowdenbeath, the team who had dumped the Methil men out of the League Cup!

For the regulars who had faithfully paid their money at the gate in recent years, the situation must have been hard to take in. Less than a decade earlier the club had commanded a position of respect not only in Scotland, but also throughout the United Kingdom and beyond. Now they were only one place above being labelled the worst team in the country. Season 1959/60 had been East Fife's worst season since joining the Scottish League almost forty years earlier. Surely matters could only improve!

Despite the continuing dire financial situation, the club boasted a potential pool of thirty players prior to the start of the 1960/61 campaign, but excluded from this number was Ian Gardiner, who had been transferred St Johnstone in March for a four-figure fee. In order to keep every player match fit, a second eleven was entered into the Combined Reserve League.

The club also announced during the summer of 1960 that a development plan had been launched at Bayview which, it was hoped, would help replenish the empty coffers.

The 1960/61 season started badly, however, with the Fifers finishing bottom of their five-team League Cup section. As for the league programme, results were little better than the previous season.

A disastrous 4-1 reverse in the first match at RecreationPark, Alloa, was followed by two further defeats before the fourth game was won 4-2 at home to Albion Rovers. Only four more wins were recorded before the end of the year, although that number included a record 8-1 thrashing of East Stirlingshire at Bayview in December.

Pictured at StationPark, Forfar, in the week leading up to Christmas 1960, where the home side cruised to a 4-1 victory. Back row, from left: Stirrat, Morrison, Allan, Moffat, Young, Bryce. Front row, from left: Tran, Scott, Yardley, Stewart, McPhee. (Dundee Courier)

Towards the end of the year, the Chairman once again appealed for support to keep the club alive. Poor form had seen attendances drop alarmingly and it was reckoned that home crowds of between 1,500 and 2,000 were needed just to break even. With the club approaching insolvency, the bank refused to increase their overdraft and the Directors were faced with having to pump their own money into the coffers. As a direct result of the appeal, donations started to roll in and sufficient funds were raised from public donations to keep the club afloat, albeit in the short term.

A derby win against Cowdenbeath on New Year's Day heralded a slight improvement in form for the remainder of the season. From the fourteen games played following the win at Central Park, eight were won and six were lost, which saw the Fifers finish seventh from bottom. It was by no means a final placing to be proud of, but it was an improvement on the previous year nonetheless!

As for the Scottish Cup, Partick Thistle proved to be the stumbling block for the second year in a row, after the first round had been successfully negotiated with a 2-1 win against Highland League side Keith at KynochPark. The gate money from the crowd of 5,500 who attended the home tie against Thistle did, however, help to ease the financial plight.

During the run-in to the end of season 1960/61, future Bayview favourite George Dewar made his first team debut at home to Stirling Albion, but as one star arrived it was time for another to depart. The end of the season saw the sad farewell of long serving right-back Sammy Stewart, who was handed a free transfer. Stewart had arrived at Bayview in 1938 and made 522 appearances during his 23 years with the club; a lengthy association that was, at the time of his departure, a club record. During his time with East Fife, Sammy also picked up three League Cup winners medals.

The start of season 1961/62 saw a marked improvement in form, with Brechin City, Arbroath and Queen of the South all put to the sword both home and away. Twenty-five goals were scored in the process and only five conceded as the Fifers entertained home crowds of up to 5,000.

Having been drawn in one of the bottom two League Cup sections, a two leg supplementary round was required to decide which club from the lower reaches of the Second Division would qualify for the quarter-finals.

A bumper crowd of 7,900 turned up at Bayview on 4th September 1961 for the first leg of the supplementary tie against Albion Rovers, where a quarter-final place was virtually secured with a 4-1 victory. Winning the return leg 2-1 for good measure at Cliftonhill two days later in front of 5,500 spectators, the Fifers were drawn to face Rangers over two legs in the following round.

As expected, the Glasgow side progressed to the semi-final, but the aggregate score of 6-2 was at least a respectful outcome for the losing side, who also benefited financially from the combined attendance of around 40,000.

A winning start was also made to the league programme with a 3-2 home win against Alloa Athletic on 9th September. The following Saturday, the points were shared in a remarkable match against Cowdenbeath at Central Park. Losing 4-1 with only six minutes remaining, goals from Bryce, Yardley and Brown secured a draw in a thrilling grandstand finish for the 4,000 spectators.

After a convincing 3-0 home win against Albion Rovers a week later, the next three games against Arbroath, Berwick and Brechin were all lost. Below-par form then took hold once again and only three more wins were recorded from the following ten fixtures. Just to rub salt in the wound, the league match against Alloa at RecreationPark on the last Saturday of the year was abandoned due to fog after 65 minutes with East Fife winning 4-0!

On a brighter note, the first round of the Scottish Cup was safely negotiated with a 3-1 home win against East of Scotland League side Gala Fairydean in mid-December.

A 5-2 home win against Cowdenbeath heralded the New Year and, from the next five league matches, only one game was lost.

Interest in the Scottish Cup was also maintained with a single goal victory against Albion Rovers in front of 3,700 at Bayview at the end of January. The match was noted not so much for the result, however, but for the fact that East Fife played in green and white jerseys. The choice of colours infuriated certain supporters so much that the following edition of the *Leven Mail* printed two letters of complaint claiming that the team looked too much like Celtic. No doubt royal blue shirts would have brought about the same response, albeit from a different set of spectators!

The cup run was halted with a 4-1 defeat against Stirling Albion at Annfield in the third round.

Back on league business, results were once again plagued by inconsistency.

A 4-1 win against mid-table East Stirlingshire at Firs Park was followed by a 3-0 defeat from lowly Dumbarton the following Saturday; successive home defeats from Arbroath and Queen of the South were followed with victory against Morton at Cappielow. It certainly wasn't the form of a promotion winning side and, although the final league position of tenth was again an improvement on the previous season, there was still a long way to go!

The Board, who only eighteen months earlier complained that the club were failing to attract the minimum of 1,500 required to break even, welcomed average home crowds of over 2,500 during the course of the season. Although the Fifers were still very much in debt, it appeared that the financial situation was gradually improving and there was now an air of optimism at Bayview that had been sadly lacking in recent years.

With the grandstand freshly painted, the terracing tidied up and new grass sown in the goal areas, the club announced in July 1962 that they were *"rarin' to show the fans that this will be their year"*.

Famous last words! The League Cup proved to be a disaster, with the first three fixtures all lost against Queen of the South, Queen's Park and Montrose; the latter winning by an embarrassing five-goal margin at Bayview. Although the three remaining sectional matches were won, including revenge against Montrose at LinksPark, the competition was exited at the first hurdle.

A losing start was also made in the league with a 4-2 defeat against Albion Rovers in Coatbridge. Although full points were taken from the next two games, against Forfar Athletic and Cowdenbeath, two defeats then followed in quick succession, including a 6-1 thumping from Stranraer.

Some faith was restored over the next six matches, when only one defeat was sustained, but the following games saw heavy losses against Dumbarton, Stirling Albion and Arbroath, which put paid to any lingering hopes that the team was ready to mount a challenge for promotion.

There was, however, the addition of silverware to the trophy cabinet in October when the Penman Cup was won by beating Stirling Albion 3-1 at Bayview. This was the last time that the cup, first played for in 1906, was competed for at senior level. The following month saw the first ever visit of a foreign side to Bayview, when Norwegian side Sportsklubben Brann were beaten 7-0 in a friendly.

The financial situation took a severe turn for the worse as the end of 1962 approached. After sharing the points with St Johnstone at Bayview on 15th December, bad weather forced the cancellation of several home matches, depriving the club of much needed income from the turnstiles. Over the following seven weeks, the only match that went ahead was the first round Scottish Cup tie against Edinburgh University at Bayview on 12th January, but only because volunteers turned out in numbers to clear the lines of snow.

A 5-0 home win was the outcome and the Fifers were rewarded with a second round tie against First Division Third Lanark at CathkinPark, where the honours were shared with a 1-1 draw.

A crowd of over 3,000 paid to see the replay in Methil on 4th February, which also finished all square at 2-2. With penalty shoot-outs still unheard of in the early 1960's, a second replay was required to decide the outcome of the tie, and the luck of the draw gave Third Lanark home advantage in the third game, which they won 2-0. Unfortunately, weather conditions in Glasgow were similar to those in Fife and the match didn't take place until 6th March, over a month later!

The series of postponed matches had put the club in dire financial straits, so a friendly was arranged against Dundee at Bayview on Saturday 2nd March in order to raise some much needed cash at the turnstiles. This brought a complaint from Raith Rovers, due to play a league match against Dundee United the same day at Stark's Park, who claimed that the counter attraction would affect their crowd. The complaint was upheld; a decision that angered one anonymous East Fife supporter so much he donated £100 to help keep the club in business! As Dundee were desperately in need of match practice prior to their forthcoming European Cup tie against Anderlecht in Belgium, the game went ahead behind closed doors.

The backlog of league fixtures meant that no fewer than fifteen matches were played during March and April. Eight wins were recorded, one match was drawn and six were lost, which saw an exhausted East Fife occupy eleventh place in the table when the curtain finally came down on season 1962/63. During the final two months of the season, Manager Charlie McCaig announced his intention to leave the club and was replaced by Jimmy Bonthrone, who took over the 'hot seat' on 14th April 1963.

Suddenly, the long suffering supporters had good reason to look forward to the forthcoming season, confident that the appointment of such an influential character would reap rewards.

Chapter Fifteen: Jimmy Bonthrone Returns

The influence of new boss Jimmy Bonthrone had an immediate impact on the team's performances. Drawn to face Arbroath, Dumbarton and newly relegated Raith Rovers in the first round of the League Cup, qualification for the latter stages of the tournament by winning the section brought a particularly pleasing start to season 1963/64. As with the same competition two years before, Rangers were the opponents in the following round and, on 11th September, the Glasgow giants were held to a 1-1 draw at Bayview in front of 14,000 spectators. A crowd of over 30,000 saw the eventual competition winners progress to the semi-final courtesy of a 2-0 second leg win, but once again the Fife had done themselves no harm at all with an extremely creditable performance at Ibrox.

The league campaign, however, got off to a poor start. Only one game was won from the opening eight fixtures, a run which included a 6-1 defeat at the hands of Morton in front of an incredible crowd of 12,000 at Cappielow.

A turnaround in fortunes brought six wins and three draws from the following eleven league games, including a record 8-0 win against Alloa Athletic at Bayview on 2nd November in which George Dewar scored six times! During this spell there was also a 6-0 drubbing of Berwick Rangers as well as a pleasing 6-1 win against Cowdenbeath in the semi-final of the Fife Cup. Raith Rovers, playing in the Second Division for the first time since 1949, were easily beaten at Bayview on New Year's Day 1964 and the favourable league form continued with a 6-0 home win against BrechinCity and a 3-1 victory against runaway league leaders Morton. Sandwiched in between the two aforementioned games, however, came an early exit from the Scottish Cup against First Division East Stirlingshire witnessed by a Bayview crowd of 5,207

The team that beat BrechinCity 6-0 at GlebePark on 18th January 1964. Back row, from left: Bob Stirrat, George Orphant, Dick Donnelly, Jimmy Walker, Jake Young, Alex Wright. Front row, from left: Eddie Meechan, Morris Aitken, George Dewar, Ian Stewart, Alex McWatt. (Dundee Courier)

The unbeaten sequence of league matches ended at Bayview on 22nd February, when victory by the odd goal in seven saw Stenhousemuir take full points. The setback was soon forgotten and the push for promotion was kick-started with three successive wins against Alloa, Queen's Park and Stranraer. With five league matches remaining, the prospect of First Division football was still very much on the agenda as the end of the season loomed, but a heavy 4-0 defeat at Berwick on 21st March knocked the confidence from the side. The end result was just one win from the remaining four fixtures and a final league placing of fourth; eight points behind runners-up Clyde.

Although promotion had not been achieved during Jimmy Bonthrone's first season in charge, an air of enthusiasm was predominant in and around Bayview prior to season 1964/65 and several supporters volunteered to carry out minor ground improvements during the summer months. A new concrete path was laid along the rear of the grandstand and in front of the stand concrete dugouts were constructed.

Commenting on how the ground had never been allowed to fall into disrepair, the *Leven Mail* commented on 22nd July:

"ever since the halcyon days of Scot Symon it has been East Fife's boast that one would have to travel far to find a ground that compares in neatness, compactness and brightness than Bayview Park".

The enthusiasm off the field of play was more than matched on the park during the opening round of League Cup fixtures. Raith Rovers were beaten 4-1 at Stark's Park in the opening match, Queen of the South were sent packing with a 5-0 defeat at Bayview four days later and, in the third sectional match, Montrose were beaten 4-2 at Bayview. Despite suffering the humiliation of a 5-1 home defeat in the return match with Raith, the section was won following a 1-1 draw against Queen of the South in Dumfries and a 5-0 win against Montrose at LinksPark.

After Forfar Athletic had been beaten 7-5 on aggregate in the following round, the Fife lined up to face Celtic in the first leg of the quarter-final at Bayview on 9th September. An injury crisis prior to the big game saw defender Bobby Broome drafted in at outside-right and, midway through the first half, the stand-in winger laid on the first goal, when he sent a corner kick into the danger zone, where the ball was only partially cleared as far as Donnelly. The midfielder's first time effort appeared to be going wide until centre-half George Christie brilliantly dived to head flick the ball into the net. The Fife still held their one goal advantage at half time, not surprising considering they had totally dominated the first 45 minutes, forcing nine corners to Celtic's one! Midway through the second half, the home side's dominance again paid off

Ian Stewart (far right) opens the scoring in East Fife's 4-2 League Cup win over Montrose at Bayview on 15th August 1964

when a Dewar shot hit Fallon and bounced to Broome, who chipped it perfectly to Andy Waddell. The left-winger controlled the ball before striking it with his left foot into the net. When the final whistle sounded, scores of black and gold bedecked supporters invaded the pitch to congratulate their heroes, convinced that the Fifers were on their way back at last! Seven days later, however, hopes of their first League Cup semi-final appearance in ten years were dashed as Celtic won through to the last four with a 6-0 second leg win. Disappointed but not disgraced, the club turned its attention to the league programme, but unfortunately inconsistency once again dogged the side. The first four league fixtures saw derby wins against Raith and Cowdenbeath countered with defeats from Montrose and Queen of the South. The big wins that followed, against Alloa Athletic and Stranraer by 7-2 and 5-2 respectively, were then countered by heavy defeats from Stirling Albion and Dumbarton. Midway through the league campaign, ten wins and two draws from eighteen matches saw the club occupy a position in the top half of the table, but a long way behind the leading pack.

The East Fife team that knocked Aberdeen out of the Scottish Cup on 10th February 1965, pictured before the home league fixture against Hamilton Accies three days later. Back row, from left: Bob Stirrat, Harold Smith, Ian Hamilton, Morris Aitken, Jimmy Walker, Frank Donnelly. Front row: Jim Rodger, George Dewar, Jake Young, Ian Stewart, JImmy Ross. (Dundee Courier)

Not one to give up hope too easily, Manager Bonthrone showed that he was determined to keep hold of his best players and, in November 1964, rejected an approach from Clyde for George Dewar. The Glasgow club, with £26,000 to spend following the sale of Harry Hood to Celtic, even asked Bonthrone to 'name his price' for the high scoring forward, but the Bayview boss still refused to part with his star man. In early February 1965, the respite of the Scottish Cup resulted in yet another giant killing act against Aberdeen. After a no-scoring draw at Pittodrie, the 'Dons' were beaten in front of a crowd of 8,001 at Bayview on 10th February. Amazingly, this was the third time that the Fifers had knocked Aberdeen out of the competition, and on each occasion they had done so as a Second Division side!

In the following round, Kilmarnock emerged 3-0 victors at RugbyPark following a no-scoring draw at Bayview.

Not long after the cup exit, it became apparent that any real chance of promotion had gone, and Jimmy Bonthrone took the opportunity to try out some younger players and trialists. One such youngster was Henry McLeish, the future First Minister of Scotland, who made his first team debut in a 3-1 home win against Dumbarton on 13th March 1965. Described by the local press as *"still a schoolboy, but a confident, strong and hard working half-back"*, the young McLeish played in all but two of the club's remaining fixtures.

Only five more victories were recorded during the second half of the league campaign and, when the season ended, the Fifers were a long way off promotion in ninth place.

Despite having recorded two memorable wins during the season, the main priority of winning back their place in the First Division had once again eluded the club. The league campaign had, once again, ended with the now familiar air of disappointment hanging over BayviewPark.

"Season 1964/65 will go down as a year of heartache," lamented the *Leven Mail,* who pointed out that injuries to key players had plagued the side throughout. George Orphant hadn't kicked a ball all season due to cartilage problems and Morris Aitken, Andy Waddell and Jim Rodger all missed several games due to injury.

During the summer of 1965, Chairman Dr Irvine Pirie stepped down after four years in charge and was replaced by John Fleming. Looking forward to the new season, the Board stated that they had complete confidence in Manager Jimmy Bonthrone and they were sure he would eventually lead the club back into the First Division.

On the playing front, Morris Aitken and George Orphant had both recovered from injury by the time training re-commenced and both were reported to be keen to win back a regular place in the side. Frank Donnelly, in an attempt to regain full fitness following hospital treatment for a shoulder injury, started training full-time at Bayview as the new season approached.

New signings for the forthcoming campaign were Hamish Watt from Forfar Athletic, Ashley Booth from St Johnstone, Eric Brodie from Dundee United, Graham Raines from Partick Thistle and Alan Guild from Forfar West End.

With the addition of Alex Rae, Willie Rutherford and Gordon Hamilton, who were all called up from the Junior and Juvenile ranks, the club were able to boast a total of 23 signed players as season 1965/66 approached. Missing from the ranks, however, was Jake Young, who had departed for St. Mirren.

Despite being roared on by healthy crowds at BayviewPark during the League Cup sectional matches, the Fifers fell at the first hurdle by winning just four points from their six fixtures. Included in the four defeats were disappointing performances at Boghead and FirsPark, where home sides Dumbarton and East Stirlingshire won by the respective scores of 6-1 and 6-2. When the first two league fixtures also ended in defeat it seemed as though the season ahead was going to be just about as disappointing as the previous campaign, but hopes were raised when full points were taken from the following three games, starting with a 3-1 win against Raith at Stark's Park on 18th September. Convincing home wins against Queen's Park and Queen of the South then followed before the inconsistent form that had plagued the side in recent years once again took hold. Before the turn of the year, only five more matches were won along with six defeats and one draw.

The poor form continued throughout January, when only three points were taken from the four fixtures against Albion Rovers, East Stirlingshire, Queen of the South and Forfar, although it has to be pointed out that all four games were played away from home.

The only match played at Bayview during the first month of the year was the narrow Scottish Cup second preliminary round victory against ElginCity on 22nd January 1966. A crowd of 2,855 turned out to see the match, fully expecting the Fifers to overcome their Highland League opponents with ease. The visitors proved to be quite a handful for the home side, however, and when the final whistle sounded it was a mightily relieved East Fife team that made its way into the pavilion following a single goal victory.

The first round proper paired the Fifers with Dundee at DensPark on 9th February and, when the referee's whistle sounded to signal the end of that particular cup tie, there must have been several visiting supporters who wished that Elgin had won the previous match.

Dundee emerged victors by nine goals to one; a drubbing, which, but for a penalty converted by Walker, would have equalled the Fifers' record defeat.

The 2-1 home win against Stranraer on 26th February kick-started the league campaign and, during a hectic March schedule, eleven points were gained from five wins and a draw to put the club right back in the promotion race. An equally hectic April saw a further eleven league points won and revenge over Dumbarton was gained with a 6-1 victory at Bayview.

Unfortunately, when the curtain finally came down on season 1965/66, a final league placing of fourth was all that could be achieved, nine points behind champions Ayr United and six behind second placed Airdrieonians.

Both East Fife and Raith Rovers, looking to develop talent for the future, entered reserve sides into the East of Scotland League for season 1966/67. The competition was split into two sections, namely the Edinburgh and District section and the Borders section. Both East Fife and Raith were members of the eight team Edinburgh section, along with Postal United, Edinburgh City Police, Spartans, Ferranti Thistle, EdinburghUniversity and Civil Service Strollers. The reserve sides of the two Scottish League clubs dominated the competition right from the start and, by the beginning of December, East Fife had won their section with ten wins, three draws and only one defeat. Meanwhile, the first eleven fell at the first hurdle in the League Cup once again, with only home draws against Arbroath and Third Lanark and a win against the latter at CathkinPark to show for their efforts.

A much better start was made to the league programme. On 21st September, following the 4-0 home win against Brechin City, the team found themselves at the top of Division Two, having dropped only two points during the first seven fixtures. Pole position was maintained with a 2-1 home win against Berwick Rangers three days later, but a 4-1 reverse against Queen's Park at Hampden on the first day of October brought the side down to earth with a bump.

The challenge for promotion was maintained during the run up to Christmas, but there were some hiccups on the way, including a 5-1 defeat against Albion Rovers at Cliftonhill. Unfortunately, the New Year once again brought about a change in fortunes as far as the league was concerned, and on New Year's Day 1967 a crowd of 7,588 saw Raith take both points with a 1-0 win at Stark's Park. Although Dumbarton were beaten in Methil the following day, further points were dropped against Queen's Park and Cowdenbeath as the quest for a place in the top two began to falter.

All thoughts of promotion were put on the back burner on Saturday 28th January 1967, when the first round of the Scottish Cup paired the Fifers with Motherwell at FirPark. Only a decade earlier, victory against the 'Steel Men' would have raised few eyebrows, but with the home side enjoying a comfortable First Division status, few gave the visitors much of a chance. When the referee signalled the end of the match, however, it was the Second Division 'minnows' who were rejoicing after Gardiner had scored the only goal of the game. Unfortunately, this 'giant killing' was almost overlooked by the media as, on the same day, little Berwick Rangers humbled their Glasgow namesakes with a single goal victory at Shielfield! Interest in the competition ended at the next hurdle against Clyde at Shawfield, where the home side won convincingly by four goals to one. It is perhaps worth adding

Pictured at Bayview in 1967 are (Back row, from left): Eric Brodie, Henry McLeish, Billy McGann, Alan Guild, Ian Gilchrist, Drew Nelson and Ian Stewart. Front row (from left): Bertie Miller, Bobby Waddell, George Dewar, Jimmy Kinsella and Andy Waddell. (Dundee Courier)

that to lose by such a margin to the 'Bully Wee' was no disgrace in 1967. Clyde went on to reach semi-final of the cup that year as well as attaining a final league placing of third, behind champions Celtic and second placed Rangers. Despite putting on a good show in the cup, the Fifers' league form continued to slump for the remainder of the season. In the fourteen league matches played following the euphoria of dumping Motherwell out of the cup, only four games were won. A final placing of fifth was achieved by beating Stranraer 3-0 at StairPark on the last Saturday of the season.

One other match worthy of mention during the run-in was the 3-2 defeat at the hands of Third Lanark at CathkinPark on 25th March which turned out to be the last ever meeting between the sides before the famous old Glasgow club were forced into liquidation.The second eleven had an equally disappointing conclusion to their East of Scotland League campaign, finishing well down the table at the end of the second phase of the competition.

Overall, failure to win promotion was put down to the lack of a dominating personality in defence and a lack of good wing-halves. Injury had, once again, played a major part, with the influential Bertie Miller plagued with an ankle injury during the second half of the season. Of the 29 players on the club's books, 27 had made first team appearances during the campaign as Manager Bonthrone tried to find the correct blend, unfortunately without success.

Financially, however, the situation at Bayview was now showing great signs of improvement, with a profit of £1663 declared for Season 1966/67, compared with a loss of £425 over the previous campaign. During the close season, the club decided that maintaining a reserve side was an essential part of the promotion jigsaw and duly entered a team into the Combined Reserve League for Season 1967/68. Other clubs competing in the competition included Glasgow University, Jordanhill, Glasgow Transport, Morton Reserves, Clydebank Reserves, Queen's Park Strollers and both Rangers and Hearts' third teams.

When training commenced at the beginning of July 1967, Jimmy Bonthrone announced that he would be able to pick from a pool of 23 players for the forthcoming season, including new signing Robert Aitchison from Hearts.

It is interesting to note that at £1-7s-6d (£1.37½p), a ground season ticket for Season 1967/68 was actually cheaper than it had been three years earlier, when the price was £1-10s-0d (£1.50). No wonder the home attendance averaged around 2,500 back in those days even though the club had been firmly rooted in the Second Division for a decade!

The Bayview faithful would also have more value for their money over future seasons in terms of comfort, as work was about to start on the erection of a cover over the north terracing. The cost of building the structure was put at around £4,000, half of which was raised by the supporters club.

An excellent start was made to the campaign, with five of the six League Cup sectional matches won against fellow group eight opponents Arbroath, Alloa Athletic and Albion Rovers. The quarter-final of the competition paired the Methil Men with Dundee over two legs. In front of a 9,000 Bayview crowd on Wednesday 13th September, the Dens Parkers won the first leg by a single goal. As expected, the dark blues secured a semi-final spot with a convincing 4-0 win in the return fixture at DensPark a week later.

A good start was also made to the league programme, with only one point dropped over the first four fixtures. The favourable run of form was more or less maintained over the first half of the season, save for one or two hiccups, including a 6-3 defeat against fellow promotion candidates Arbroath on 28th October at Gayfield. Home crowd figures also showed signs of improvement over the first half of the season, with average attendances of almost 3,000 now enjoying the benefit of shelter from the wind and rain.

New Year's Day 1968 started with an entertaining 3-3 draw with Cowdenbeath at Bayview, closely followed by another share of the points against Dumbarton at Boghead.

The push for promotion was given an enormous boost over the following four league matches, with victories against Albion Rovers, Berwick, Alloa and Stranraer.

The winning form was maintained in the first round of the Scottish Cup on 27th January, when Alloa Athletic fell victim to the Fifers' formidable home record for the second week in a row as the Methil Men romped home 4-0. The second round of the competition saw the previous season's Second Division champions Morton visit Bayview. The Greenock side, who were at the time proving to be more than a match for most of their First Division counterparts, were held to a no scoring draw in front of a 5,515 crowd. Unfortunately, home advantage in the replay saw Morton progress to the third round with a 5-2 victory.

The distraction of the Scottish Cup, however, had an adverse effect on league form. In between the first and second rounds, defeat was suffered against Ayr United at SomersetPark and, following the Scottish Cup exit, a crucial fixture against league leaders St. Mirren was lost at Love Street.

Still very much in with a chance of top-flight football, however, the team rallied and dropped only one point over the next six games. As well as a 2-0 home win against fellow promotion candidates Arbroath, the winning streak included impressive 6-0 victories against both East Stirlingshire and Clydebank, the latter result being helped considerably by the dismissal of three 'Bankies' players.

Unfortunately, the winning form could not be maintained and, on 13th April, a 3-0 defeat at the hands of Queen's Park put a severe dent in the promotion dream. Although only one more point was dropped over the remaining three matches, the Fifers finished in third place, four points behind Arbroath and thirteen behind St. Mirren.

Yet again the team had come agonisingly close to achieving their dream of a return to the First Division. Of the eighteen league fixtures played at Bayview, not one had been lost and in only five home fixtures were the points shared. In addition, the Fifers had proved that they were the only side in the league capable of beating champions St Mirren over the course of the season.

During the summer of 1968, the Board of Directors demonstrated that they were determined to take the club back into the 'big time' by increasing the share capital to £10,000. The additional 38,000 shares created by the increase in capital were entirely taken up by existing shareholders.

Surprisingly, despite a slight increase in home attendances during season 1967/68, a loss of £606 for the financial year ending 31st March 1968 was announced compared with the previous season's profit of £1,663. The club were quick to point out, however, that the figure quoted included their contribution towards the cost of erecting the cover over the north terrace.

On the playing front, it was announced that rather than enter a team into the reserve league, fringe players would be kept match fit by participating in a new 'Midweek Floodlit League'. This competition, which was expected to include teams representing Celtic, Rangers, Raith Rovers, Morton, Cowdenbeath, East Stirlingshire and Clydebank in its membership, would give the club the opportunity to field trialists and a sprinkling of first team members. The proposal for the new league was put forward for approval by the appropriate governing bodies in July 1968, but unfortunately the ambitious proposal never got beyond the planning stage.

The new season got under way on the first day of August, when English Third Division side ShrewsburyTown visited Methil as part of a two game visit to Scotland. A 2-0 home win set the Fifers up nicely for the series of first round League Cup matches against Clydebank, Queen of the South and Berwick Rangers.

Only two points were dropped, both against Queen of the South, as the quarter-final of the competition was reached for the second season in succession.

The quarter-final, however, was a disappointing affair, with Hibernian winning the first leg at Bayview 4-1 in front of a healthy 6,728 attendance. With the outcome of the tie already a foregone conclusion, the Methil Men held the Edinburgh side to the more respectable score of 2-1 in the return leg at Easter Road.

Only one point was dropped in the three opening league matches, but the promising run was halted by a 2-0 defeat from Berwick Rangers at Shielfield on 14th September. Only one win from the following five league matches, including a 4-0 defeat at the hands of newly relegated Motherwell, saw the team occupying a mid-table position by mid-October. Indeed, the position could have been even worse had it not been for a last minute Guild penalty that won a point in the home fixture against Queen of the South on 21st September and a last minute winner from Bobby Waddell against Hamilton Academical the following Saturday!

Unhappy at the disappointing state of affairs at the club, Andy Waddell, younger brother of Bobby, asked to be placed on the transfer list.

A complete turnaround in fortunes started with a morale boosting 1-0 home win against promotion chasing Ayr United in the next match and was followed by an emphatic 6-1 victory against Montrose at the beginning of November. A further four wins against Stirling Albion, Stranraer, Clydebank and Stenhousemuir, which produced thirteen goals against three conceded, brought the winning sequence to six matches and put the Fifers right back in the promotion race.

No prizes for guessing what happened next. Only one point was gained from the next three games, during which only two goals were scored and eight conceded! The supporters had, in recent years, learned to take the rough with the smooth, but this latest state of affairs prompted a flurry of angry letters to the Sports Editor of the *East Fife Mail*.

The year was rounded off with a 5-0 home win against Alloa Athletic on 28th December which attracted a crowd of only 500, such was the despondency of the Bayview faithful.

The month of January 1969 brought mixed fortunes, with two convincing home league wins against Berwick Rangers and Hamilton Academical countered by defeat in Dumfries against Queen of the South and an early exit from the Scottish Cup at Stranraer.

The cup defeat was all but forgotten two weeks later, however, when runaway league leaders Motherwell were convincingly beaten 3-1 at Bayview thanks to a Dewar brace and a Guild penalty. Perhaps the promotion dream wasn't over after all!

Only one win from the following five fixtures, however, brought the club and its long suffering supporters, once again, down to earth with a bump, and even that one win had looked extremely unlikely on the day! Two goals down at home to fellow promotion hopefuls Stirling Albion with twelve minutes to go, a brace from George Dewar and a single counter from Alex Rae turned the game around.

With a finish in the top two now beginning to look unlikely, the club announced in March that, in order to reduce the wage bill, all four full time players were to be placed on the transfer list, which meant that Jim Kinsella, Alex Rae, Walter Borthwick and Dave Gorman could soon be plying their trade elsewhere. On a brighter note, Alan Guild was selected for the Scotland Amateur International side for the match against England at CelticPark on 28th March.

At the end of March, with eight league matches remaining, one last desperate effort to challenge the teams at the top of the league was made. A seven match winning run started with a 4-1 win at Stenhousemuir, closely followed by a 6-1 midweek victory against BrechinCity at Bayview. Further wins against East Stirlingshire, Brechin and Cowdenbeath meant that there was still a slight chance of making the step up to Division One as the season reached its conclusion. With three games remaining, the Fifers were sitting in third place with 44 points, two behind second placed Stirling Albion, who had the added advantage of a game in hand. The 'Honest Men' of Ayr, however, sitting two points behind in fourth place, had four games in hand. All the Fifers could do was to keep on winning and hope their rivals would slip up during the run in.

The following Saturday evening, 12th April, the chance was still there, albeit slight. Albion Rovers had been beaten 2-0 at Bayview, but Ayr United's 3-0 win at Brechin the same afternoon coupled with their midweek victory at Stenhousemuir put the SomersetPark outfit level on points with the Fifers in equal third place, a point behind Stirling Albion. United, however, still had five matches remaining compared to East Fife's two.

A week later the chance of promotion was all but gone. All three of the clubs fighting for the second promotion place behind champions Motherwell had 48 points, but East Fife had only one game to go. Stirling still had two matches to play and Ayr had four.

On Saturday 26th April 1969, the promotion race was finally decided. Although Ayr were beaten by Queen of the South, both East Fife and Stirling Albion also lost, which meant that the single point won by Ayr in the preceding midweek against Motherwell was enough to secure a place in the top flight. When the last competitive game of the season was finally out of the way, the club bid a sad farewell to Manager Jimmy Bonthrone, who had been appointed coach of Aberdeen. Bill Baxter, who had taken over as coach at Bayview from Johnny Gear just twelve months previously, filled the position vacated by Mr Bonthrone and almost immediately set about the task of re-organising his playing staff. As a result, free transfers were handed to Drew Nelson, Henry McLeish, Danny Burke and Brian Smyth. Midway through the following month, one of the full-time players who had been placed on the transfer list, Alex Rae, joined Bury for a 'five figure sum'.

During the summer of 1969 there was a major ground improvement at Bayview, when the old wooden dressing rooms were demolished and a new pavilion constructed. The old dressing rooms were over 50 years old and had actually been formed from an old army hut, which, as mentioned in an earlier chapter, had been surplus to requirements following the First World War.

The financial situation, however, was not looking healthy. A loss of £4,500 was made during season 1968/69 and the club now had an overdraft of £11,888.

As part of the agreement that saw Alex Rae move to Bury, the 1969/70 season kicked off with a friendly against the newly relegated English Third Division side at Gigg Lane on 26th July, where a crowd of 15,000 witnessed a 1-1 draw. Two days later, the two match English tour concluded with a 3-1 defeat at Rochdale. Preparations for the forthcoming campaign were rounded off with a 2-2 draw against Oldham Athletic at Bayview, during which Pat Quinn, signed from Motherwell during the close season, scored his first goal for the club.

A first round exit was made from the League Cup as eventual semi-finalists Motherwell won the first round section with ease. Although the club had once again announced that a determined bid would be made for promotion, the 1969/70 league campaign proved to be a huge disappointment. The first three league matches of the season against Albion Rovers, Queen's Park and Falkirk were all lost and, to make matters worse, two of the defeats were at Bayview. After Queen of the South were defeated on their own soil by the odd goal in seven on 10th September followed by wins against Dumbarton, Alloa Athletic and Montrose, it seemed as if the poor start could be overcome. The winning form could not be sustained, however, and although full points were taken from two of the next three games, only three more victories were recorded before the end of the year.

The gloom deepened on New Year's Day 1970, when promotion-chasing Cowdenbeath won the local derby at Bayview by a single goal. Although the following two games against Alloa and Forfar were both won, it was to be mid-March before the next league victory was recorded, against Berwick Rangers in Methil.

During the poor league run, however, there were two remarkable Scottish Cup wins at Bayview against higher league opposition. On 24th January, the club's record of never having lost a Scottish Cup tie to Raith Rovers was maintained with an impressive 3-0 victory thanks to a Finlayson brace and a single counter from Waddell. The 6,893 crowd would have been treated to an even greater winning margin if Soutar hadn't missed from the penalty spot! Round two saw Morton travel east to Methil, where over 7,000 saw the Fifers progress to round three thanks to a Peter McQuade effort which was deflected into the net by Morton's Rankine. Interest in the competition ended at DensPark on 21st February when home side Dundee won by a single goal.

All hopes of promotion were long gone as the league programme entered its final phase. When the curtain finally came down on season 1969/70, East Fife occupied tenth place in the nineteen team league, a full twenty-two points behind champions Falkirk, who only just pipped Cowdenbeath for the title.

Would East Fife ever make it back to the top flight? It was now twelve years since the likes of Rangers and Celtic had visited Methil on league business. During those twelve years the club had come close to promotion, but had either fallen at the final hurdle or failed to leave the starting gate with the rest of the field.

Jubilant scenes in the Bayview home dressing room following the 3-0 Scottish Cup victory over Raith Rovers on 24th January 1970 (Dundee Courier).

The Bayview faithful could be forgiven for feeling despondent. They had regularly paid their money at the turnstiles year after year and were, by now, beginning to resign themselves to the ever increasing opinion that East Fife were, and always would be, a Second Division club.
If only they knew what lay just around the corner!

Chapter Sixteen: Back in the Big Time

Pictured in Holland in 1970 wearing the colours of Dutch side Go Ahead Deventer (the training jerseys having been accidentally left behind in the team hotel!). Back row, from left: Doug Soutar, John Martis, Rab Cairns, Brian McNicoll, Jim Wood, John Brown, Walter Borthwick and Peter McQuade. Front row: Eddie Thomson, Billy McPhee, Pat Quinn, Dave Gorman, John Bernard and Colin McDonald. (John Brown)

Despite still having a substantial overdraft, the club found the necessary finance to embark on a tour of Holland and Germany in May 1970. After drawing 1-1 with Oldham Athletic in a friendly at BoundaryPark on 2nd May, the touring party flew out from ManchesterAirport and shared four goals in their first continental game against Rot Weiss Essen in Germany a week later. Amateur side Haltern were then convincingly beaten in a 'bounce' game, before the honours were shared with Dutch league sides Go Ahead Deventer and MVV Maastricht.

"The game against Maastricht was a real cracker", recalled former player John Brown, now a columnist with the Dundee Evening Telegraph. *"It was played in a very impressive open-plan stadium and, if my memory serves me well, we were ahead for most of the game, which finished in yet another draw".*

On their return to Scotland, Chairman John Fleming announced that the club were considering the possibility of moving to a new stadium in Glenrothes. The Chairman also hinted that a merger with neighbours Raith Rovers was a possibility. Following the Annual General Meeting at the beginning of August, it was announced that the proposed move had been 'stalled for a year' to allow shareholders to make their minds up on the issue.

One notable arrival at Bayview in 1970 was Billy McPhee from Rangers who, over the coming seasons, was to prove a valuable asset with his deadly free kicks from the edge of the penalty area.

Following a return match with Go Ahead Deventer at Bayview on 3rd August, in which the honours were once again shared with a 1-1 draw, the 1970/71 season got under way with first round League Cup matches against Partick Thistle, Queen of the South and Stirling Albion.

Once again, interest in the competition was ended at the first hurdle, although this time only on goal difference from newly-relegated Partick.

A good start was made to the latest quest for promotion, with the Fifers winning six of their opening nine league fixtures, including a 5-1 victory over Raith Rovers; the points being shared in the other three games. The unbeaten run was eventually brought to halt with a 2-0 defeat from Queen's Park at Hampden on 10th October.

No doubt still reeling from their trouncing during the opening series of league fixtures, near neighbours Raith Rovers tempted Manager Bill Baxter to Stark's Park in October. Baxter's position at Bayview was filled by the promotion of Pat Quinn, who took up the role of Player/Manager. The departure of Baxter signalled a slight downturn in fortunes, with only one league point won from the two fixtures played before October drew to a close.

On 2nd November, top English side StokeCity appeared at Bayview in a benefit match for George Dewar. A crowd of 6,000 paid to see the game, which also marked the end of Dewar's playing days at Bayview. In goal for the visitors, who emerged 1-0 winners on the night, was the legendary England goalkeeper Gordon Banks.

Pat Quinn's first home league match in charge of the side ended with a resounding 5-1 win against Stirling Albion, which was followed by a 5-3 victory against East Stirlingshire at Firs Park a week later.

Although Stranraer ended the Fifers unbeaten home league record on 21st November, the promotion challenge was maintained with three wins and a draw from the following matches against Brechin, Dumbarton, Queen of the South and Albion Rovers, helped in no small way by new signing Joe Hughes from Stirling Albion.

Raith Rovers gained a little revenge for their earlier humiliation at Bayview by winning the New Year derby 2-1 at Stark's Park in front of 8,000 spectators, but the Methil Men bounced back with a 3-1 home win against Alloa the following day.

The satisfaction of taking full points from the RecreationPark side was overshadowed following the final whistle, however, when news of the Ibrox disaster started to filter through. As the evening wore on and the death toll started to rise, it became clear that this was a tragedy of huge proportions, which had also claimed the lives of a party of youngsters from the nearby Fifevillage of Markinch.

After sharing the points with fellow promotion challengers Arbroath at Gayfield a week later, then taking full points from the home fixture with Montrose, the players' confidence was sky-high for the Scottish Cup tie with St. Mirren at Bayview on 23rd January 1971.

A crowd of 7,031 turned out to see the Fifers share the honours with the 'Buddies' in a 1-1 draw, a result that was repeated at Love Street in the replayed match three days later. Two energy-sapping matches against First Division opposition, however, was hardly the ideal preparation for the clash with league leaders Partick Thistle at Firhill on 30th January, where team spirit took a huge nosedive with a 4-0 defeat in front of a crowd of 10,000.

Not surprisingly, the exhausted Fifers went down 3-1 to St Mirren two days later in the second replay of their Scottish Cup tie in front of 9,413 at Love Street.

Four of the next five league matches were played at Bayview, where home advantage resulted in all four games being won convincingly against Berwick Rangers, Queen's Park, Hamilton Academical and Stenhousemuir. The home supporters were treated to no fewer than eighteen goals in the process with only two conceded as East Fife took over at the top of the league. The only hiccup during the rise to the top of the table was a 3-0 reverse against fellow promotion hopefuls Clydebank at New Kilbowie on 20th February.

After sharing the points with Stirling Albion at Annfield on 13th March, an emphatic 6-2 home victory against East Stirlingshire followed by wins against Stranraer and BrechinCity virtually secured promotion by the beginning of April.

Unfortunately, the following Saturday was a free week for the Fifers, a situation brought about by the fact that there were an odd number of teams in the league back in the early 70's. This meant that, with league leaders Partick due to face promotion rivals Arbroath, the opportunity to secure promotion by winning a match might not present itself.

In order to keep the momentum going, a two-match tour of the Highlands was arranged. On Friday 9th April, Inverness Thistle were defeated 5-2 at Kingsmills and, the following afternoon, RossCounty inflicted defeat at Victoria Park by a single goal. Despite losing, however, it was celebration time when the final whistle sounded. With the match between Arbroath and Partick ending all square, East Fife's return to the big time was confirmed. The long wait was over at last!

East Fife in 1971. Back row, from left: Dave Clarke, Rab Cairns, Walter Borthwick, Dave Gorman, John Martis, Peter McQuade, Jim Finlayson. Front Row: Bertie Miller, Pat Quinn, Joe Hughes, Graham Honeyman, Billy McPhee. (Dundee Courier)

The remaining league matches were played out with a home victory against Queen of the South and defeat at Berwick, either side of a friendly against Eintracht Brunswick at Bayview on 20th April. Although outclassed by their German visitors, the narrow 2-1 defeat was no disgrace as Brunswick were, at the time, a top league side containing several international players.

As part of the preparations for First Division football, a glass fronted Directors' Box was built on top of the pavilion during summer of 1971. The new structure would be a 'status symbol' according to the club and fitting for their return to the top flight. When asked if the new box would block the Wellesley Road residents' view of the west goal, the club's reply was "probably"!

Once again, preparations for the new season took the form of a continental tour. On 20th July a return match with Eintracht Brunswick in Germany resulted in another 2-1 victory for the home side. The following day, the mini-tour concluded with a single goal defeat against Holstien Kiel. On their return to Scotland, the Fife played host to Aberdeen in the first round of the Drybrough Cup at Bayview on the last day of July. Anyone using this match to judge how the Methil Men would fare during the forthcoming league campaign would be rather concerned, as the 'Dons' cruised to a comfortable 3-0 victory. Although some confidence was restored with a 5-1 friendly win at Dumbarton a week later, the programme of League Cup first round fixtures that followed proved disastrous. Near neighbours Raith won the opening game 2-1 at Stark's Park, followed by a home defeat against Partick Thistle by the odd goal in five.

Draws against Arbroath, Partick and Raith then followed and, when Arbroath won the last sectional game 2-0, a bottom of the section final position was confirmed.

The opening First Division league match against Dunfermline Athletic at Bayview on 4th September resulted in a disappointing 1-0 defeat. The following Saturday Hibernian emerged winners of the second fixture, although the narrow 2-1 defeat at least brought some credit to the side. Any renewed confidence was lost a week later, however, when Dundee trounced the Fifers 5-2 in Methil. Yes, it looked like being a tough season!

The first victory of season 1971/72 came courtesy of a single goal win against Clyde at Shawfield on 25th September. Would this result ease the nerves and signal a turnaround in fortunes? The healthy crowd of 4,150 who turned out the following week for the visit of Morton must have thought so.

Unfortunately, the home supporters were left feeling bitterly disappointed at the end of a dire ninety minutes, as the Greenock side found the net six times without reply to record their biggest-ever victory at Bayview.

The annihilation was hardly the ideal preparation for the visit to Ibrox the following Saturday, where Rangers took both points with a 3-0 win.

On Saturday 16th October the first home win of the season finally arrived in the form of a 2-0 win against a poor Kilmarnock side, which signalled the beginning of a four match unbeaten run during which the points were shared with Airdrieonians, Hearts and Ayr United.

The improvement in form was brought to an abrupt halt in mid-November, with a 5-0 defeat from Aberdeen at Pittodrie. Only one point was taken from the following four league games, although the side's confidence was boosted when they lost narrowly to Celtic, who were at the time on the way to recording their seventh successive league title, at Parkhead on 11th December.

Following the visit of Preston North End to Methil three days later for the official opening of Bayview's new floodlights, the Fifers embarked on a seven match unbeaten run, although the honours were shared in all but one of the games.

After the points were shared in the New Year Derby with Dunfermline Athletic at East End Park, the best result of the season was recorded at Bayview on 3rd January 1972, where Hibernian were humbled in front of 8,217 spectators.

Traditionally East Fife's 'bogey team' during the halcyon days of the late 1940's and throughout the 1950's, the 2-1 win marked the first home league success against the Easter Road men since February 1931!

What made the victory even more satisfying was the fact that during the early 1970's Hibs were a side to be reckoned with. The team who lost at Bayview that afternoon contained no fewer than three Scottish internationalists, namely Pat

Stanton, John Brownlie and Alex Cropley. Three future Scotland players; Erich Schaedler, John Blackley and Arthur Duncan, were also in the side along with Jim Herriot, the goalkeeper who had previously won eight Scotland caps whilst with Birmingham City!

The next game resulted in a highly creditable no-scoring draw against high-flying Dundee at DensPark, and was followed with another share of the points against Clyde at Bayview on 15th January.

The visitors' defence looks on despairingly as Billy McPhee's stunning first half free kick opens the scoring against Hibs on 3rd January 1972. The Fife eventually won the match 2-1 thanks to a Joe Hughes strike ten minutes from time. (Ricky Janetta)

Morton, who had trounced the Fifers on their own soil earlier in the season, were held to a no-scoring draw at Cappielow a week later. Although the point gained was very welcome and put the team into fifth bottom place, a point ahead of Dundee United, the match could have been won. In the dying seconds, substitute Doug Dailey was sent clean through on goal and seemed certain to score when the referee blew for full-time!

The visit of Rangers to Methil on 29th January 1972 was an eagerly anticipated event, with many of the Bayview faithful in the 12,000 crowd believing that an upset could well be on the cards considering their favourites' recent form. Although the Glasgow giants won the match by a single goal, the home team's reputation as a vastly improved side remained intact following the game.

The Scottish Cup brought a welcome respite from the pressures of league business at the beginning of February, but hopes of progressing in the competition were ended by Clydebank with a 1-0 defeat in a replayed match at Bayview after the first game at New Kilbowie ended in deadlock. When the league programme resumed, the fourth win of the season was recorded against Kilmarnock by the odd goal in five at RugbyPark on 12th February.

After the points were shared in the next two games against Airdrieonians and Hearts, Bayview played host to yet another foreign side on Wednesday 8th March when Danish outfit Aarhus visited Methil for a friendly and took the honours with a 3-1 win.

Three days later the Fifers' chances of avoiding the drop were dealt a severe blow when fellow relegation candidates Ayr United inflicted a 4-0 defeat SomersetPark.

With the following league fixture against Aberdeen at Bayview also ending in defeat, it was imperative that something was taken from the next two matches, against fellow relegation battlers Dundee United and Falkirk. At Tannadice on 25th March, the points were shared in a 2-2 draw and, the following Saturday, the home clash with Falkirk resulted in the same score-line, although home supporters were extremely disappointed at sharing the points with the 'Bairns'. Two Billy McPhee goals in 32 and 65 minutes looked to have won the match, but the visitors scored twice in the final ten minutes to force a draw.

With four games to go, East Fife, Airdrieonians, Falkirk and Morton were all sitting on 21 points, only one point ahead of Clyde and three clear of bottom club Dunfermline. It was the Methil Men who remained favourites for the step down to Division Two, however, as three of their remaining fixtures were away from home, with the only game scheduled for Bayview being a visit from title-chasing Celtic.

A single goal defeat against Partick Thistle at Firhill on 8th April was followed by a 3-0 home defeat at the hands of Celtic, who secured the League Championship in the process. As the Celtic fans cheered their heroes off the park, there was a definite air of despondency amongst the home fans as they left the ground, convinced that relegation was now a certainty. The following week, however, a 1-0 win against St Johnstone at Muirton thanks to a Billy McPhee free kick gave the Fifers a glimmer of hope. They now occupied third bottom place on 24 points, only a single point clear of Clyde and Dunfermline, who both had a better goal difference. A win against Motherwell in the final match would ensure another season of First Division football at Methil, but if the match against the 'Steel Men' was lost and either Clyde or Dunfermline picked up a point, then the Fifers would be relegated.

On a tense and nail biting afternoon, a point was won at Fir Park thanks to a Joe Hughes goal and, when news drifted through at full-time that Dunfermline had lost at home to Dundee United and Clyde had only managed to draw with Airdrieonians, the Fifers began to celebrate. Against all the odds, relegation had been avoided on the last day of the season!

Did the club deserve another chance in the top flight? Some would argue that the team had struggled for the entire season and that the same struggle to avoid relegation would present itself again the following year.

If, however, we consider the fact that East Fife lost only three more league matches than third-placed Rangers, perhaps the

Methil Men did deserve another chance in Division One. After all, Airdrieonians, Clyde, Falkirk, Hearts, Kilmarnock, Motherwell and St Johnstone had all failed to beat the Fifers either at home or away over the course of the season!

Season 1972/73 kicked off on 29th July when Sheffield Wednesday paid a friendly visit to Methil and took the honours with a 3-1 win, before the team set off on their foreign travels once again, this time to Holland, where a 2-0 win against Dordrech in Rotterdam on 2nd August was followed up four days later with a 3-2 victory against Haarlem.

The team had only just returned to home soil when they played host to Dutch Premier League side Den Haag on 6th August. A no-scoring draw was the outcome; a very respectable result considering the visitors were of a similar calibre to fellow countrymen Feyonoord and European Cup holders Ajax.

The serious business of the League Cup started on 12th August with the visit of newly promoted Arbroath, who were beaten 2-1.

A 1-1 draw against Celtic at Parkhead in the next fixture set the Fifers up nicely for the visit of Second Division Stirling Albion on 19th August, who surprisingly held their hosts to a no scoring draw.

Defeat from both Celtic and Arbroath in the next two games put qualification for the second round in doubt, but a 2-0 win against Stirling Albion at Annfield on 30th August saw the Fifers safely through.

A single goal win over Partick Thistle at Bayview followed by stalemate at Firhill in the second leg was enough to secure a quarter-final meeting with Aberdeen, but all hopes the team had of progressing to their first League Cup semi-final since 1954 were well and truly extinguished as the Dons comfortably won the tie by an aggregate score of 7-1.

The 1972/73 league programme kicked off on 2nd September with a highly entertaining 4-3 win against Morton at Bayview. Favourable results in the following fixtures, including victories over Kilmarnock, Hearts and Falkirk, secured a respectable mid-table position by the middle of October.

In early November, revenge was almost gained against Aberdeen in a league match at Pittodrie, when goals from Billy McPhee and Graham Honeyman gave the Fifers a 2-0 half-time lead. Making his debut for East Fife that afternoon was former Scotland international goalkeeper Ernie McGarr, who must have had high hopes during the interval of getting one over his former team. Unfortunately, McGarr had to pick the ball out of his own net four times during the second half as the 'Dons' fought back to win 4-3.

The team were, by now, proving that they were capable of giving most sides in the First Division a run for their money and, for the first time in several years, East Fife players were being considered for international honours. In mid-November, both Davie Clarke and Graham Honeyman were selected to play for the Scotland Under-23 side in a trial match at Easter Road.

Full points were taken from the league matches against Dundee United, Motherwell and Airdrieonians before the end of the year, but heavy 4-0 defeats were suffered against Dundee and Rangers over the same period.

New Year's Day 1973 was celebrated with a 2-0 home win against Arbroath at Bayview. A single goal defeat against Hibernian at Easter Road five days later was made up for with a convincing 3-0 home win against Kilmarnock and a share of the points with Hearts at Tynecastle over the following two weeks.

At the beginning of February, Billy McPhee netted his fiftieth goal for the club as the Fifers were knocked out of the Scottish Cup with a 4-1 defeat at CelticPark.

Two weeks later, on 17th February 1973, the Fifers had the opportunity to gain revenge when the 'Hoops' came to Methil on league business, and the 11,577 spectators who lined the terraces on that bright but chilly afternoon witnessed a spectacle that was to be talked about for years to come. Picture the scene before the match: a young Kenny Dalglish warms up alongside the advertisement hoardings with the screams of young female admirers in his ears. Lisbon Lions Bobby Murdoch, Billy McNeill, Jimmy Johnstone and Bobby Lennox go through their paces still looking good after their European Cup success five years before.

Billy McPhee equalises from the penalty spot minutes into the second half in the league clash with Celtic at Bayview on 17th February 1973. (Ricky Janetta)

With other household names such as Dixie Deans, Harry Hood, Tommy Callaghan and Danny McGrain in the Celtic team, few gave the Fifers a snowball's chance in hell of taking anything from the match.

The visitors started well and, had it not been for a series of good saves from Ernie McGarr in the home goal, Celtic could well have taken a commanding lead during the early stages. The Fifers slowly came into the game and, when half time arrived, the team could be reasonably satisfied their first half performance despite having gone behind to a Dixie Deans goal after 21 minutes.

The second half had only just got under way when Kevin Hegarty was brought down just inside the penalty area. After the referee had ascertained that the foul had been committed inside the box, he pointed to the penalty spot to the delight of the home supporters. Billy McPhee blasted the ball home and the Fifers were level.

The cheers had hardly died down when Bayview erupted in jubilation once again as Walter Borthwick shot home past the outstretched arms of Celtic 'keeper Ally Hunter. Black and

The moment Bayview erupted! Celtic 'keeper Ally Hunter lies helpless as Walter Borthwick's shot puts East Fife 2-1 ahead against league leaders Celtic in February 1973. (Ricky Janetta)

Gold bedecked supporters hugged each other and schoolboys leapt over the hoardings to dance around on the park. East Fife had taken the lead against the league leaders, the mighty Glasgow Celtic! But would it last?

The visitors piled on the pressure with wave upon wave of attack as the game progressed and, midway through the second half, Kenny Dalglish was sent clean through on goal. Just when it looked like an equaliser was on the cards, the young striker hesitated and his weak shot was saved on the line by the hand of defender Bobby Duncan.

Bobby Murdoch stepped up to take the resulting penalty kick only to send the ball high over the bar. The referee, having decided that some East Fife players had strayed into the penalty area when the kick was taken, ordered a retake!

This time Ernie McGarr saved with his foot from Harry Hood to maintain the Fifers' lead.

Celtic continued to pressurise the home goal and, with time running out, Davie Clarke brought down Deans inside the box. Once again the referee pointed to the spot.

The home supporters could hardly bear to watch as Dalglish stepped up to take his side's third penalty, but once again home 'keeper McGarr was equal to the task and saved the spot-kick.

With two minutes to go, just as it looked as if the Fifers were destined to hold out for a famous victory, Dixie Deans squeezed a header just inside the left post to square the match at two goals apiece.

When the final whistle finally went, it was a mightily relieved Celtic support that streamed out of the ground. The home support on the other hand, although a little disappointed that victory had been snatched from their grasp, made their way home delighted to have witnessed such a spectacle. For many (including the author) it was, and still is, the best match they had ever seen.

Over a month was to pass following the Celtic match before the side next tasted defeat, when Aberdeen emerged narrow victors in a closely fought encounter at Bayview on the evening of Tuesday 27th March.

Four days later, Motherwell visited Methil on a bright but breezy afternoon and, with a strong wind blowing up the park from west to east, the Fifers took full advantage of the conditions during the second half. Every clearance from 'keeper Ernie McGarr was carried by the wind before dropping in his opposite number's goal area, where the Fife forwards were waiting to pounce. At the end of the 90 minutes the 'Steel Men' could consider themselves fortunate to have lost by only three goals to one!

As the end of the league season approached, Dundee were lucky to take full points from a midweek game at Bayview on 18th April in which intense pressure from the home side during the final quarter of an hour failed to cancel the Dens Park side's single goal advantage.

In the final home match of the season against St Johnstone three days later, Johnny Love scored one of the quickest goals ever seen at Bayview after only 25 seconds. When Billy McPhee added a second just over ten minutes later, one veteran was heard to remark "ah think wur in fur a barryload". It was not to be, however, and the Perth side struck twice to level the match and complete the scoring before half time.

The final league game of the season was played on 28th April against Rangers at Ibrox. The Glasgow side, trailing league leaders Celtic by a single point but with a vastly inferior goal difference, had to win the match and hope their rivals lost against Hibernian at Easter Road in order to win the title. Although the 'Gers did the business on the day with a 2-0 victory against the Fife, Celtic won their eighth championship in succession with a 3-0 win in Edinburgh.

With Motherwell winning their final match at Arbroath, the Ibrox defeat meant that East Fife slipped down the league table to finish in ninth place.

All things considered, however, it had been a great season. The faithful supporters who had seen their favourites battle through the dark days of the late 1950's and witnessed the failed promotion bids of the 1960's had finally got their reward, with fast and entertaining football now considered to be the order of the day in Methil.

Finishing in the top half of the league table also had its benefits, with the reward of a match with a top English side to look forward to in the following season's Texaco Cup competition.

Almost as soon as the last competitive ball had been kicked, the Fifers embarked on a three game continental tour at the beginning of May, during which Danish sides Horsens and Aarhus were beaten 5-1 and 2-0 respectively before Germans BU Hamburg won the final tour match by the odd goal in seven.

Back home, the season was wound up with a benefit game for Dave Clarke, Dave Gorman, Walter Borthwick and Peter McQuade at Bayview on 7th May against Wolverhampton Wanderers.

The match, which ended in a no scoring draw, was rather disappointing according to the *East Fife Mail*. Despite Wolves having finished fifth in the English League as well as reaching the semi-final of the F.A. Cup, a 'disappointing' crowd of only 3,379 turned out for the event. The local newspaper concluded that the poor performance from both sides was due to the lack of atmosphere in the ground caused by the 'poor' crowd!

With a pool of over thirty signed players at the beginning of season 1973/74, including the nucleus of the previous season's side, regular Bayview patrons could look forward to the forthcoming campaign with confidence. Some even went as far as to say that the club would emulate their respectable final league position of the previous campaign as well as reach the latter stages of one or both of the main cup competitions. With names such as Kevin Hegarty, Drew Rutherford, Walter Borthwick, Jim Hamilton, Billy McPhee, Doug Dailey, Bobby Duncan, Bobby Cairns, Dave Clarke, Graham Honeyman, Ernie McGarr, Dave Gorman, John Martis and Johnny Love now familiar even beyond the realms of the local pubs and clubs, it seemed a foregone conclusion that a good season was in store.

Only weeks after their previous European trip, two pre-season matches were played in Holland at the end of July. The first game, against ADO den Haag, resulted in a disappointing 4-0 defeat on 25th July, but three days later confidence was restored with a 3-2 win over Telstar.

On returning home, friendly wins were recorded against Southend United and Tranmere Rovers before the League Cup started with a visit from Dundee United on Saturday 11th August.

The 'Arabs' returned home with a 2-1 win under their belts and, when Motherwell romped home with a 5-0 victory four days later, it looked like exit from League Cup at the first hurdle was a foregone conclusion.

A share of the points against Aberdeen at Pittodrie followed by revenge over Motherwell at Bayview restored a little pride, but defeat in the remaining two fixtures against Aberdeen and Dundee United ensured that the Fifers finished bottom of their section.

The first two league fixtures resulted in defeats from the two sides newly promoted from Division Two, Clyde and Dunfermline Athletic. Despite the arrival of Alex Rae from Partick Thistle for a reported fee of £7,500 on 7th September, form didn't improve and the third league game, against Hibernian at Easter Road on the following Saturday, was also lost.

In mid-September, the first game of the much-awaited Texaco Cup was played against English top league side Burnley at Turf Moor. The small band of East Fife supporters who made the trip south knew they would be in for a tough time, but few expected the 7-0 thrashing which resulted!

Only 1,657 spectators turned out for the meaningless second leg in Methil two weeks later, but those who did witnessed an entertaining match in which the Fifers took a 2-0 lead through Billy McPhee and Graham Ritchie. Burnley, with Welsh international wizard Leighton James and England's Keith Newton in their ranks, refused to lie down and eventually turned the game around with goals from Fletcher, Hankin and Noble to win on the night by the odd goal in five.

The first league win of the season came on 29th September with a 1-0 victory over Dundee at DensPark thanks to a Billy McPhee penalty.

Poor overall league form, however, resulted in the sacking of Manager Pat Quinn, who was replaced at the helm by former midfield stalwart Frank Christie, a great club servant during the 1950's.

With Christie not due to take over the reins until Morton's visit to Methil the following week, the Fifers travelled to Ibrox without a Manager for the league fixture with Rangers on 13th October 1973. Kit man Alex Doig, the longest serving member of the backroom staff to travel with the squad that afternoon, knew more about the individual merits of the East Fife players than most and duly volunteered to assist by picking the team. With only one win from the six league matches played, the Fifers weren't expected to take anything from the game and a resounding victory for the Glasgow giants was expected, but the eleven players who ran out on to the Ibrox turf that afternoon thought otherwise. After only seven minutes play, Jim Hamilton scored the only goal of the game to give East Fife their first, and so far only, competitive win against Rangers at Ibrox.

Frank Christie's first game in charge, against Morton at Bayview on 20th October, proved to be a damp squib. On an extremely wet and miserable afternoon in Methil, almost the entire crowd of 2,329 huddled under the covered enclosure as the players slipped around on the treacherous surface. When half time arrived, both teams changed their entire kit, but to no avail as all twenty-two players were once again soaked to the skin within minutes of the re-start. Morton rounded off a truly miserable afternoon by scoring the only goal of the game through McIlmoyle.

The first home league win of the season was only delayed for a week, however, as Partick Thistle were beaten 2-1 on 27th October thanks to goals from McPhee and Love.

Rather than signal a turnaround in fortunes, the victory marked the start of a sequence of seven games without a win, although it has to be said that the points were shared with Dundee United, Aberdeen and Hearts over the same period. Despite the club's lowly league standing, ambitious proposals were put forward in November 1973 for major ground improvements at Bayview. Chairman Jim Baxter revealed that the club intended building a new grandstand with a capacity of 2,000, new dressing rooms, a treatment room, an administration block and a licensed restaurant. The terracing at either end of the ground was to be covered and the total cost of the project was estimated to be £100,000. The proposals were 'not pie in the sky' according to Chairman Baxter, and would put Bayview 'in the big time'. Unfortunately, just like all the ambitious schemes previously considered, the plan fell by the wayside.

The end of the year was marked with a single goal victory over Clyde in which Bertie Miller made his first appearance after returning from Aberdeen for a club record fee of £10,000 and, on New Year's Day 1974, full points were taken in the crucial derby with Dunfermline Athletic at East EndPark. Were things about to take a turn for the better? Unfortunately not.

The next three league games against Hibernian, Dundee and Rangers were all lost 3-0 as East Fife went to the bottom of the league with the unenviable reputation of having the worst goal scoring record in Britain. An early exit from the Scottish Cup against Second Division promotion challengers Queen of the South in Dumfries during the same period simply added to the gloom.

Despite the team's poor performances in January, at least one player was attracting attention south of the border, and

Graham Honeyman was invited south for trials with NottinghamForest.

The signing of Harry Kinnear from Hearts at the beginning of February was expected to rectify the poor scoring record and, in only his second game, he scored his side's only goal in a 1-1 draw with Dumbarton at Boghead. Just as Kinnear arrived at Bayview, it looked like the club might be on the verge of losing another player capable scoring goals, with Billy McPhee attracting interest from Dundee United. Fortunately, the fans' favourite remained at Bayview.

A delighted Davie Clarke looks on as Ron McIvor's effort beats the Motherwell 'keeper to record a much-needed victory over Steel Men at Bayview on 20th April 1974 (Ricky Janetta)

The signing of Miller and Kinnear started to have the desired effect in March, with both players finding the net as Partick Thistle, St Johnstone and Arbroath were all beaten on their own soil to push the team up to thirteenth place in the table.

From his debut against Rangers on 9th February until the end of the season, Kinnear claimed the No.9 shirt as his and, although there was still a place in the forward line for Kevin

Hegarty, the former Hearts player signed on a free transfer from Carlisle United in 1971 joined Morton on 14th March for £8,000.

The two games that followed the three match winning sequence, against Dundee United and Aberdeen, were both lost and, when fellow relegation candidates Falkirk won 2-1 at Bayview on 6th April, the Fifers sank back into the relegation quagmire.

A share of the points with Hearts at Tynecastle was followed by a crushing 6-1 home defeat at the hands of Celtic, but when Motherwell were beaten on 20th April by a Ronnie McIvor strike, there appeared to be a glimmer of light at the end of the tunnel.

With two matches to go, against bottom club Falkirk at Brockville and against Ayr United in Methil, it looked as if the drop could be avoided.

Even after the points were shared with Falkirk, hopes were high that safety would be secured with victory over Ayr, but on 27th April the 'Honest Men' scored the only goal of the game through Mitchell to take both points.

All was not lost, however. Having completed their fixtures, the Fifers were still sitting third from bottom and would still beat the drop if second bottom Clyde, a point behind and with a vastly inferior goal difference, only picked up a single point from their two outstanding matches with Hibernian and Hearts.

After sharing the points with Hibs at Shawfield on 1st May, defeat at Tynecastle three days later would send the 'Bully Wee' down to Division Two, but the hopes of the East Fife supporters were dashed as Clyde held out for a no scoring draw against Hearts to retain their top flight status.

The fight had been lost. Methil would now have play host to Second Division football for at least the following season.

The axing of the reserve team at the end of the campaign resulted in a radical clear out of playing staff. Free transfers were handed to no fewer than fifteen players, including Ibrox goal hero Jim Hamilton, stalwart defender Bobby Duncan and long serving goalkeeper Dave Gorman along with familiar names such as Davie Cairns and Doug Dailey. In addition, both Alex Rae and Walter Borthwick were placed on the transfer list.

"We will build again", vowed manager Christie.

The continental pre-season tours of recent years must have seemed like distant memories, as preparations for season 1974/75 got under way. Instead of visiting Denmark, Holland or Germany, the farthest the Fifers travelled was the north east of England, where victory against Darlington on 3rd August was countered with defeat against non-league Gateshead United two days later.

The League Cup campaign started well enough with a 2-1 win at Alloa on 10th August, but when a 4-1 defeat was sustained at home to Falkirk four days later, the chance of winning the section and progressing in the competition seemed remote. Cowdenbeath were beaten 2-1 in the next fixture, but defeat at Falkirk on 21st August all but ensured a quarter-final place for the 'Bairns', who went on to defeat Hearts before losing to Hibernian at the semi-final stage.

After losing the return fixture against Cowdenbeath at Central Park, the series of first round League Cup games was rounded off with a 5-1 home win against Alloa Athletic.

With league re-construction due to take place at the end of the season, a final place in the top six of the table would ensure promotion to the new fourteen-club First Division.

It was widely expected that this would be achieved with ease and when Forfar Athletic, who had finished their previous campaign second bottom of the league, visited Methil on the last day of August for the first league fixture, a home victory seemed certain. Forfar had other ideas and, as the home supporters were still assembling behind the east goal, the visitors stunned their hosts by scoring in the opening minute. The Fifers rallied, however, and turned the game around with goals from McPhee and Kinnear to get their league campaign off to a winning start.

When Derek O'Connor scored a brace at Stark's Park the following week to secure both points against Raith Rovers, it looked increasingly likely that a successful season lay ahead. Only one match was lost from the following thirteen league fixtures as East Fife claimed pole position; a run which included a 5-0 home win against Albion Rovers and a 3-0 victory over St Mirren at Love Street, aided by an own goal from former Fifer Walter Borthwick.

It was not all plain sailing during the successful run, however. Returning home from the victory against Hamilton Academical on 9th November, four players were hurt in a car crash near Falkirk. The most seriously hurt was Billy McPhee, who sustained a dislocated right hip, a broken finger and an arm wound, and was taken to Falkirk Infirmary. The other players involved were Mark Clougherty, Drew Rutherford and Harry Kinnear. With McPhee expected to watch from the sidelines for the remainder of the season, the club didn't have its troubles to seek.

Almost immediately, the player's absence had a detrimental effect on performances.

On 22nd November the Fifers and league newcomers Meadowbank Thistle met for the first time at the Commonwealth Stadium. The Edinburgh side, formerly known as Ferranti Thistle, had struggled since joining the Scottish League and an easy win for the visitors was anticipated, but when the referee's whistle signalled the end of the game it was the Methil Men who left the field with red faces following a 2-1 defeat.

A win in the next outing was imperative if the challenge for the league title was to be maintained, but defeat at Montrose on the last day in November saw the team slip down to third place in the table.

When mid-table Stenhousemuir forced a draw at Bayview the following week, it looked like the form slump wasn't going to be temporary, but two goals from trialist Sammy Frickleton against Stirling Albion on 14th December helped to send the Fifers back to the top of the league with a 3-1 win.

The 2-1 derby win over Raith Rovers at Bayview on New Year's Day 1975 proved to be an entertaining match, with Sammy Frickleton's second half winner delighting the bumper 5,292 crowd.

Exactly two weeks later, English football legend Bobby Charlton graced the Bayview turf as part of an 'All-Star Select' side who took on a Fife Select in a testimonial for Bayview favourite John Martis. Appearing beside Charlton was Martis himself along with other household names such as Willie Mathieson, Tommy Gemmell, Pat Stanton and Dixie Deans. The crowd of 3,073 were treated to an entertaining match in which goals from Charlton and Hearts' Aird were not enough to overcome a plucky Fife side, who won 6-2 thanks to doubles from Raith's Conn and Dunfermline's Mackie along with further goals from Cowdenbeath's Laing and Dunfermline's Kinninmonth.

The top of the table position was maintained until the beginning of February 1975, despite losing to both BrechinCity and East Stirlingshire in January. Once again exit from the Scottish Cup at the first hurdle was sustained with a 1-0 defeat from St Johnstone in Perth.

As the season entered its crucial stage, league defeats from fellow championship contenders St Mirren and Falkirk knocked the Fifers from their perch and panic set in at Bayview.

Only one win from the following five fixtures saw the club slip down to fifth place and, instead of challenging for the league title, a battle for a place in the top six was now on the cards.

Convincing wins against Meadowbank Thistle and Cowdenbeath looked to have put the team back on the rails, but a 4-0 home defeat from Montrose on 5th April cast serious doubt over the ability to win promotion. Only two points were required from the remaining three games, but considering the poor form shown over the second half of the season, it was just possible that all would be lost.

The fears of the Bayview faithful were proved to be unfounded when, at Ochilview the following Saturday, a Harry Kinnear goal secured a place in the new First Division with a 1-0 win. The huge sigh of relief in the visitors' dressing room after the game almost drowned out the sound of the champagne corks popping!

With little at stake, only one point was gained from the final two fixtures against Stirling Albion and Stranraer, and the Fifers finished in fifth place.

Preparations for season 1975/76 came in the form of four wins against English opposition. On 26th July, non-league Bishop Auckland were beaten 4-1 at Bayview and, on the last day of the month, the Fifers went one better against Hartlepools United with a 5-1 victory.

The series of pre-season fixtures was rounded off with wins both home and away against English Fourth Division side WorkingtonTown.

A poor start to the League Cup was made with defeat from St Mirren at Love Street on 9th August, followed by a 2-2 draw at home to Raith Rovers on a foggy Wednesday evening four days later.

Hopes of progressing to the second round were all but extinguished with a 4-0 defeat at Montrose on 16th August and, although the remaining three sectional games produced convincing wins against Raith and St Mirren and a share of the points against Montrose, it was the LinksPark side who won the right to face Hibernian in the quarter-finals.

For the record, the 'Gable Endies' went on to produce one of their most famous victories by beating the Edinburgh giants 3-1 at home on 24th September to win the tie 3-2 on aggregate and progress to a semi-final clash with Rangers. Predictably, Rangers ended Montrose's run with a 5-1 win at Hampden on 8th October.

When the league campaign kicked off, the Fifers still couldn't get the better of the LinksPark side, and went down 3-0 at Montrose on 30th August.

When Dunfermline Athletic were soundly thrashed 5-1 at Bayview in the first home league game on 6th September and Falkirk were beaten at Brockville the following Saturday, however, it looked like a challenge could be made at the top of the table after all.

Although points were dropped over the following six league matches, a reasonably healthy league position of fifth was maintained until the end of October, but the following month heralded the start of a rapid slip down the league. Helped in no small way by a 5-0 defeat from Partick Thistle, the team were well and truly embedded in the relegation zone by mid-December.

An unbeaten run of six matches then ensued, which was halted abruptly with a 3-0 Scottish Cup defeat against Rangers at Ibrox on 24th January 1976.

The league programme resumed with a narrow defeat at Kilmarnock, but the disappointment of losing the first league match in almost two months was completely overshadowed at Bayview a week later.

Montrose, still in with an outside chance of promotion to the Premier League, humiliated their hosts by inflicting the Fifers' record home defeat of 7-1, helped in no small way by the inclusion of former Bayview favourites Bertie Miller and Dave Gorman in their line-up!

Victory against Queen of the South in the penultimate league match on 21st February ensured safety from relegation, but defeat at Morton seven days later confirmed a final league placing of third bottom.

With the league programme having consisted of only twenty-six matches, a new tournament was introduced to fill the blank Saturdays until the end of the season.

The Spring Cup, which involved only clubs from the First and Second Divisions, took a form similar to the League Cup, where teams competed in mini-leagues of four with both the winners and runners-up progressing to the second round. The Fifers were drawn to play against Stranraer, Airdrieonians and BrechinCity.

After starting poorly with a single goal defeat at Stranraer, a convincing 3-0 home win against Airdrieonians followed by a 2-0 victory over Brechin put the Fifers in the driving seat. Despite losing at Broomfield in the next game, a win and a draw against Stranraer and Brechin meant a final position of second in the table and a second round clash with Division One champions Partick Thistle.

After losing the first leg by a single goal at Firhill on 14th April, a 2-0 home victory three days later set up a quarter-final meeting with Clydebank. With the tie all square following both legs, the Fife ended their season by exiting the competition 4-2 on penalties at Bayview on 24th April.

Although Manager Christie pursued the signatures of one or two players during the summer of 1976, there were no significant arrivals at Bayview during the close season. As the new season approached, speculation surrounded the future of Derek O'Connor who, it had been rumoured, was set to sign for Ayr United. When the new season got under way, however, O'Connor was still an East Fife player.

Unbeaten in their six pre-season matches against St Johnstone, Hartlepool United, Alloa Athletic, Ross County, Brora Rangers and Inverness Clachnacuddin, it was a confident East Fife side that lined up to face Stranraer at Bayview in the first of the sectional League Cup first round games on 14th August 1976. With newly signed former Rangers star Quinton Young making his first appearance in black and gold, a 3-0 home win was the outcome, but the joy was short lived.

The only other first round win, an impressive 2-1 victory over Falkirk at Brockville, was accompanied by humiliating 5-0 defeats at both Hamilton and Stranraer and a 5-1 reverse against Falkirk at Bayview.

The league programme opened on 4th September and, although the results were not quite so embarrassing, only one win from the first seven matches resulted in the resignation of Manager Frank Christie following the home defeat from Morton on 25th September.

Ironically, Christie's last game in charge turned out to be identical to his first. Both games were against Morton at Bayview and both finished 1-0 to the visitors!

Roy Barry was appointed Player/Manager in time to take charge of the side for the visit to Montrose on 20th October, but failed to halt the run of poor form and a 2-0 win for the home side was the outcome.

As the season progressed, things went from bad to worse. By the end of November, only eight league points had been amassed from eighteen matches leaving the team firmly anchored at the foot of the table.

Anyone thinking that the home game against Clydebank might bring an end to the miserable run would be sorely disappointed. On a snow covered Bayview Park, with future Scotland star Davie Cooper in their ranks, the 'Bankies' scored six without reply to record their best-ever win over the Fifers and, in doing so, set a new record for the home side of sixteen consecutive matches without a win!

After the disastrous run was finally halted with a 1-0 home victory against Montrose on 18th December, a slight improvement in form ensued and, helped by a 2-1 win against Raith Rovers in the New Year derby, a league position of third bottom was achieved by mid-January 1977.

The Scottish Cup brought a brief respite from the battle to escape relegation and the visit of Second Division Clyde on 29th January resulted in a 2-1 win and a home tie with Albion Rovers in round four. A similar score-line in front of 2,514 in Methil on 26th February brought the reward of a quarter-final clash with Hearts.

The Fifers belied their league status at Tynecastle on 12th March and forced a no-scoring draw in front of 13,350 to bring the Edinburgh side back to Methil for the replay on the following Tuesday evening. With a semi-final clash against Rangers at stake, cup fever hit Methil and its environs and 8,658 paid to see the match. With time running out, the score was still level at 2-2 thanks to goals from Love and Kinnear for the home side and Gibson and Prentice for the visitors. In 84 minutes, however, John Gallagher scored to break the hearts of the home supporters and win the match by the odd goal in five for the visitors.

Although favourable form during the run in to the end of the season resulted in fifth bottom position with just two games to play, defeat in the penultimate game coupled with unfavourable results elsewhere meant that only one point separated the Fife from joint second bottom St Johnstone and Raith Rovers going into the last match.

Safety was ensured with a 3-3 draw at Dumbarton on the last day of April, but when the dust settled it transpired that the result from Boghead was unimportant. Raith's home defeat against Morton meant that East Fife would have been safe in any case and, with St Johnstone winning handsomely in Dumfries, the Kirkcaldy side were relegated along with Falkirk.

Despite their poor league showing, a profit of £8,656 was made over the 1976/77 season, thanks mainly to the revenue generated from the Scottish Cup run. Coupled with the profit of over £10,000 for the previous season, the club reported that they were now almost £4,000 in the black. Oh, for a similar situation today!

In preparation for the 1977/78 season, the Fifers embarked on a three-match tour of Ireland. Earlier in the year, manager Roy Barry had hinted at the possibility of a short summer tour of Saudi Arabia, which was to be organised with the help of his 'old pal' Jimmy Hill, who was at the time responsible for the development of soccer in Saudi. Unfortunately the tour never materialised and, after proposals for a tour of Holland also fell through, the club embarked on their first ever trip across the Irish Sea. All three games in the 'Emerald Isle', against Galway Rovers, Coleraine and Irish Champions Sligo Rovers, ended in draws.

The league programme got off to a poor start with a home defeat at the hands of newly promoted Stirling Albion on 13th August 1977.

Four days later, an early exit from the newly re-formatted League Cup was virtually assured following a 5-0 first-leg defeat from Clydebank at New Kilbowie. The 'Bankies' completed the job with a 1 0 win at Bayview a week later.

The poor start to the league campaign went from bad to worse as the weeks progressed and, by mid-September, the Fife found themselves sitting at the foot of the table still seeking their first win. The deadlock was finally broken with a 3-1 victory against Dumbarton on 28th September but, although the next two games produced a draw with Arbroath and full points from the home fixture with Queen of the South, a run of five straight defeats restored the gloom by mid-November. Few would have expected the Fifers to take anything from the home league fixture with Hearts on 12th November but, as so often happens when the chips are down, the underdogs upset the applecart! Goals from Quinton Young and Ken Mackie without reply from the promotion chasing Edinburgh side delighted the home supporters in the 3,898 crowd as East Fife recorded only their third league win of the season.

Unfortunately, the turnaround in fortunes proved to be only temporary.

A home defeat from Morton in the next match followed by defeat against bottom club Alloa a week later saw the Fifers exchange places with the RecreationPark side at the foot of the table. When the end of the year arrived without a further win and with the club still bottom of the league, the departure of manager Roy Barry was inevitable.

Davie Clarke replaced Barry in January 1978, but even a new man at the helm didn't bring an immediate turnaround in fortunes.

Every match played in January and February 1978, including the Scottish Cup tie with Hibernian, was lost. Relegation now seemed probable rather than just possible.

Omitting the 5-0 Fife Cup win against Burntisland Shipyard in December 1977, the home defeat at the hands of Alloa Athletic on 8th March 1978 was the club's fifteenth competitive game without a win.

Davie Clarke's first victory as East Fife Manager came on 12th March in the form of a 2-0 home success against Queen of the South, a game that was also significant in that it was the first time the club had ever played on a Sunday.

The eternal optimists who believed that the corner had finally been turned, however, were to be proved sadly wrong. Not another win was recorded before the end of the season and, although relegation could still theoretically be avoided with six matches to play, manager Clarke accepted the inevitability of taking the drop down to the Second Division following the defeat at Hamilton on 25th March. East Fife were, once again, back in the basement.

Chapter Seventeen: Dark Days Again

Determined to return to Division One at the first attempt, the club decided to re-instate their reserve team at the beginning of Season 1978/79. The second string were entered into the Scottish Reserve League East and former coach Mike Marshall, who had resigned when Roy Barry departed from Bayview, returned to the club as reserve coach.

Former Bayview favourite George Dewar was installed as first team coach and in July the club's hopes for the season were boosted with the signing of 27 year-old former Celtic player Johnny Gibson.

Unlike recent years, all preparations for the forthcoming campaign were played out at Bayview, with friendly wins recorded against Gateshead United, Hartlepool United and a strong Dundee United side.

After Dunfermline Athletic were knocked out of the Fife Cup following a penalty shoot-out on 7th August, the league season got under way with a visit from Albion Rovers five days later. Hopes for an impressive start to the league programme were dashed, however, as the Coatbridge side scored twice to take the points and, when Forfar Athletic claimed both points in the next match at Station Park, it looked as if a long, hard season was once again on the cards. An early exit from the League Cup following defeat in both legs of the second round tie with Arbroath simply added to the air of despondency.

The season was kick-started with victory by the odd goal in five against Queen's Park at Bayview on 26th August and, following further wins against East Stirlingshire, Berwick Rangers and Stenhousemuir, the promotion challenge was well and truly back on track by mid-September.

At the beginning of October, however, a 5-1 defeat from fellow promotion hopefuls Dunfermline Athletic severely dented the players' confidence and only one further victory was recorded before the end of November as the Fifers slipped down to mid-table.

December proved to be infinitely more successful, producing four good wins against clubs all involved in the hunt for promotion, but just when it looked like the winning run could be maintained, Scotland was hit by one of the severest winters for years. With Bayview and many other Scottish grounds totally unplayable and with many Fife roads blocked by drifting snow, football was simply out of the question.

The Fife eventually got back into action with a Scottish Cup tie against lowly BrechinCity at Bayview on 16th January 1979, which was won 2-1 thanks to a Dickson brace. In the following round, also at Bayview, hopes of progressing to the later stages of the competition were ended by Berwick Rangers, who won the right to face Celtic at Parkhead with a single goal victory.

The home fixture against Cowdenbeath on 20th January was the only league match played that month and, with conditions still far from perfect, the visitors won by a single goal.

Only two games went ahead during February, but full points were taken from both with a 3-0 home win over Stenhousemuir and an impressive 1-0 victory against Falkirk at Brockville.

Most of the outstanding league fixtures were played out during March and only two games were lost in the process, both against Albion Rovers. With a favourable goals tally into the bargain, hopes were high of qualifying for the following season's Drybrough Cup, for which the eight highest scoring sides in the Premier, First and Second Divisions were entered. It wasn't long before the full cost of the two defeats against Albion Rovers was realised.

A 5-2 win against fellow promotion challengers Falkirk at Brockville on 18th April, described by the *East Fife Mail* as *"the best away performance for many years"*, would have placed the

Fifers in a challenging position had their performances during March been more favourable.

Instead, with the promotion chance all but gone, an air of despondency hung over Bayview during the final weeks of the season and only a single point was won from the final three games, resulting in a final league position of fourth, nine points behind second placed Dunfermline Athletic and eleven behind champions Berwick Rangers.

A Fife Cup final win against Raith Rovers in May did little to lift the gloom of having to face the certainty of at least another season in the Second Division and, to add to the disappointment, the club failed to qualify for the Drybrough Cup by just two goals.

On a brighter note, the ever-present midfield player Colin Methven was picked to play for Scotland in a semi-professional tournament held in Manchester from 31st May to 4th June 1979. Players for the semi-pro team were picked from Scottish Second Division and Highland League clubs. During the tournament, Methven attracted attention from several English clubs and general feeling following the tournament was that his days at Bayview were numbered.

A total of seventeen players were retained at the end of the 1978/79 season although the club announced that they were willing to listen to offers for Johnny Gibson, who had been at Bayview for less than a year. Jim George, Ken Halley, Gordon Heaney and Robert Morris were all handed free transfers.

In July 1979, the Fifers were off on their travels once again, this time as guests of the Fourth Royal Tank Regiment in Munster, Germany.

No fewer than six games were played in as many days, starting on 23rd July with a challenge match against their hosts. The army lads proved to be no match for their guests, who scored eight times without reply. Over the border in Holland the following day, Dutch First Division outfit

Cambuur Leewarden provided a stiffer test and were held to a no scoring draw.

On 25th July, the toughest game of the tour was played against top Dutch side F.C. Utrecht, and the difference in class was apparent as the Fifers failed to score against their hosts, who found the net six times.

Despite feeling the exhaustion of having played three games in three days, the Fife went nap in their fourth fixture against F.C. Pleimtje Helgelo from the Dutch Second Division, who were beaten 5-0. On day five of the tour, the fatigue was beginning to show as a Dutch Amateur Select scored the only goal of the game on 27th July to send the tourists back over the border to Munster with the record of having won only one match in Holland along with one draw and two defeats. In the final tour game, the Second Division of the Fourth Royal Tank Regiment were defeated 3-0.

Back on home soil, Wigan Athletic were beaten 2-0 in a friendly at Bayview and Cowdenbeath were beaten 2-1 in the semi-final of the Fife Cup before the League campaign started with a trip to Forfar on 11th August.

Although the opening match was lost by a single goal, league results from the opening quarter of the season were reasonably satisfactory. Only three games were lost from the ten played during August and September, and a 4-0 win against Cowdenbeath was recorded in the process. One match played during this spell, against Meadowbank Thistle at the Commonwealth Stadium on 24th August, was significant in that it marked the debut of future star Stevie Kirk, who replaced Jim Brown during the second half.

As one promising player was beginning his Bayview career, however, it was time for another to depart.

In September 1979, midfield stalwart Colin Methven, who had played in every competitive East Fife game since replacing John Martis in 1975 until the end of the 1978/79 season, was sold to Wigan Athletic for £30,000. Although the club were sorry to lose Methven, who had been at Bayview since signing from Leven Juniors in 1973, the transfer fee was more than enough to wipe out their overdraft with plenty left over!

Back on the field of play, an early exit was made from the League Cup in early September following defeat both home and away against local rivals Raith Rovers, followed by a form slump in October which saw only one point gained from four league matches.

In the midst of the run of poor form, George Dewar resigned as first team coach and was replaced by reserve coach Mike Marshall. The appointment of Marshall saw little change in the team's performances, and only two points were taken from the four matches played during November as the Fifers slid to third bottom of the league.

As the end of the year loomed, it looked as if the corner had finally been turned with a 4-2 win against bottom club Queen of the South in Dumfries on 8th December followed by a home win against Alloa Athletic a week later.

A heavy defeat from promotion chasing East Stirlingshire at Bayview on 20th December followed by defeat from BrechinCity at GlebePark two days later, however, saw the end of the year arrive with an air of despondency hanging around Bayview once again. Just to add to the gloom, the club announced that Ron McIvor had joined Colin Methven at Wigan Athletic following a successful loan period.

The first day of January 1980 saw local rivals Cowdenbeath beaten 2-1 at Bayview and, when second top Falkirk were denied pole position with a 1-0 defeat courtesy of a 30 yard John Lumsden free kick in the next league match, the future looked a little brighter. Sandwiched between the two aforementioned games, however, an early exit was made from the Scottish Cup thanks to a 1-0 home defeat from fellow strugglers Alloa Athletic.

Any promising player plying his trade in the lower reaches of the Scottish League is always going to attract the attentions of bigger, wealthier clubs. John 'Roxy' Lumsden, who had only arrived at Bayview seven months previously, fell into this category and became the second big-money departure of the season when he signed for StokeCity for a record £40,000 fee following the home draw with Stranraer on 19th January. The following series of eight league matches produced only one win and one draw, with eight goals scored against nineteen conceded in the process.

All hopes of promotion were now long gone, but as winter gave way to spring, hopes for the future were high with the steady improvement of teenager Stevie Kirk.

As the season drew to a close, the Fifers embarked on a three game winning run which started on 29th March with a 4-0 win over Forfar Athletic at StationPark, during which Kirk scored his first goal for the club. Not surprisingly, the promising youngster was by this time attracting attention from south of the border and, only a week after the Forfar match, Kirk was on trial with Stoke City, during which he played in a youth tournament in France. Although Newcastle United were also interested in signing the player, the move to the 'Potteries' was made permanent four weeks later when a fee of £10,000 was received for the teenage starlet.

When the curtain finally came down on season 1979/80, the Fifers found themselves occupying tenth place in the league table.

Despite the lack of success on the park, the club were able to report a profit of £68,637 for the season, thanks mainly to the sale of players. Only time would tell if the healthy bank balance would be put to good use in order to lift the club out of the lower reaches of the Scottish League.

Veteran Quinton Young decided to call it a day during the summer of 1980 and returned to playing junior football with Western League side Whitletts Victoria.

For the second year in a row, the Fife travelled to Germany as guests of the Fourth Royal Tank Regiment in July. Unlike the hectic schedule of the previous tour, however, only two matches were played against club sides. On 20th July the Fifers were narrowly beaten by German league side Preussen Munster, but managed a 2-0 win against Dutch league side S.V. Heek three days later.

Shortly after returning home, the *East Fife Mail* reported that a young player currently on the books of Real Madrid, described as 'of slight build but with fantastic ball skills', had been on trial with the club. It later transpired that the player in question, Angelo Ortega, was anxious to sign for the Fifers in order to avoid doing his Spanish National Service! The club decided not to pursue the Spaniard's signature.

As usual, the Bayview faithful turned out for the beginning of the competitive season expecting the club to shake off their troubles of recent years and make a serious challenge at returning to the First Division.

Unfortunately, season 1980/81 turned out to be just as disastrous as the previous campaign. The opening two league matches were lost; a 3-1 reverse against Clyde at Shawfield followed by defeat by the odd goal in five against Forfar Athletic at StationPark. Either side of the Forfar game a first round exit from the League Cup arrived in the form of a 9-2 aggregate defeat from Dundee United.

When the next two home games against Cowdenbeath and Meadowbank Thistle were won 3-2 and 2-1 respectively, the home support had reason to believe that the good times were just around the corner, but once again it was not to be.

The end of the year arrived with the club once again languishing in the lower reaches of the league, with only five wins and eighteen points to show for their efforts.

The fact that Falkirk paid out a record £25,000 to take impressive youngster Willie Herd to Brockville in September didn't help matters on the field of play and the transfer of Dave Berry to Raith Rovers during the same month had a similar detrimental effect.

One arrival at Bayview the following month, however, would eventually have a huge impact on the club, although the true value of the signing would not be appreciated until well into the following season. In October 1980, manager Dave Clarke pulled off what would turn out to be probably his greatest ever signing, when he persuaded 16 year-old Gordon Durie from Hill of Beath Under 16's to put pen to paper.

The Scottish Cup campaign provided the Bayview faithful with some welcome cheer either side of the festive season. A home win against non-league Civil Service Strollers on 13th December was followed by an impressive 2-1 victory over promotion chasing Queen of the South at Palmerston on 10th January 1981. The third round of the competition paired the Fifers with First Division Clydebank and, following stalemate at Bayview, the Methil Men exited the competition after putting up a great fight in the replay at New Kilbowie on 28th January, where the home side eventually won by the odd goal in nine after extra time!

As far as the league was concerned, the second half of the season saw things go from bad to worse. Only four wins materialised from eighteen league games which, along with seven draws, meant a final league position of fourth bottom, one place lower than the previous season.

On the financial side, the club were still reporting a healthy bank balance at the end of the 1980/81 season and decided to replace the railway sleepers on the north and east terraces with concrete. Unfortunately, the opportunity was not taken to replace the crush barriers at the same time; a decision which eventually caused the ground's official capacity to be set at the ridiculously low figure of 5,433 despite being one of the neatest grounds in the lower divisions.

The healthy financial situation also allowed the club to announce that there would be no increase in the cost of an adult season ticket for the forthcoming campaign and prices were set at £15 for the stand and £12 for ground only. The situation for youngsters was even better, with the price halved from £8 to £4. Normal match-day admission prices were set at £1 for adults and 70p for children and OAP's.

After facing Hibernian and Raith Rovers in pre-season matches, the first competitive game of season 1981/82 finished with an encouraging 3-1 victory over Stranraer in the first round of the League Cup.

The tournament had reverted to its traditional format of mini-leagues for the first round and the Fifers found themselves playing in a six team section along with Albion Rovers, Arbroath, Meadowbank Thistle and Stenhousemuir as well as their opening day opponents. Although just one match was lost during the opening series, only two wins were chalked up which resulted in a final group position of second and a first round exit from the tournament.

Once again a poor start was made to the league programme, with the first two fixtures against Stranraer and Stenhousemuir ending in defeat.

Form improved over the next four games, which produced two wins and two draws, including convincing victories against Stirling Albion and Albion Rovers at Bayview, both won by three goals without reply. The following five fixtures, however, were all lost and once again the lower reaches of the league table beckoned.

After the points were shared on New Year's Day 1982 against Cowdenbeath at Bayview, the second round of the Scottish Cup was reached with a convincing 4-1 home win against Stranraer, but in the following round Forfar Athletic visited Methil and dumped the Fifers out of the tournament on 18th January.

The 'Loons' went on to send shock waves through Scottish football by reaching the last four of the competition following wins against Hamilton Academical, Hearts and Queen's Park in rounds three, four and five. Few gave the Second Division minnows much of a chance against Rangers in the semi-final, but amazingly they held the Glasgow giants to a no-scoring draw at Hampden before going down 3-1 in the replay!

Back on league business, hopes of mounting a challenge for promotion during the second half of the season were boosted with victory against promotion hopefuls Alloa Athletic at RecreationPark on 2nd February, which set the team up nicely for the visit of league leaders Clyde four days later. The table toppers, who included a young Pat Nevin in their ranks, were held to a 2-2 draw and, although the Fifers were still sitting in the bottom half of the table, it looked like the move upstairs was still possible.

Amazingly, after such favourable results against two of the promotion favourites, a crowd of only 367 turned out for the next home fixture against Montrose. Perhaps the Bayview regulars realised that the upturn in form was too good to last, and the 'Gable Endies' took full points with a single goal win. When the next game was lost 3-1 at Arbroath, Manager Davie Clarke decided the time was right to make radical changes in the line up – and changes there certainly were!

Regular 'keeper Dave Gorman was dropped in favour of reserve custodian Christensen, several players in defence and midfield were switched around and, most significantly, a young player by the name of Gordon Durie was given his chance in the first eleven.

Almost straight away, the changes started to reap rewards.

A 2-1 victory at Stranraer on 20th February was followed by a home victory against Forfar Athletic a week later, in which the outstanding Durie scored the only goal of the game midway through the second half.

"A Star is Born", proclaimed the *East Fife Mail* on Wednesday 3rd March, reporting that the teenage starlet had been the most outstanding player on the field. *"The cheers at full time were not merely for an unexpected victory"*, they went on, *"but also for the emergence of a possible star"*.

The change in fortunes didn't end there. The following two fixtures brought wins against Cowdenbeath at Central Park and against Meadowbank at Bayview and suddenly the future seemed a whole lot brighter.

Hopes for promotion were finally ended with a four game losing streak at the end of March and the beginning of April which saw the club slip back down to fourth bottom, but hopes for the forthcoming season remained high. Not one of the final seven league matches was lost; a sequence which included wins against Stirling Albion, Stenhousemuir and Montrose and a draw against league winners Clyde at Bayview on Sunday 25th April.

The 'Bully Wee' had won the championship only the previous week, and a large support travelled through from Glasgow intent on making the match one to remember.

The afternoon was not remembered so much for the visitors' celebrations, however, but more for an incident that occurred that same afternoon on the other side of the world. At half-time, the announcement was made over the loudspeaker system that British forces had attacked a submarine in the south Atlantic; the conflict with Argentina over the sovereignty of the Falkland Islands had started in earnest and a huge shadow was cast over the afternoon's celebrations.

"We hate corned beef," chanted both sets of supporters as the teams lined up for the start of the second half!

Fortunately, the conflict lasted only a matter of weeks and, by the time season 1982/83 was ready to get under way, the Falklands War was consigned to history.

For the second year in succession, season 1982/83's competitive programme started with a series of six sectional League Cup fixtures. If failure to qualify from the weakest section in the previous season's tournament was disappointing, the 1982/83 series of first round games proved to be truly disastrous!

Despite having been drawn in the same section as Partick Thistle, newly relegated from the Premier League, the Fifers were expected to perform reasonably well against the other teams in the group; namely East Stirlingshire and BrechinCity. The first two matches finished goal-less, but included an impressive share of the points against Partick Thistle at Firhill. The following three games, however, against East Stirlingshire, Partick and Brechin, were lost by the respective scores of 1-0, 3-0 and 4-0 and, with the final match against 'Shire ending in yet another no-scoring draw, East Fife finished at the bottom of the four team section without having scored a single goal!

The league programme kicked off with a home fixture against East Stirlingshire at Bayview on 4th September, where the home side gained revenge with a 3-1 win.

The early part of the league programme then proceeded to follow a pattern similar to previous years, with a mixture of wins, draws and defeats bringing hope one week then despair the next. However, two impressive performances during the first half of the campaign resulted in a 5-1 victory over Queen of the South in Dumfries and a 5-0 home win against promotion candidates Meadowbank Thistle.

Steve Kirk returned from StokeCity on 3rd November 1982 and, although the influential player took several weeks to settle back into the side, his presence began to have an effect as the year drew to a close.

The second half of the league season proved to be more successful than the first. Victory by the odd goal in seven against Albion Rovers at Bayview two days after Christmas was followed by a 4-2 win over Cowdenbeath in the New Year derby at Central Park as the push for promotion was stepped up.

The Scottish Cup brought plenty good reasons to be cheerful during January and February 1983. After recording a single goal second round victory against high-flying BrechinCity, the third round draw brought near neighbours Raith Rovers to Methil on 29th January.

This was the third time that the two sides had been drawn to play each other in the tournament and, on each previous occasion, East Fife had emerged victorious. With the Methil side now sitting mid-table in the Second Division and the Kirkcaldy side playing in the First Division, however, there were several East Fife supporters who seriously doubted their side's ability to maintain their impressive record.

Their fears proved unfounded. The healthy crowd of 5,760 who lined the Bayview terraces on that blustery afternoon witnessed a competent display of football by the home side, in which Robin Thomson scored the only goal of the game to dump his former club out of the tournament.

The fourth round draw produced a tie against Hearts at Tynecastle on Sunday 20th February and, with the draw for the quarter-finals having been made the previous evening, a money-spinning encounter against Celtic awaited the winners. Although the Fife rose to the occasion and made their Edinburgh hosts fight every step of the way, the Tynecastle side emerged 2-1 winners on the day and the cup dream was over for another year.

The challenge for promotion was maintained throughout January and February despite defeats at the hands of Berwick Rangers and Stenhousemuir, but was effectively ended when both Cowdenbeath and Forfar Athletic took full points from their trips to Methil at the beginning of March. Although convincing wins against Montrose, Berwick and Stenhousemuir were to follow, the pack leaders were always just out of reach and the two promotion places were eventually filled by champions BrechinCity and second placed Meadowbank Thistle, who finished eleven points ahead of the Methil Men.

Despite failing to take the step upstairs yet again, the team had proved it was starting to come together. Having beaten runners-up Meadowbank convincingly on every occasion the sides had met during the 1982/83 season, East Fife proved that they were worthy of a promotion place. It wasn't so much a case of _if_ First Division football would return to Methil, but _when_!

Chapter Eighteen: Pushing for the Premier

The beginning of the 1983/84 season saw the format of the League Cup first round stage return to a single tie played over two legs. A single goal win against Arbroath at Gayfield, followed by a draw at Bayview, was rewarded with a second round meeting against Premier League side St Johnstone. After losing the first leg by the narrow margin of 2-1 at Bayview on Wednesday 24th August, the return game was played at Muirton three days later. Although the second leg was lost 6-3, the East Fife supporters in the meagre 1,848 crowd had reason to be proud of their favourites on the day. The Methil Men made their Premier Division opponents work hard for their win, and twice took the lead before the full-time Perth side finally took control of the game late in the second half.

Meanwhile, the league campaign started with a satisfactory 1-0 win against Montrose at Bayview and was followed up with a share of the points against newly relegated Dunfermline Athletic at East EndPark. After Stranraer were beaten 1-0 in Methil and East Stirlingshire disposed of by the convincing score of 4-1 at FirsPark over the next two matches, the Bayview faithful felt confident that the challenge for promotion could be maintained.

Once again, however, the supporters were left feeling let down.

Arbroath gained revenge for their early League Cup exit by recording a single goal win in Methil on 17th September and, a week later, the players' confidence took another nose-dive with a 5-2 defeat against the previous season's First Division wooden spoon winners Queen's Park at Hampden.

Only four games were won during the following three months as the club slithered back down the table, although the victory against East Stirlingshire on 12th November was notable for the superb solo effort scored by debutant Tom McCafferty, signed on loan from St Johnstone. The following month, McCafferty's move to Bayview was made permanent as part of the deal that took Gordon Scott to Muirton.

By now convinced that the season was yet another lost cause, the week between Christmas and New Year brought an unexpected treat for the supporters.

On Boxing Day, a 3-1 home win against Queen's Park not only gained revenge over the 'Spiders', but boosted the team's confidence just in time for the visit of near neighbours Dunfermline Athletic on the last day of the year. The 'Pars' were beaten 3-1 thanks to a Gordon Durie brace and a satisfying counter from Graham Hutt over his former club as East Fife moved back up to fourth place in the table.

After full points were taken from the next two games against Montrose and Albion Rovers either side of a 5-0 Scottish Cup victory against Queen of the South at Palmerston, confidence was sky-high for the Scottish Cup tie against Hibernian at Easter Road on 28th January 1984.

Although the Bayview die-hards expected their favourites to put up a good fight on the day, few seriously expected anything but a home victory, but against all the odds the tie finished goal-less. Indeed, the edited highlights shown on the BBC's *Sportscene* programme that evening proved that the Fifers had certainly given Hibs a match to remember, with Gordon Durie a continuous thorn in the side of the Premier League outfit. However, not even the most wildly enthusiastic East Fife supporter would have correctly predicted the outcome of the replay in Methil three days later.

The home supporters in the huge Bayview crowd (no attendance figure was given in the following edition of the *East Fife Mail!*) went wild when Tommy McCafferty calmly slotted the ball home from close range during the first half and, when Steve Kirk ghosted into the box to bullet a header into the net midway through the second, the cheer from the Aberhill school end could almost be heard in Edinburgh! With Hibernian failing to make any impact on the home defence whatsoever during the remainder of the match, the game finished 2-0, and East Fife became the first Second Division side to knock a Premier League club out of the Scottish Cup. Drawn to face Celtic at Bayview in the fourth round, the excitement of the forthcoming tie had a detrimental effect on form over the following two weeks and the league fixtures against Stenhousemuir and Stranraer were both lost.

A capacity crowd of 10,000 (it would have been more had it not been for the seizure of a large quantity of counterfeit tickets immediately prior to the game!) lined the terraces for the visit of Celtic on 18th February 1984. Nobody seriously expected the home side to pull off a double against Premier League opposition and, not surprisingly, the Glasgow side won comfortably by six goals without reply. Interestingly, all the goals were scored by Scottish internationalists, with Tommy Burns (twice), Murdo MacLeod, Frank McGarvey, John Colquhoun and Brian McClair all finding the net.

The following Tuesday, the exhaustion caused by playing a full-time side only three days earlier took its toll when Albion Rovers, struggling at the foot of the table, won 4-1 at Bayview. It didn't take long for the form to return, and the following four league fixtures included a share of the points with both league leaders Forfar Athletic and second placed Queen of the South, as well as a win against promotion chasing Stirling Albion at Annfield.

A hat-trick from Bobby Russell, on loan from Raith Rovers, helped the Methil Men record a morale boosting 5-1 'demolition derby' against Cowdenbeath at Central Park on 17th March, which resulted in the resignation of Cowden Manager Willie McCulloch.

The Fifers were keen to hold on to Russell following his goal scoring feat and offered their Kirkcaldy rivals cash plus Colin

O'Brien for the player. Raith declined the offer, saying that they would only part with Russell for £5,000 cash, and the player returned to Stark's Park.

After beating Stirling Albion 4-2 at Bayview in the following fixture, the Fifers drew level on points with the Annfield side, although still five points adrift of second placed Queen of the South. When Berwick Rangers scored two late goals to win the following match 2-1 on the last day of March at Shielfield, the team slipped back to sixth place and it looked as if their slim chance of promotion had gone. The jitters were also starting to set in with the other promotion clubs, however, and results elsewhere started to work in the Fifers' favour.

Two successive home wins against Stenhousemuir and East Stirlingshire, coupled with defeats for the other clubs in the promotion chasing pack, resulted in a league position of fourth by mid-April. Two points behind Queen of the South with four games remaining, the supporters started to believe that promotion to the First Division was not beyond the capabilities of the team after all!

Against Dunfermline Athletic at East EndPark on 21st April, with time running out and the match still goal-less, East Fife were awarded a penalty. The visiting supporters on the east terracing held their breath as Gordon Durie took the kick; the Dunfermline 'keeper blocked the effort, but in doing so knocked the ball straight back to Durie, who shot home to win the game.

Heading out of the exits after the final whistle and with ears pressed firmly against their transistor radios, the supporters could hardly believe their ears. Second placed Queen of the South had lost 6-3 at Arbroath and third placed Stirling Albion had only managed to draw with Montrose. East Fife were in second place!

Still in with a chance of promotion themselves, it was a determined Arbroath side who lined up the face the Fife at Gayfield the following week, but the visitors were equal to the task. Once again Gordon Durie was on hand to score the only goal of the game and, with the other promotion hopefuls slipping up yet again, a two point gap was opened up over third placed Berwick Rangers. The significance of Player/Manager Dave Clarke's 500th appearance for the club was almost forgotten as the jubilant supporters made their way back across the TayBridge!

On 5th May 1984, promotion was finally achieved after six long seasons in the Second Division with a convincing 3-0 home win against Queen's Park, coupled with defeat for nearest challengers Berwick Rangers at Montrose. Two Gordon Durie penalties along with a Hutt strike sent the 1,315 crowd home happy, convinced that having finally escaped the clutches of the bottom league, the club were more than capable of maintaining First Division status in the season that lay ahead.

With Raith Rovers dropping down from the First Division to join both Dunfermline Athletic and Cowdenbeath in the second, the Methil Men could once again claim to be the 'Kings of Fife'!

Club and supporters alike looked forward to season 1984/85 with eager anticipation. General Manager Jimmy Bonthrone, now back working behind the scenes at Bayview following a six year spell as coach and manager of Aberdeen and a five year spell out of the game, was keen to boost the home crowds. *"Bring the family for a pleasant afternoon to Bayview"*, he enthused, *"and I am sure you will not be disappointed"*.

Whatever the outcome of the home fixtures over the coming season, visitors to Bayview could be certain of one thing: Gordon Durie's ability to find the net!

In the build up to the new campaign, Durie scored all four in a friendly with Dalkeith Juniors and followed up by scoring his side's only goal in the 1-1 draw with Dunfermline Athletic in the semi-final of the Fife Cup at Bayview, which the home side won 5-4 on penalties. On Tuesday 7th August 1984, the series of pre-season matches concluded with a visit from Rangers on a pleasant evening in front of a 1,100 crowd at Bayview. The game, which finished 1-0 to the home side thanks to a Graham Hutt goal, doubled as a benefit for long serving goalkeeper Dave Gorman.

Gordon Durie chases a through ball in the Dave Gorman testimonial match against Rangers at Bayview on 7th August 1984. (Jim Corstorphine)

The Fifers' return to the First Division kicked off with a visit from Falkirk four days later, when opening day jitters were a deciding factor as the 'Bairns' took full points with a 4-2 win. Were the Methil Men out of their depth? Certainly not! The following Saturday, the Fifers travelled to play St Johnstone at Muirton, where they took both points with a thrilling 4-3 victory over the side newly relegated from the Premier League.
During the following midweek, an early exit was made from the League Cup, although the team put up a brave fight as they went down by a single goal to Hibernian at Easter Road.
On their travels once more on Saturday 25th August, Hamilton Academical were demolished almost single handed by

Gordon Durie, who once again scored all four goals in a 4-2 victory at Douglas Park.

Unfortunately, although the team's form away from home was impressive, victory at Bayview continuously eluded the side.Following defeat from Falkirk on the opening day of the season, three home matches were drawn and a further two were lost before BrechinCity were finally beaten 2-0 on 10th November. Over this same period no fewer than three games had been won away from home, three had been drawn and only one game had ended in defeat!

As well as being the Fifers' first home league win of the season, the Brechin match was significant in that it marked the first team debut of teenager Paul Hunter, who came on as substitute in place of Derek Hyslop.

The year was rounded off by gaining revenge over the 'Bairns' of Falkirk with a 2-1 win at Brockville and, on the first day of January 1985, an unimpressive St Johnstone side were convincingly beaten 3-0 at Bayview.

The improved form continued, and a share of the points with Kilmarnock at RugbyPark was followed by a 3-1 home win against Partick Thistle.

The Fife were widely expected to make progress in the Scottish Cup after their third round tie at Brechin finished all-square. A crowd of 2,143 turned out for the replay at Bayview on the evening of Tuesday 29th January, only to be let down in spectacular fashion as the Glebe Park side ran riot and scored four without reply to win through to the fourth round and a home tie against Hearts.

Back on league business, the Fifers bounced back from their Scottish Cup disappointment in style by beating Airdrieonians 3-1 at Bayview on 2nd February.

The following six games produced two wins, two draws and two defeats by the end of March and, although relegation was still possible, little sleep was lost over the prospect.

291

Gordon Durie sends the Hamilton 'keeper the wrong way to put the Fifers two goals ahead in their 4-2 victory at Douglas Park on 25th August 1984. (Jim Corstorphine)

Gordon Durie, on the right of the picture, completes his hat trick against Hamilton Academical on 25th August 1984 with a tremendous drive from the edge of the penalty area. Waiting in the goal-mouth to capitalise on any goalkeeping errors is Stevie Kirk.
(Jim Corstorphine)

In fact, promotion to the Premier League seemed more of a possibility than a return to the Second Division with the club sitting just six points off second place with seven games to play!

Although the side was boosted by the signing of 38 year-old former Rangers and Scotland star Willie Johnston in late March, the spectre of relegation returned when all five league matches played during April were lost. With two fixtures remaining, East Fife found themselves sitting in tenth place; three points clear of the second bottom club with a difficult trip to Airdrieonians on the agenda followed by a visit from promotion favourites Clydebank.

Realising that victory over Airdrieonians at Broomfield was imperative, Manager Davie Clarke arranged a practice match against a Fife Under-18 Select side at Bayview three days before the game in order to overcome the team's recent inability to find the net. The idea had the desired effect.

The East Fife forwards scored no fewer than sixteen times during the practice match and, with renewed confidence in front of goal, scored four against Airdrieonians to ensure First Division football remained at Bayview for at least another year.

For the record, the final match against Clydebank, who had already won promotion to the Premier League, finished goalless.

The following midweek saw silverware return to the Bayview trophy cabinet for the first time since 1979 when the Fife Cup was won by beating Cowdenbeath 3-2 at Central Park.

Although the 1984/85 season ended happily, the campaign was tinged with sadness as the club mourned the loss of three well known former associates during the course of the campaign.

In mid-October 1984 former outside-right Tommy Adams died aged 69. Ironically, the wee player who had entertained the crowds with his darting runs down the right wing almost half a Century earlier, ended his days confined to a wheelchair.

The following Spring former goalkeeper Johnny Curran, a member of the 1953 League Cup winning side, died in Aberdeen aged just 60 then, on 30th April 1985, the football world bid farewell to former East Fife and Rangers Manager Scot Symon.

Preparations for season 1985/86 consisted of practice games against Junior opposition from Fife and the Lothians along with friendlies against Meadowbank Thistle, Raith Rovers and Swedish outfit Asmuntorp.

The latter side, managed by former East Fife boss Bill Baxter, were no match for the Fifers and were soundly beaten 5-0 at Bayview on 30th July. The convincing win was not, however, a sign of what was to come when the competitive season commenced.

Supporters who were relieved that relegation had been avoided at the end of the previous campaign could be forgiven for believing that the club was destined for the drop as early as the Autumn of 1985.

The league season started in disastrous style with a 4-0 drubbing from BrechinCity at GlebePark on 10th August, quickly followed by an early exit from the League Cup at Douglas Park, Hamilton.

Although only three of the following nine games were lost, the remainder finished all-square and, by losing to Ayr United at SomersetPark on 19th October, the Fife earned the unenviable reputation of being the only senior club in Britain still to record a win. It was a status they were to retain for a further three weeks!

Although the 'duck' was finally broken with a 2-0 victory over a strong Forfar Athletic side at StationPark on 9th November, the remainder of the year produced just three more wins.

The second half of the season was a complete contrast to the first, with only two league matches lost from the eighteen played. A goal-less encounter with Montrose at Bayview on New Year's Day 1986 was followed by revenge against BrechinCity in the following league match with a 4-2 win at the same venue. The next fixture against Falkirk at Brockville on 18th January was lost by a single goal, but turned out to be the Fifers' last league defeat for almost three months!

The Falkirk match was followed by a third round Scottish Cup tie against St Mirren at Bayview, which the home side were unfortunate not to win. A 1-1 draw was the outcome after 90 minutes play, but the Paisley side progressed to the fourth round thanks to a 3-1 replay victory at the beginning of February. Over the remainder of the league season a truly remarkable turnaround was achieved. From being the last British senior club to record a victory, East Fife were transformed into a side who were, in the end, unfortunate not to win promotion to the Premier League.

From the fourteen league fixtures played between the Scottish Cup exit and the end of the season, the only defeat came against fellow promotion hopefuls Kilmarnock at RugbyPark in early April.

Eight games were won over the same period, including a four goal victory against runaway league leaders Hamilton Academical as East Fife made a determined bid to become the first Fife club to play in the Premier League.

With only one match to play, however, the Fifers were still two points behind second placed Falkirk with a vastly inferior goal difference, but by strange co-incidence the Methil Men were due to visit Brockville for the final league match of the season. If the 'Bairns' could be defeated by six clear goals, promotion would still be achieved providing both Kilmarnock and Forfar Athletic dropped points on the same day.

A large travelling support descended on Brockville on 3rd May 1986, where the honours were shared with a 2-2 draw.

The single point was just enough to win promotion for the home side and, although nobody seriously expected a six-goal win for the Methil Men, the visiting supporters in the 6,600 crowd returned home solemnly reflecting on what might have been.

East Fife had been the form side over the second half of season 1985/86 and the Bayview faithful firmly believed that the momentum would be maintained over the forthcoming campaign. Would Bayview host top-flight football once again in the foreseeable future? Only time would tell!

One thing was certain, however. The early kick off's during the winter months that had been endured since the previous November due to the poor condition of the Bayview floodlights would not be a feature of the coming season. During the summer of 1986 a new floodlighting system was installed at the ground in the form of four pylons along each side of the park.

Although the new floodlights were welcomed by the supporters on the terracing, the same could not be said for the patrons of the grandstand, where the positioning of the new lighting towers had made the already restricted view even worse! Those supporters who chose to pay that little extra for a seat might not have to wait long for conditions to improve, however, as the club announced that negotiations were under way for the construction of a 'major new stand' to replace the 65 year-old corrugated iron structure.

In an effort to strengthen the squad, an attempt was made to bring John Lumsden back to Bayview. The player who had netted the club £40,000 when he signed for StokeCity back in 1980 was now a free agent and living in London. Unfortunately, 'Roxy' decided not to return north.

Another player who would not be pulling on a black and gold jersey during the coming season was Brian Jenkins, although not through choice. Sadly, the player who had almost made the No.3 jersey his own since arriving from Stenhousemuir in

1983, was forced to retire from the game due to a knee injury sustained earlier in the year.

The first competitive matches of season 1986/87 came in the form of the Fife Cup. Unlike previous years, the competition was played in the shape of a four-team mini-tournament at Stark's Park on Saturday 2nd and Sunday 3rd August.

After host club Raith Rovers disposed of Burntisland Shipyard in the curtain raiser, the big match of the afternoon was played out between East Fife and Second Division champions Dunfermline Athletic.

The resurgence of the west Fife club during the previous season had resulted in much larger crowds lining the terraces at East EndPark and wherever the team travelled. By the time the match kicked off at three o'clock the attendance had swelled to around three thousand and a tense contest got under way.

Playing down the infamous Stark's Park slope during the first half, the Methil Men scored the only goal of the game through Paul Hunter and returned to Kirkcaldy the following day to face Raith in the final. Confident of landing the silverware, the visitors perhaps underestimated the club who had finished the previous campaign in the lower reaches of the Second Division and went down 3-1!

The start of the league programme also proved disappointing, with Kilmarnock running out convincing 4-1 winners at Bayview on the opening day. After sharing the points against both Montrose and Clyde in the following two matches, it seemed once again as though the dream of promotion to the Premier League might be over for another year with the season just weeks old.

Confidence in the side was restored with victory against Partick Thistle at Firhill in the second round of the League Cup on 20th August. When the draw for the third round handed the Fifers a home tie with Rangers, football fever once again came to Methil!

As well as testing the new floodlight system, the visit of the Glasgow giants on the evening of 27th August 1986 would also give a fair indication of the home side's ability to compete alongside the best in the land. The East Fife supporters in the all-ticket 10,000 crowd were not to be disappointed; the critics were about to be well and truly silenced.

The Rangers team, who included England internationalists Terry Butcher and Chris Woods in their number, were held to a no-scoring draw on the night. After 120 minutes of nail-biting drama, including a penalty miss from 'Gers golden boy Ally McCoist, supporters of both sides could hardly bear to watch the penalty shoot-out which was to decide the outcome of the tie.

After the Fife had converted four penalties through Burgess, Marshall, McCafferty and Mitchell, the score stood at four goals each with McMinn, McCoist, Butcher and Durrant having netted for the visitors.

As Hugh Hill made his way forward to take the fifth kick, the atmosphere was so tense that some East Fife supporters standing immediately behind Chris Woods' goal couldn't bring themselves to watch and turned their backs to the field. Whether the sight of this had an effect on the player's confidence we shall never know, but the fact of the matter is that the kick was missed.

Ibrox legend Davie Cooper calmly netted his side's fifth kick and the large travelling support erupted in a mixture of joy and relief.

"We'll probably go on to win the competition now", taunted one Rangers fan as he made his way through the lines of East Fife supporters making their way down Wellesley Road, and right he was. Two months later the 'Gers lifted the trophy by beating Celtic 2-1 at Hampden.

Although the outcome was disappointing, the performance against Rangers proved that the Fifers were no push-over for the bigger clubs and 4,448 spectators turned out to witness the

4-2 demolition of table toppers Dunfermline Athletic at East EndPark three days later.

A league position of fourth was achieved by mid-September following wins against Morton, Brechin City and Partick Thistle, but a sequence of four matches followed during which only two points were picked up.

By mid-October the club had slipped down into the lower half of the table, but a 3-0 win over Airdrieonians at Broomfield signalled the start of a mini-revival and, by the time league leaders Dunfermline Athletic visited Bayview on 8th November, a league position of fourth had been regained. On a bitterly cold afternoon, a crowd of almost 4,000 witnessed an impressive performance by the home side against a somewhat nervous looking 'Pars' eleven, and a 2-1 win moved the Methil Men up to third place.

Although just one of the following four league fixtures was won, a 2-1 victory against Kilmarnock at Bayview, the other three games were drawn and, when the teams lined up at Links Park, Montrose, on 13th December 1986, East Fife boasted the proud record of having lost not one of their previous twelve competitive matches.

All good things come to an end, however, and on the day the 'Gable Endies' belied their lowly league position by winning 2-1.

During the unbeaten spell, a benefit match was played at Bayview against a Celtic XI in aid of popular left-back Brian Jenkins who, as mentioned previously, had been forced to quit the game due to a knee injury. The Fifers won the match 2-1 in front of a healthy crowd of 1,300, who were also treated to an exhibition match between former Celtic and Rangers stars at half-time.

Manager Dave Clarke's claim that his men had had "a genuine off day" at Montrose seemed to be backed up as, following a no scoring home draw with Airdrieonians, Clyde were beaten at Firhill in the last game of the year.

New Year's Day 1987 dawned dull and extremely wet and, as the car-loads of football fans left Methil and its environs bound for East End Park and the local derby with Dunfermline Athletic, conditions started to get even worse. The scene that greeted the supporters making their way into the ground looked anything but promising. Large pools of water covered the entire park and, with the ground notorious for its poor drainage, it started to look increasingly likely that the game would not start.

About thirty minutes before kick-off, referee McVicar appeared with the match ball and dropped it on to the playing surface in order to see how high it would bounce, only for the ball to stick in the mud! The spectators already through the turnstiles braced themselves for the announcement over the loudspeaker system that the match was off. But no such announcement came. To the utter amazement of all present, the game kicked off as scheduled at three o'clock with 4,956 spectators inside the ground!

Although exciting in its own way, the game turned out to be a farce, with players unable to control the ball as it floated on the large puddle that had formed in front of the covered enclosure. With the home side leading by a Grant Jenkins goal at half-time, the East EndPark ground staff desperately tried to sweep the water off the park in order to prevent the game being abandoned. The visiting support on the other hand, realising that their favourites were unlikely to turn the game around on the sodden surface, started to wish that the teams wouldn't re-appear for the second 45 minutes.

But re-appear they did, and almost immediately Jenkins should have scored his second goal of the afternoon following a defensive error. To the relief of the travelling supporters, his effort stuck in the mud, allowing 'keeper Gordon Marshall to gather easily. Three minutes later the Dunfermline man's anguish turned to despair as he turned the ball into his own net to square the game! With no further scoring it was a cold and wet but mightily relieved East Fife team that made their way towards the dressing room, rather fortunate to have gained a point in such dreadful conditions.

A week later it was the turn of second-placed Morton to visit Bayview, where a 2-1 win for the home side maintained the promotion challenge and a league position of fourth, just two points behind second placed Airdrieonians.

Having successfully negotiated two of the toughest games of the season in the space of only a few days, it looked like the push for promotion to the Premier League was about to step up a gear. Once again, however, the club failed to take advantage of the situation and the following four games ended in draws. If all four fixtures had been won, the team would have been sharing first place in the table with Dunfermline and Morton by mid-February!

The club also exited the Scottish Cup at the first hurdle during the same period, although it has to be said that the 4-1 defeat from Dundee at Bayview followed a highly creditable 2-2 draw at DensPark.

As if the disappointing run of results wasn't bad enough, the Bayview faithful were dealt a huge blow during the same month when Manager Dave Clarke left to take charge of Premier League club Falkirk.

Clarke was replaced at the helm by Gavin Murray and, although the new Manager's first game in charge resulted in a 1-0 win against Queen of the South at Palmerston, the chance of Premier League football coming to Methil started to look increasingly unlikely as the season progressed.

By the end of March, supporters started to accuse the club of having no ambition as player after player was allowed to leave. Goalkeeper Gordon Marshall followed Dave Clarke to Falkirk for £65,000 along with Stuart Burgess and Hugh Hill. Next to depart was Davie Kirkwood, who was transferred to Rangers for £30,000.

As part of the Kirkwood deal, Scott Nisbet came to East Fife on loan until the end of the season and the money received from Rangers was used to sign goalkeeper Ray Charles from

Montrose. Despite the protests, Gavin Murray insisted that the transfers were justified and that the replacements were adequate.

The supporters were far from happy at the situation and even the announcement by Chairman Jim Baxter that construction of a new £300,000 grandstand could possibly begin during the summer of 1987 did little to appease the disgruntled fans.

The promotion dream was all but ended following defeat by the odd goal in five against relegation candidates BrechinCity on 11th April at GlebePark.

Three victories from the last four fixtures, including a 5-0 win against Queen of the South at Bayview, resulted in a final league position of fourth.

The club announced a profit of £56,905 for season 1986/87, but plans for the new grandstand were shelved after the application to the Football Grounds Improvement Trust for £180,000 to assist with its construction was turned down.

The healthy financial situation did allow for a foreign tour to take place during the summer of 1987, however, and both Aigaleo and Poseidon were defeated in Greece during July.

The first competitive match of season 1987/88 took the form of a first round Fife Cup tie at Bayview, where Raith Rovers progressed to the semi-final with a 2-0 win.

Although the League Cup campaign ended in embarrassment at the first hurdle when lowly Albion Rovers dumped the Fifers out of the tournament on penalty kicks following a 1-1 draw at Cliftonhill, the league programme started reasonably well.

The side tasted defeat only once during the first six matches, against Airdrieonians on the opening day of the campaign. Home wins against Kilmarnock and newly promoted Raith Rovers were also recorded over the same period.

A 3-0 defeat from Queen of the South at Bayview on 12th September, however, sparked off a miserable run of results and, by the middle of October, the club were firmly rooted at the bottom of the table.

The Fifers' troubles didn't end there. A report on ground safety in September concluded that Bayview's grandstand, west terrace and certain crush barriers were in a dangerous condition and the ground's capacity would have to be cut accordingly. Never again would five-figure crowds line the Bayview terraces.

Although there were signs of an improvement in form towards the end of the month with wins against the two thistles, Partick and Meadowbank, the first week in November saw the club suffer one of its most humiliating defeats ever. A crowd of 2,958 turned out to witness the first league match between Raith and East Fife at Stark's Park for over ten years. When the final whistle sounded at quarter-to-five, the only spectators left inside the ground were wearing blue and white scarves; the visiting supporters having long since departed. A hat-trick from Dalziel, a brace from Harris and singles from McStay and Brash were countered by a solitary goal from David Graham as the Methil Men were swept aside to the tune of 7-1. It was the Kirkcaldy side's record victory against their local rivals and, discounting a 7-2 win in a wartime league match in 1942, the first time that Rovers had found the net seven times in the local derby.

Understandably, the reaction from the disgruntled supporters was one of anger.

The *East Fife Mail* became inundated with letters to the Sports Editor, who responded by printing a full-page article on 18th November in which Chairman Jim Baxter replied to the many complaints. The answers given by Mr Baxter did little to appease the supporters and, when no change in performances materialised, further letters appeared demanding the Chairman's resignation.

Ironically, the second string topped the Reserve League during November 1987 - at the same time that the first team were firmly rooted to the bottom of Division One!

The year ended with the team showing slight signs of improvement but, although full points were taken from the home game against Kilmarnock along with a share of the spoils against Queen of the South and Forfar Athletic, the club remained at the foot of the table.

A bumper crowd of 4,161 paid to see the derby against Raith Rovers at Bayview on 2nd January 1988. With the Methil Men dominating the game for long periods, it looked like a welcome victory could be on the cards but, against the run of play, the visitors emerged victorious with a narrow 2-1 win, which the following edition of the *East Fife Mail* claimed was 'daylight robbery'.

Despite playing better football, results continued to go against the team and, by the end of January, the club found themselves six points adrift at the bottom of the league and out of the Scottish Cup after losing at home to Airdrieonians. At long last, things began to improve during the month of February.

After sharing the points with high-flying Meadowbank Thistle, successive wins were recorded against Clyde and Airdrieonians and the gap at the foot of the table began to narrow.

Although the following two matches at Clydebank and Queen of the South were lost, home wins against Forfar and Partick followed by a revenge win against Raith at Stark's Park gave the club a glimmer of hope. Relegation might be avoided after all!

Only one of the six remaining league matches was lost, against promotion-chasing Meadowbank Thistle at the Commonwealth Stadium. After beating Clyde and drawing with Hamilton Academical and Dumbarton, the penultimate match of the season saw fellow relegation candidates

Dave Clarke, a loyal servant to the club both as player and manager, was signed from Tynecastle Boys Club in January 1968 and was at Bayview until March 1987, when he left to become manager of Falkirk. During his eighteen years with East Fife, Dave Clarke made a record 517 first team appearances for the club. (Author's Collection)

Kilmarnock visit Methil on the last day of April. A 3-1 win for the Fifers meant that the relegation battle was to go right down to the wire and, almost unbelievably considering their position earlier in the campaign, East Fife actually looked like they would avoid the drop going into the last game!

On the morning of 7th May 1988, any two from three clubs could be relegated. Both East Fife and Kilmarnock were on 35 points, although the Ayrshire side had a vastly superior goal difference. If the Fifers could beat Clydebank at Bayview and Killie were to lose to Partick Thistle at Firhill, then Dumbarton and Kilmarnock would be relegated. Dumbarton, on the other hand, had to beat Raith Rovers and hope that both East Fife and Kilmarnock lost in order to avoid the drop.

In the event, the Fifers only managed to draw with Clydebank and, against the odds, Kilmarnock beat Partick by a single goal to ensure First Division football would be played at RugbyPark for another season. Dumbarton, despite managing a fine 3-0 victory against Raith Rovers, joined East Fife on their way down to Division Two.

For the Bayview faithful, it was all too hard to take. How could their side have been so close to winning promotion to the Premier League one season, then find themselves in Scottish football's basement just twelve months later?

Of course, the answer was simple. One of the most promising young Managers in Scottish football had been allowed to leave Bayview to take over at Falkirk, a club of similar standing, and take the nucleus of the team with him.

During the 1987/88 season, no fewer than five players who had featured in Dave Clarke's promotion challenging sides of recent years were playing Premier League football.

If Clarke had been persuaded to stay with the club he had loyally served since 1968, things could have been so different. Instead, BayviewPark was destined to host Second Division football for the foreseeable future.

Chapter Nineteen: Down in the Doldrums

"I aim to take East Fife back into the First Division in one season", claimed Manager Gavin Murray at the beginning of the 1988/89 campaign, adding that a run of results matching those of the previous season's latter stages would surely reward the club with promotion.

Although the league programme started badly with a 3-1 defeat at Dumbarton, the Manager was almost correct with his claim that the League Cup encounter at Bayview against Dunfermline Athletic, just relegated from the Premier League, would be a 'cracking game' with every possibility of progressing into the following round. The home side put up a great fight against their higher league opponents and, when the referee signalled the end of open play, the teams were tied at a goal apiece. Following a penalty shoot-out, however, it was the 'Pars' who won the right to face Motherwell in round three by converting four spot-kicks compared to East Fife's three.

Back on league business, the Fife looked anything but promotion material during the first quarter of the season. Following defeat in the opening two matches, a resounding 4-1 victory against Cowdenbeath was recorded at the end of August, but the convincing win didn't signal the start of a successful run.

From the first ten matches of the thirty-nine game programme, just three games were won along with four draws and three defeats. It was hardly the form expected from a promotion challenging side.

Of the matches played during the first quarter of the season, the 2-1 home win against Stenhousemuir on 15th October was significant in that it marked the first team debut of future star Ally Mitchell. Two days after Mitchell's debut, Jim McLaren's eight years at Bayview was commemorated with a match against Rangers which attracted a healthy testimonial attendance of 1,800.

The following ten league fixtures produced similar results to the first ten, but concluded with a victory against Stirling Albion on the last day of the year that was far more convincing than the 2-0 score-line suggests. Watching the game that afternoon were two Nigerian footballers named Emmanuel Karmah and Augustine Diopko, who had arrived at Bayview on trial. The players wanted to give up their amateur status with Nigerian league side Nepa in order to carve out a career in Scottish Football, but neither player impressed Gavin Murray and both returned to Nigeria a few weeks later.

Meanwhile, although league form had been largely disappointing overall, progress was made in the Scottish Cup at the beginning of December with a 4-1 home win against non-league side Spartans from Edinburgh. The cup run only lasted until the second round, however, as lowly Stranraer disposed of their more fancied opponents with a 2-1 win at StairPark on 7th January 1988.

Unfortunately, the convincing league win against Stirling Albion on Hogmanay 1987 didn't signal the start of a winning run and, even with the influential figure of Davie Kirkwood back in the side on loan from Rangers, the next five league games were all drawn. Indeed, it was a Kirkwood brace that helped save the side from embarrassment when the honours were shared in a 2-2 draw with East Stirlingshire at Bayview on 14th January. The visitors looked like taking full points at one stage when 'keeper Ray Charles was stretchered off and replaced in goal by Andy Harrow. Fortunately, the veteran utility player, signed the previous summer from Raith Rovers, was equal to the task and pulled off some fine saves to deny the visitors.

As if sharing the points with clubs from the lower reaches of the league wasn't bad enough for a side seeking a quick return to the First Division, the run of draws was ended with yet another defeat from Stranraer followed by a disastrous 4-0 hammering at the hands of Dumbarton, who were at the time sitting near the bottom of the table.

Then, just when all hope seemed lost, a winning run was strung together.

After Cowdenbeath were beaten 1-0 at Bayview on 25th February, the debut of the legendary 'Wullie Broon' was marked with a 2-1 victory over runaway league leaders Albion Rovers in Coatbridge. Brown, signed from Forfar Athletic in exchange for Brian McNaughton, scored the winning goal and added fresh impetus to the team with his robust, influential presence.

When fellow promotion hopefuls Alloa Athletic were beaten at Bayview in the next match, the gap between the Fifers and second placed BrechinCity was narrowed to just three points. Perhaps Manager Murray's prediction would prove correct after all!

A 3-1 win against Arbroath at Gayfield was then followed by a 3-0 home victory against Stirling Albion at Bayview, where renewed confidence amongst the supporters resulted in the attendance breaking into four figures once again.

Appropriately, it was on April Fool's Day that the winning sequence was abruptly halted. Confidence was high for the trip through to Falkirk to face East Stirlingshire at FirsPark, but a superb second half performance from the home side ripped the Fifers apart and the 'Shire deservedly ran out 4-2 winners.

With four of the remaining six league matches scheduled for Bayview, however, hopes were still high that promotion was still well within reach.

The following three games produced home wins against Stranraer and Queen's Park, either side of a share of the points with Stenhousemuir at Ochilview. With results elsewhere going their way, the club suddenly found themselves in second place in the table with three games remaining. A point ahead of nearest challengers Alloa Athletic and Brechin City, the Fifers' destiny was now entirely in their own hands.

After failing to take full points from Berwick Rangers at Bayview in the next game, the team headed north on 6th May for a showdown with fellow promotion challengers BrechinCity. A closely fought game resulted in a single goal win for the home side, and suddenly the chance of promotion had all but disappeared once again.

In order to bring First Division football back to Methil, East Fife now faced the unenviable task of having to beat Montrose by a 'barrow-load' of goals at Bayview and hope that both Alloa Athletic and Brechin lost by a considerable margin. In the event, it was Montrose that scored the 'barrow-load' at Bayview on the last day of the season, and any lingering hopes of promotion were finally laid to rest.

Alloa Athletic, who looked the least likely bet to finish as runners-up with two matches to play, took full points from their trips to Queen's Park and Dumbarton and were promoted along with champions Albion Rovers.

The final push for promotion certainly wasn't helped by the departure of Steve Pittman to ShrewsburyTown for a reported fee of £30,000 in March, but the move was more about the player's ambitions than club loyalty. With the 1990 World Cup in Italy looming, Pittman reckoned that playing in England would give him a better chance of being selected for the USA international squad.

Preparations for season 1989/90 took the form of a tour of the north of England, where defeat against BillinghamTown was followed by wins over Barrow and Netherfield. On the way home, Gala Fairydean were beaten 4-1 at Netherdale.

The pre-season programme concluded with home wins against both Hibernian and Inverness Clachnacuddin before the first competitive match, a League Cup tie against Queen's Park, was played at Bayview on the evening of 9th August.

The Queen's Park game was memorable not so much for events during open play, but more for the way in which the outcome of the tie was decided. With the score standing at 2-2 after 120 minutes play, a penalty shoot-out was required to decide which team would progress to the following round. After both teams had converted six penalties each, the visitors missed their seventh kick. East Fife then scored from the spot and, with the cheers of the home supporters ringing in their ears, both teams started to make their way back to the pavilion.

Referee Brian McGinlay, however, had other ideas and halted the players in their tracks with a sharp blow on his whistle. For some reason which was never properly explained (but rumoured to be because the ball had not been sitting centrally on the penalty spot), the official ordered the winning kick to be re-taken.

This time the penalty was missed and, with the 'Spiders' converting their next kick before the Fifers missed for a second time, it was the Glasgow side who made it through to the second round!

Off the field of play, the club didn't have its troubles to seek as once again the condition of BayviewPark came under scrutiny and the standing capacity was reduced from 5,950 to 5,147.

The league programme got off to a reasonable start, with only one of the opening nine matches lost, although the fact that the points were shared in five of the games meant that the Fifers were still in a mid-table position at the beginning of October.

Two of the toughest fixtures on the card, both against promotion chasing clubs, then presented themselves in quick succession. On 14th October a trip to RugbyPark resulted in a single goal victory for home side Kilmarnock then, a week later, a 3-1 defeat from Stirling Albion on the Annfield 'astroturf' saw the Fifers slip into the lower half of the table.

Convincing home wins against Montrose and Arbroath were then followed by a dismal five game losing run that ended with a 5-1 hammering from Queen of the South in Dumfries. With former Celtic and Scotland star Tommy Burns making his debut for Kilmarnock, few thought that the home fixture against the full-time Ayrshire outfit on 16th December would result in anything else but a convincing win for the visitors. On a bitterly cold Saturday afternoon, things didn't go quite to plan for the promotion favourites and, with time running out at the end of the game, the Fifers were leading 2-1 with goals from Ally Mitchell and Paul Hunter.

With eighty minutes on the clock, all twenty-two players were soaked to the skin due to the incessant rain and sleet and, when one of the Kilmarnock team complained to the referee that he was suffering from hypothermia, the whistler decided it was time for all to have a hot shower.

The home supporters were irate that the referee had decided to abandon the game when victory was well and truly within sight and many were of the opinion that the player in question had feigned his condition in order to save his side from embarrassment!

Following a share of the points in the next three league games, including a goal-less New Year derby encounter with Cowdenbeath at Bayview, Kilmarnock returned to Methil on the evening of 10th January 1990 to replay the abandoned game.

On a cold, crisp evening, the visitors had no answer to the home side's enthusiasm and a Brown brace along with further goals from Mitchell and Hunter resulted in a 4-2 win for the Fifers. Justice had been done!

Three days prior to the Kilmarnock visit, the Scottish Cup campaign started with a trip north to face non-league RossCounty on Sunday 7th January. The match should have been played at the end of December, but was postponed several times due to the state of the Victoria Park playing surface.

With the home side missing one of their key players due to his strict religious belief that football should not be played on the Lord's day, East Fife ran out convincing 4-1 winners despite having gone a goal behind during the first half.

Action from the RossCounty v East Fife Scottish Cup tie at Victoria Park, Dingwall, on Sunday 7th January 1990, when County were still a Highland League club. Since County were admitted to the Scottish League in 1994, Victoria Park has undergone a complete transformation, with the old rickety grandstand seen in this photograph replaced by a modern structure. (Jim Corstorphine)

Two weeks later a Paul Hunter hat-trick was enough to overcome First Division Meadowbank Thistle at Bayview and the winners were rewarded with a fourth round tie against Hibernian in Edinburgh.

The morning of 24th February 1990 dawned dull and overcast and, by mid afternoon, conditions had deteriorated to the point where many of the travelling supporters making their way to Easter Road on foot found themselves soaked through. Once inside the ground, visiting supporters were confined to the open south terrace, where the wet conditions had to be endured throughout the game.

The match itself proved to be as disappointing as the weather as far as East Fife supporters were concerned, with Hibs winning 5-1. Hibs 'keeper Andy Goram managed to add to the misery by saving a second half penalty, before Ally Mitchell brought a little cheer to the rain soaked south terrace with a late consolation goal.

Depths of Despair! Cold, wet and miserable, the author wonders if the trip to Easter Road on 24th February 1990 was such a good idea after all! (Bob Hunter)

By this stage in the season it had become clear that the chance of promotion was once again slipping from the club's grasp. Although favourable results had been recorded against promotion chasing Kilmarnock, Berwick Rangers and Stirling Albion during January, defeats from clubs struggling at the other end of the table proved to be the Fifers' downfall. A 'flu bug was blamed for poor form at the beginning of March and, although a league position of fifth was achieved before the end of the month following wins against Dumbarton and Montrose, the final push for promotion never materialised. The situation wasn't helped by the loss of three key players during March 1990. Paul Hunter, who had represented Scotland at Under-21 level during his five years at Bayview, netted the club a record £150,000 when he was transferred to HullCity.

Along with the respected striker's departure, Englishmen Tom Connor and Tony Hall announced that they were finding travelling up from south of the border for every game too much to handle and asked to be released.

The final five league matches were all played against promotion candidates, including BrechinCity and Kilmarnock, who were respectively destined for the Championship and second promotion place. The fact that four of these games were lost speaks for itself; East Fife just weren't good enough for the step up to the First Division.

Off the park, the club were still reporting a healthy financial situation and, during the summer of 1990, Manager Gavin Murray reported that he was hopeful of adding to the squad and was currently investigating the possibility of bringing a number of foreign players to Bayview. One of the players interesting the club was Swedish forward Mats Lundgren, who was invited to accompany the Fifers on their pre-season tour of the north of England along with summer signings Robert Scott and Jim Moffat.

Mixed fortunes were encountered during the pre-season tour, with victories against GooleTown and WhitleyBay countered by defeat at both Scarborough and North Ferriby.

At the end of the tour, Lundgren returned to Sweden claiming he was homesick.

Home friendlies against ChesterCity and Dundee both ended in defeat before the competitive season got under way with a League Cup encounter against Queen's Park at Hampden on 14th August. For the fourth year in succession, the tie was lost on penalty kicks following a 3-3 draw.

In the league, the club got off to their best start for years and quickly established themselves as league leaders by winning seven of their first ten fixtures and drawing the other three.

Paul Hunter, signed in 1984 from Leven Royals, went on to play for Scotland at Under-21 level during his five years at Bayview. He netted the club a record £150,000 when he was transferred to HullCity in March 1990 (Author's Collection).

During this time the Fifers also beat Clydebank and Stranraer in the new Centenary Cup competition before going down 2-1 to Kilmarnock in the quarter-final at Bayview.

The first league defeat of the campaign arrived on 20th October against Berwick Rangers at Shielfield and signalled the start of a slump in form that saw just one point taken from five matches.

In an effort to win back their place at the top of the table, Dave Beaton and Jim Cowell were signed from Falkirk at the end of November for the combined price of £55,000. The new signings had little immediate impact on the side, however, and only one further game was won before the end of the year, against Albion Rovers at Cliftonhill.

A dreadful winter forced the cancellation of several games during December 1990 and January 1991 and only three league games were played over a two-month period from which only two points were gained.

The months of December and January did, however, provide some very exciting drama in the Scottish Cup. In the first round of the competition, East of Scotland League side Whitehill Welfare were soundly beaten 4-0 at Ferguson Park, Rosewell, thanks to a Dougie Hope brace along with goals from Mitchell and Wilson.

A long trip north was the reward for the winning side and in round two the honours were shared with Inverness Thistle at Kingsmills on Saturday 5th January. In the replay at Bayview two days later, a Robert Scott strike was enough to win a place in the third round and a home tie against Premier Division title challengers Dundee United.

Considering the gulf that existed between the two clubs at the time, the drama that unfolded on Saturday 26th January and in the days which followed was quite remarkable.

With an all-ticket 'capacity' crowd lining the Bayview terraces, recent signing Jim Cowell sent the home supporters wild by opening the scoring after half-an-hour. It was no less than the home side deserved, with full-time United struggling to cope with the sheer determination of the Second Division part-timers.

The visitors desperately tried to push forward during the second half without success and, when the game eventually went into injury time, the Bayview faithful waited for the referee's whistle to signal a famous victory. They waited and waited, but still no whistle sounded. Puzzled, the home

Dundee United 'keeper Alan Main rises to safely clutch the ball as East Fife pressurise United's goal during the Scottish Cup tie at Bayview on 26th January 1991. (Jim Corstorphine)

supporters checked their watches over and over again and exchanged glances. Still there was no whistle.

Fully seven minutes into time added on, Paddy Connolly spared United's blushes by squeezing the ball just inside the post to earn his side a replay they scarcely deserved.

The fact that United managed only three shots on target (including their goal) throughout the entire game speaks for itself. East Fife considered themselves robbed, and rightly so! 'Lucky United' proclaimed one Sunday newspaper, who were at a loss to explain where referee McVicar found the extra seven minutes from.

In complete contrast to newspaper reports, however, United claimed that the added time was justified as the Fifers had spent most of the game time-wasting and kicking the ball out of the park whenever the opportunity arose. Sour grapes indeed!

Of course, there was absolutely no truth in the 'time-wasting' claim, and the afternoon's drama was summed up perfectly by United's Maurice Malpas as he left the ground to board the team coach.

"A bit lucky there, weren't you?" shouted one disappointed Fifer. "What do you mean, lucky?" replied Malpas. "That was daylight robbery!"

Of course, everyone expected the replay at Tannadice three days later to be nothing more than a comfortable home win. Everyone, that is, except for East Fife and their loyal band of travelling supporters.

Once again the Fifers took a first half lead, this time through Stuart Wilson, who sent a cracking volley past helpless United custodian Alan Main from the edge of the penalty area. Such was the quality of the strike, it was nominated for the BBC Sportscene 'Goal of the Month' competition.

Although it has to be said that the home side were perhaps the better team on the night, when the allotted 90 minutes were over the teams were level at a goal apiece.

In extra time, the visitors' hearts were broken when Duncan Ferguson drove the ball into the net to claim his first goal for the 'Tangerines' and knock the Fifers out of the tournament. United went on to reach the Scottish Cup final at Hampden that year, where they lost a thrilling match 4-3 to Motherwell after extra time. Ironically for the losing finalists, the man who scored the winning goal that afternoon was none other than former Bayview favourite Stevie Kirk. Yes, there was many a wry smile down Methil way that evening!

Back on league duties, the renewed confidence gained from the cup experience lasted just four matches, from which six points were gained from two wins and two draws. Following the 4-1 demolition of Berwick Rangers on 19th February, a run of four defeats ensued which, once again, virtually ended all hopes of promotion.

The team eventually got back to winning ways with a single goal win over Stenhousemuir at Bayview on 9th March, followed three days later by an impressive 6-3 win against Alloa at RecreationPark.

Another run of defeats was just around the corner, however, and acute embarrassment for the club arrived in the form of a 5-1 hammering from lowly East Stirlingshire at Firs Park on 6th April during which home striker Danny Diver netted four times.

As if that wasn't bad enough, local rivals and promotion hopefuls Cowdenbeath handed out a 5-0 thumping at Bayview two weeks later!

After having made such a promising start to the season, the Fife ended the campaign in tenth place, only ten points clear of bottom club Arbroath and seventeen points behind Second Division Champions Stirling Albion.

Looking back over the season as a whole, however, the club's reputation had been done no harm at all during the Scottish Cup run and the players were rewarded with a trip to Florida at the end of May.

Talk during the summer of 1991 was centred on a proposed move from Methil to Kirkcaldy, where it was anticipated East Fife would share a new 10,000 seat stadium with Raith Rovers at Chapel Level. Fortunately, with many Bayview regulars voicing the opinion that such a move could only be detrimental to the club, the idea was shelved.

Towards the end of the close-season, history was made when John Sludden became the most expensive player ever to join East Fife when he was signed from Kilmarnock for a reported fee of £70,000. Other summer arrivals at Bayview were Tom Spence, a team-mate of Sludden's at RugbyPark, and Joe McBride from Dundee.

Following home friendlies against English Second Division side Charlton Athletic and non-League outfit Witton Albion, season 1991/92 kicked off on 10th August with a narrow defeat against newly-relegated Clyde at their temporary home of Douglas Park, Hamilton.

Three days later East Stirlingshire visited Methil for a first round League Cup tie, the outcome of which was almost predictable. With the score standing at two goals apiece after extra time, the visitors finished the job from the penalty spot to send the Fifers tumbling out of the competition.

Reasonably consistent form in the league saw the club maintain a challenging position in the top half of the table for most of the first half of the campaign, with eight wins, six draws and six defeats recorded from the twenty games played before the end of the year.

A vital 1-0 home win against fellow promotion hopefuls Cowdenbeath on New Year's Day 1992 signalled the start of a seven game unbeaten run which was halted abruptly with a 4-0 defeat from Clyde on 15th February.

By winning their first and second round Scottish Cup ties against Queen's Park and BrechinCity by the respective scores of 6-0 and 3-1 during December and January, the Fifers won the right to face First Division Morton at Cappielow in round three. Despite putting up a brave fight on the day, the home side found the net four times compared to East Fife's two and the Greenock club progressed to the fourth round.

The main priority, however, was the challenge for promotion and four of the five league matches played between mid-February and the beginning of April were won, including a 5-1 victory against Queen of the South.

The only defeat sustained during this five game spell, against Cowdenbeath at Central Park, proved crucial. When the end of the season arrived, following a further five matches during which the only defeat suffered was at the hands of eventual champions Dumbarton, East Fife found themselves occupying fourth place, just two points behind second placed Cowdenbeath. If victory had been recorded at Central Park, then it would have been East Fife taking the step up to Division One as runners-up and not their local rivals. Instead, the Methil club found themselves in the unenviable situation of being the only Fife club in the bottom league, a situation that hadn't befallen the Methil Men since 1928! During the summer of 1992, Raith Rovers announced that they were pulling out of plans to ground-share with East Fife, as the latest proposals on the table would mean a move to Glenrothes. The Methil club, however, still thought that re-locating to the new town was in their best interests and decided to go it alone with the proposed new stadium opposite the Fife Sports Institute. The proposed move once again fuelled much debate in local pubs and clubs, with most supporters vociferously opposed to the move.

Following home friendlies against Hibernian and Dundee United in the build up to the 1992/93 season, the semi-finals and final of the Fife Cup were all played at BayviewPark in the form of a four team mini-tournament.

The hosts were drawn to face Raith Rovers and went down 3-1 on Saturday 25th July, with Dunfermline recording a narrow victory against Cowdenbeath later that afternoon. The following day, Raith landed the trophy with a single goal win against the 'Pars'.

The League Cup got under way on the first day of August against Stranraer at StairPark where the tie was once again decided on penalty kicks. The home side emerged victorious following the shoot-out, which meant that East Fife had exited the tournament in exactly the same manner for an amazing seven consecutive seasons!

Once again, the league programme started reasonably well, with the team suffering only one defeat, at home to Forfar Athletic, during the eight matches played during August and September. October was an entirely different story with a straight run of four defeats against Stranraer, Queen of the South, BrechinCity and Montrose, although the month ended on a high note with a 5-0 win against Albion Rovers at Cliftonhill.

The month of November was a bag of mixed fortunes, although a superb 6-1 win against East Stirlingshire at FirsPark went a long way towards restoring confidence in the side. As usual, inconsistency proved to be the team's downfall and the rout in Falkirk was closely followed by defeat in the only two league matches played during December against Stenhousemuir and Stranraer. On 28th December, the second round of the Scottish Cup was reached by beating Alloa Athletic 6-5 on penalties after the two sides couldn't be separated in open play at both Bayview and RecreationPark. The year 1993 started well with a 2-0 league victory against Alloa Athletic when the Fifers visited RecreationPark for the second time in less than a week on 2nd January. The following week First Division Stirling Albion were dumped out of the Scottish Cup thanks to a 2-1 win at Albion's temporary home of Ochilview.

With confidence now fully restored, the next two league matches against Albion Rovers and Montrose were won in convincing style and it suddenly looked like a fresh challenge for promotion was on the cards.

The unbeaten run was maintained with a share of the points against Clyde at Bayview on 26th January, but when fellow promotion hopefuls Berwick Rangers emerged 3-0 victors from the league match at Shielfield four days later the bubble was well and truly burst.

The third round Scottish Cup tie against Arbroath at Gayfield on 6th February brought a welcome break from league duties and a healthy crowd of 2,984 paid to see the match, highlights of which were screened that evening on *BBC Sportscene*.

The match finished goal-less, but the travelling supporters standing behind the north goal were convinced their favourites had been denied a certain penalty when Dougie Hope was brought down in the penalty box towards the end of the game.

The draw for the fourth round of the competition handed the eventual winners a home game against Rangers, which resulted in a crowd of 3,722 paying to see the replay at Bayview on Tuesday 16th February. Again the television cameras were present, but the match proved to be nightmare viewing for the home supporters as the 'Lichties' ran in four goals to the Fifers one during a bad tempered encounter. Although league form had been reasonably good either side of the cup replay with wins recorded against promotion challengers Brechin City and Forfar Athletic along with a share of the points with Queen of the South at Palmerston, defeat by the odd goal in five against Clyde at Bayview on 27th February proved to be the straw that broke the camel's back as far as Manager Gavin Murray was concerned and the board received his letter of resignation on the following Monday. Former St Johnstone Manager Alex Totten was appointed to replace Murray on 15th March 1993 with applications also received from Cammy Fraser, Bert Paton and player Willie Brown.

After the points were shared in the following two games against Alloa Athletic and Queen's Park, new boss Totten took charge of the side for the trip to East Stirlingshire on 20th March 1993, where full points were taken with a 3-1 victory. An 'open day' was then arranged at Bayview where the new Manager took the opportunity to speak to supporters and explain how his re-organisation of the playing staff and training arrangements would eventually reap rewards.

"Every Manager in the Second Division knows that East Fife can only play for eighty minutes", explained Mr Totten, an opinion backed up by the fact that precious points had been lost over the course of the season to late goals. *"We have players at this club who are not prepared to travel to Methil for midweek training.*

That is no good to me", remarked the new boss, who went on to say that players who didn't show commitment to the club would find themselves on the transfer list.

The rest of the league season proved to be disappointing, although it has to be said that the poor form was largely down to the new Manager's experimentation and re-organisation of the side. In the eight league fixtures that remained following the win at FirsPark, only one further game was won and two were drawn.

The team finished ninth in the league table, sixteen points behind Champions Clyde and sixteen points clear of bottom club Albion Rovers, but the supporters were not too downhearted. After all, with Alex Totten at the helm the good times were just around the corner, were they not? Perhaps, but the Fifers would possibly have to start the new campaign without Totten as rumours started to circulate towards the end of May that the recently installed Methil boss was about to take over at the helm of Dunfermline Athletic.

When training re-started at the beginning of July, however, Alex Totten was still in charge and the Bayview boss announced that he was pleased with the fitness of his players after their summer break. Missing from the training sessions was local hero 'Wullie Broon', who had returned to junior football with Dundee St. Joseph's, but the squad was strengthened with the arrival of Andy Williamson from Dunfermline Athletic. Also expected to put pen to paper was former Fifer Paul Hunter but, despite being made a good offer, the striker mysteriously opted to join newly-relegated Cowdenbeath.

After travelling to the north of England to face Darlington and Gateshead United on a mini pre-season tour, the Fife played host to newly relegated English Premier League side Middlesborough at Bayview on 26th July 1993, where the only difference between the teams was a 76th minute strike from future Aberdeen player Craig Hignett for the English club.

Two days later, the first competitive game of the new campaign ended with a single goal defeat from near neighbours Dunfermline Athletic in the first round of the Fife Cup.

A home defeat from Albion Rovers in the first round of the League Cup on 3rd August had some supporters wondering if the appointment of Alex Totten had been a good thing after all, but the critics were to be silenced when the programme of league fixtures commenced.

A single goal win against Berwick Rangers at Shielfield was followed up with a 3-0 home victory against Stenhousemuir. Newly relegated Cowdenbeath were then beaten on their own soil before Alloa Athletic were confidently pushed aside with a 4-1 win at Bayview on 28th August as the Fifers went to the top of the league.

With home crowds once again creeping into four figures, it looked as though the club were about to go from strength to strength and, with league reconstruction due at the end of the season, the one promotion place on offer looked like it might just be coming to Bayview. But then it all went horribly wrong. On 4th September, Queen of the South made their long trip north from Dumfries worthwhile with a 2-0 win and, seven days later, a single goal defeat against Meadowbank Thistle in Edinburgh took the shine right off what had been a promising start. Unfortunately, the disappointment didn't end there.

On 18th September, any remaining confidence was all but wiped out with a 4-2 defeat from Queen's Park at Hampden and, a week later, few eyebrows were raised when East Stirlingshire inflicted an embarrassing home defeat on Alex Totten's side.

Suddenly it looked as though the Fifers could even struggle to hang on to their Second Division status when league reconstruction was implemented at the end of the season, as even a finish in the top six looked beyond the capabilities of the team!

Still the debate regarding the proposed re-location to Glenrothes raged on, with Chairman Jim Baxter stating in September that a new stadium at Methil Docks was out of the question as the club were not in the sort of financial situation to fund such a move. The preferred option was still to re-locate to a new 10,000 seat stadium in Glenrothes costing £4.5 Million.

At a supporters meeting held in a local hostelry towards the end of the month, Chairman Baxter was left in no doubt as to what the feelings of the supporters were regarding the move.

"Glenrothes is only nine miles away. Nine miles is nothing to travel these days", claimed the Chairman, in reply to claims that East Fife's rightful place was in Methil.

"It may be only nine miles from Methil to Glenrothes", replied one supporter, *"but added to the distance from the East Neuk, where a fair percentage of East Fife's support comes from, that distance becomes twenty-five miles. If East Fife were to move to Glenrothes, then both Dundee and Dundee United would be closer to the East Neuk villages and therefore a more feasible destination on Saturday afternoons. What do you have to say to that?"*

Mr Baxter considered the point, before replying: *"Well, if that's the way the supporters want it, then that's the way it'll have to be"*. The proposed move to the new town was never mentioned again.

The team finally got back to winning ways in October, when three wins, one draw and only one defeat in five games restored faith in Mr Totten and his players.

In November, a single goal win against East Stirlingshire at FirsPark was followed with a thrilling home encounter with Queen's Park in which the honours were shared in an amazing 5-5 draw. For long periods during the match it looked as if the visitors had the game sewn up with their commanding lead, but the Fifers refused to lie down and kept battling away until the end. With only three minutes remaining, the 'Spiders' still had a 5-3 advantage, but goals right at the death from Joe McBride and Robert Scott had the home supporters dancing with joy!

Inconsistent form then plagued the side until the end of the year, which drew to a close with a 3-2 defeat against Arbroath at Gayfield on a bitterly cold evening in which the Fifers came back from being two goals down only to lose to a late strike from the home side.

The Scottish Cup campaign started well with a 5-0 win against Highland League side Rothes at Bayview in which Robert Scott grabbed a hat-trick and was presented with the match ball.

The first match played in 1994 was the second round Scottish Cup tie against Berwick Rangers at Shielfield on 8th January which was lost by a single goal thanks to a mistake from 'keeper Ray Charles.

During the following midweek, Cowdenbeath were beaten 2-0 as the push for promotion was kick-started, but unfortunately the win proved to be the last victory until the beginning of March.

Over the following seven league fixtures only five points were gained from five drawn matches which, along with defeats from Meadowbank Thistle and Montrose, looked to have scuppered the club's championship hopes once and for all.

Despite recording three wins from the four games played in March against Berwick Rangers, Queen's Park and East Stirlingshire, the chance of landing the Second Division Championship all but slipped away by the beginning of April. All that now remained open to Alex Totten's side was to try to finish in the top six in order to avoid relegation to the new Third Division.

With seven games to go, a home win against Albion Rovers at the beginning of April should have set the team up nicely for the run in to the end of the season, but instead a nervous finish to the campaign ensued. After sharing the honours with Meadowbank Thistle in Edinburgh, a home defeat from Queen of the South on 16th April set the alarm bells ringing at Bayview.

Fortunately for East Fife, Cowdenbeath were having a bad season after having been relegated from the First Division at the end of the previous campaign and the 2-1 win at Central Park a week later was to prove vital. On the last day of April, Arbroath took full points from the league fixture at Bayview, which left the Fifers chances of avoiding the drop into Division Three balancing on a knife-edge. After sharing the points with Stenhousemuir in the penultimate game, the Fifers' fate was decided in a showdown with Alloa Athletic at RecreationPark on the last day of the season. Before the match, both clubs were on 40 points although the Fifers had a better goal difference. An East Fife victory or a share of the points would mean basement league football for the 'Wasps', but a win for the home side would mean Third Division football at Methil for at least the following season.

On the warm and sunny afternoon of 14th May 1994, Alloa took a first half lead to the delight of the home supporters in the 1,156 crowd. With the RecreationPark outfit retaining their advantage until half time, things didn't look good for the Methil Men. Only a minute into the second period, however, Alan Sneddon equalised for the Fifers and the travelling support started to nervously count the seconds to the final whistle even though almost half of the match remained!

The home side threw everything at the visitors' defence throughout the second half and on more than one occasion Alloa looked certain to regain the lead. East Fife held out, however, and when the referee's whistle signalled the end of the match the pitch was invaded by a mightily relieved horde of black and gold clad supporters.

The jubilant fans chanted Alex Totten's name until he re-appeared from the dressing room to take the plaudits. Anyone not familiar with the situation would have thought that the Fifers had won promotion instead of having managed to avoid the drop into Division Three; indeed many supporters considered the feat to be just that!

No matter how the situation was viewed, however, the fact of the matter was that East Fife, Berwick Rangers, Stenhousemuir, Meadowbank Thistle and Queen of the South would now take their place in the newly re-formed Second Division along with relegated First Division clubs Dumbarton, Stirling Albion, Clyde, Morton and BrechinCity. The three-league set up which had been in place for the past nineteen years was about to be replaced by four leagues of ten clubs as the Scottish Football League entered a new chapter in its history.

Chapter Twenty: Enter Steve Archibald

The summer of 1994 saw Jimmy Bonthrone end his long official association with the club when he decided to retire from his position as General Manager. Other comings and goings at Bayview were few and far between, with Manager Alex Totten electing to stick largely with the previous season's squad, although one notable arrival was Paul Hunter, who decided to return to the club following a miserable year with Cowdenbeath.

After a brief visit to the north of England, preparations for the coming campaign were rounded off with home games against Rangers and Hibernian. Before the pre-season matches against the Premier League sides were played, however, it became clear that the club would soon be searching once again for a new Manager. Speculation surrounding the future of the Alex Totten was finally ended on 1st August when the East Fife supremo was appointed Manager of Kilmarnock. The lure of becoming involved with a Premier League club also proved too much to resist for second-in-command Kenny Thomson, who followed Totten to RugbyPark a week later. Players Alan Sneddon and Ronnie Hildersley took charge on a temporary basis until a replacement could be found.

For the Rangers match on 1st August, the visitors included Ally McCoist and the £4,000,000 rated Duncan Ferguson in their side and predictably ran out 3-0 winners. Three days later the gulf between the Fifers and visitors Hibernian was clearly not so great, with the Edinburgh side winning by just a single goal.

The serious business of the League Cup started well with a home win against Forfar Athletic, the prize for which was a second round meeting with Alex Totten's Kilmarnock. Unfortunately, the re-construction of RugbyPark forced an early evening midweek kick-off, and few East Fife supporters were able to make the long journey south to Ayrshire for the match on Wednesday 17th August, which finished 4-1 to the home side.

Not long after the League Cup exit, the Fife certainly managed to raise a few eyebrows when former Aberdeen, Tottenham, Barcelona and Scotland star Steve Archibald was appointed Manager. Chairman Jim Baxter claimed that those supporters who had in the past claimed the club showed no ambition would surely now be silenced!

Archibald's first game at the helm was a Fife Cup tie against Dunfermline Athletic at East End Park on 24th August, by which time the first two league matches had netted a win and a share of the points against Stirling Albion and Stenhousemuir respectively. Predictably, the Fife Cup tie was lost against the First Division 'Pars', but the new Manager went on to take full points from Queen of the South and Clyde and share the spoils with Brechin City in his first three league games in charge.

At this early stage in the season, it is interesting to note that the top five clubs in the ten-team league had all played in the Second Division during the previous campaign and thebottom five were the teams relegated from the First Division.

Speaking on the *BBC Sportscene* programme, however, Dumbarton Manager Murdo MacLeod was quick to point out that the previous season's Second Division teams had all raised their game to face the challenge of 'big' clubs such as Dumbarton, Stirling Albion, Clyde, Morton and BrechinCity!

League newcomers Ross County made their first-ever visit to Bayview on 17th September for a first round B & Q Cup tie; a hard fought encounter that the home side eventually won 2-1. The second round of the competition handed the Fife a match with Third Division strugglers Cowdenbeath at Bayview and an easy home win was anticipated. Thanks to a hat-trick from Mark Yardley, however, the visitors won convincingly by three goals without reply. What made the defeat even more embarrassing was that Cowden hero Yardley had been rejected by East Fife only the previous season!

Meanwhile, league form took a dip when Morton inflicted the first home league defeat on 24th September, which was followed up with a share of the points against Berwick Rangers at Shielfield and defeat by the odd goal in five at home to Dumbarton.

Inconsistent form plagued the side for the remainder of the year, with the following run of eight league matches including a convincing 3-0 win against league leaders Berwick Rangers, but also defeat against bottom club BrechinCity.

Boxing Day 1994 will be remembered by the loyal band of supporters who made their way through to Boghead for the fixture against Dumbarton as one of the wettest and most miserable afternoons they ever had the misfortune to suffer standing on a football terrace. The spirit of the travelling support was anything but lifted by the football on offer, with the home side scoring four times without reply. The Fifers barely had a shot at goal during the entire game and it was an extremely depressed number that made their way back east that night, but faith in the side was restored when the following two games against struggling Meadowbank and Brechin were won by the respective scores of 2-1 and 4-0.

The Scottish Cup campaign got under way with a superb 6-2 win against Gala Fairydean at Netherdale on 7th January 1995 and was rewarded with a second visit of the season from RossCounty. A bumper crowd of over 2,000 turned out for the third round cup-tie, which was won by a single goal thanks to a Gilbert Allan penalty. The fourth round draw produced a second trip of the season to Kilmarnock on 18th February, where the home side ended the Fifers' interest in the competition with a 4-0 win.

The league matches played out during early 1995 proved disastrous, with only one point gained from the four fixtures against Stirling Albion, Stenhousemuir, Clyde and Queen of the South. At the beginning of the year there was still an outside chance of promotion to the First Division, but league results during January and February put paid to any slim hopes there may have been.

Gilbert Allan almost scores with a close range effort against Meadowbank Thistle at Bayview on 31st December 1994. (Jim Corstorphine)

It was during early 1995 that the club officially announced its intention to build a new stadium within the Levenmouth area and, on 22nd February, the *East Fife Mail* reported that the intended location for the new stadium was at Ashgrove, Methilhill.

Although the plans for the 3,000 seat stadium and associated training facilities werewelcomed by the supporters, the same cannot be said for the residents of Methilhill. Almost as soon as the proposals were made public, residents of the streets adjacent to the intended location started a campaign to force the club to abandon its plans.

One argument against the proposed venture came from the unlikely source of Raith Rovers Chairman Alex Penman, who stated that East Fife would be far better selling Bayview and using the money raised to help build a new 10,000 stadium in Kirkcaldy, which could be shared with Raith. Needless to say,

Penman's remarks were treated with contempt by the Bayview faithful. One angry supporter even went as far as to state in a letter to the local press that Raith Rovers should move to Methil if they wanted to ground-share with East Fife! Eventually, after a much-publicised effort involving Councillors and the local Residents Association, the plans for the ground at Ashgrove were shelved.

The first league win since the new-year victory against BrechinCity came in the form of a 3-1 success against Meadowbank Thistle in Edinburgh on 11th March in what turned out to be East Fife's last-ever game at the Commonwealth Stadium.

Although the chance of promotion was now gone, bottom clubs Meadowbank Thistle and Brechin City were so far detached from the pack by mid-March that there was also little likelihood of relegation and the remainder of the season was played out in a relatively relaxed manner.

One notable arrival at Bayview towards the end of the season was Trinidad and Tobago Internationalist Arnold Dwarika who, after putting in an impressive performance for the reserves, made his first team debut against Berwick Rangers at Bayview on the first day of April. With several promising players now in his squad, Steve Archibald had a sound platform on which to build for the forthcoming campaign.

The beginning of the 1995/96 season will be remembered not so much as for the impressive start made to the league campaign, but more for the visit to BayviewPark of one of the most famous sides in British football. On Sunday 13th August 1995, the day after a winning start was made to the league programme with a 2-0 victory at Forfar, Manchester United graced the Bayview turf in honour of long standing East Fife servant Jimmy Bonthrone.

Jimmy's eventful career with East Fife has been well documented within earlier chapters of this book and, taking into account his successful days at the helm of Aberdeen and his involvement with the Scottish international squad, few would argue against the claim that a visit from United was an appropriate farewell to such a well-respected figure. Manchester United boss Alex Ferguson did his old friend proud and fielded the strongest side available to him on the

Lee Sharpe congratulates Brian McClair after the latter had scored Manchester United's second goal in the Jimmy Bonthrone testimonial at Bayview on 13th August 1995. The East Fife players nearest the camera are John McStay and goalkeeper Lindsay Hamilton. (Jim Corstorphine)

day. Players wearing the famous red jerseys that afternoon included household names such as Paul Parker, Dennis Irwin, Steve Bruce, Roy Keane, Brian McClair, and Lee Sharpe. Future stars included Gary and Phil Neville, Paul Scholes and a certain promising youngster by the name of David Beckham. On a bright and sunny afternoon, a 'capacity' crowd of 5,385 lined the terraces as East Fife took on their undoubtedly superior opponents. As the visitors strutted confidently over the Bayview turf, David Beckham ably demonstrated that he was on the verge of becoming a first team regular with two superb long-range goals in 29 and 73 minutes, with United's other strikes coming from McClair and Sharpe.

Back on domestic duties the following Saturday, Airdrieonians visited Methil on League Cup business. The Fifers, having disposed of Brechin City by the odd goal in five in round one, found themselves on the receiving end of the same score as the 'Diamonds' progressed to the third round. After exiting the Challenge Cup to Dundee three days later, the more serious business of league football resumed with a home game against Ayr United on 26th August.

Full points were taken once again with a single goal victory, and Steve Archibald was named Bell's 'Manager of the Month' for August.

Convincing wins against Stirling Albion and Montrose in the following two league matches saw the team firmly installed as league leaders and, although the following match at Stranraer ended in defeat, pole position was maintained.

Indeed, the club was destined to remain at the top of the league until the following January, but not without a few slip-ups along the way. Following the defeat at Stranraer, a seven game unbeaten run produced four wins and three draws, although it has to be said that the winning margin was never greater than a single goal. Another interesting statistic is that all four victories during the seven-match run were achieved away from home; the remaining three drawn games being played out at Bayview.

What had caused the poor home form? General opinion was that unrest within a certain faction of the home support had instilled a lack of confidence in the players. This theory was proved when, on 18th November, unfair criticism aimed at certain players throughout the home game with Stenhousemuir resulted in a 2-0 win for the visitors.

The following edition of the East Fife Mail contained letters appealing for the hecklers to have more respect for their side, and the result was almost immediately apparent.After defeating Queen of the South 2-0 at Palmerston in the following fixture, second placed Berwick Rangers were defeated at Bayview; the Fifers' first home league win in well over two months!

Unfortunately, bad weather coupled with a bye in the first round of the Scottish Cup meant that the only other game played before the end of the year was a single goal victory against Clyde at Broadwood on 16th December, but there was certainly a lot of activity off the field of play during the month of December 1995.

A second Trinidad and Tobago Internationalist, Craig Demmin, put pen to paper the day before the Clyde match and, during the following midweek, press speculation suggested that former Bayview favourite Steve Kirk was set to return to Methil. Chairman Jim Baxter was quick to point out that the rumour surrounding the signing of Kirk was unfounded.

As 1995 drew to a close, the question of re-locating the club to a new stadium within the local area once again cropped up and, on the evening of Monday 18th December, building firm Morrison Construction unveiled their plans for a new 3,000 seat stadium at Methil Docks, along with plans to build new houses, a nursing home, a railway heritage centre and a marina. Although some local residents voiced concerns about car parking and noise levels, the club decided to proceed with the proposals and duly submitted their planning application to Fife Council.

With the bad weather continuing throughout the Christmas and New Year period, the Fifers remained out of action until their Scottish Cup second round tie with Spartans in Edinburgh on 6th January 1996.

In what was East Fife's first game at City Park since Edinburgh City were Scottish League members almost 60 years earlier, the players slid around the muddy surface for the entire 90 minutes and were almost unable to string two passes together. Playing up the steep slope for the second half, few chances were created and the match finished goal-less.

A six-point gap at the top of the league was opened up with a 2-0 win against Forfar Athletic at StationPark during the following midweek, before the cup replay went ahead at Bayview on Saturday 13th January. Goals from Richard Gibb, his first for the club, and Gilbert Allan, proved just enough to overcome a plucky Spartans side and win a place in the third round.

Steve Archibald (8) and Gilbert Allan (10) look on as a second half effort goes narrowly wide in the Scottish Cup tie against Spartans at CityPark, Edinburgh, on 6th January 1996. The ground's bad slope and badly cut up playing surface are evident in the photograph (Jim Corstorphine)

Wednesday 17th January saw the much awaited league fixture between the Fife and nearest rivals Stirling Albion take place at Bayview and, although the result was disappointing for the home supporters, from the quality of football on display it was clear that both sides were worthy of their league positions. After sustaining early pressure from the home team, Albion scored twice just before the interval and from then until the end of the match never looked like losing. A third goal two minutes from the end secured a 3-0 win which cut the Fifers' lead to just two points.

Despite taking full points three days later from the crucial fixture against promotion challengers Berwick Rangers at

Shielfield and sharing the spoils with Stenhousemuir at Ochilview, the Fifers finally relinquished their position at the top of the league to StirlingAlbion on 24th January.

Poor form then ensued, during which only two points were taken from three games, all of which were played against teams in the lower reaches of the table. It looked like the bubble had burst!

As if the poor league form wasn't bad enough, league newcomers Caledonian Thistle inflicted further pain by knocking the Fifers out of the Scottish Cup. After drawing the first game at Telford Street, the sides still couldn't be separated following 120 minutes play in the replay at Bayview, and the Inverness side eventually progressed to round four following a penalty shoot-out.

When league business finally resumed on the evening of Wednesday 21st February, the critics were well and truly silenced when Montrose were convincingly beaten 7-0 at Bayview. A Robert Scott hat-trick along with goals from Allan, Chalmers, Donaghy and Gartshore did the damage as the home side recorded their biggest league win for 33 years. Unfortunately, the victory against the 'Gable Endies' didn't spark off a return to wining form and once again only two points were gained from the following three fixtures, although it has to be said that the sequence included a share of the spoils against league leaders Stirling Albion at Forthbank, where the Fife were denied victory by a controversial equaliser deep into injury time.

By this stage in the season, however, both East Fife and Stirling Albion were so far ahead of the pack that promotion for both clubs looked inevitable. After taking full points from the following three fixtures against Stenhousemuir, Stranraer and Montrose, the Fife went into their home fixture against Berwick Rangers on 6th April knowing that victory would ensure promotion to the First Division. With a crowd of 1,943 lining the terraces, Steve Archibald was once again presented with the 'Manager of the Month' award, but a goal-less draw meant that the champagne had to remain on ice for at least another week.

On 13th April 1996 promotion was finally secured against Clyde at Broadwood when two late headed goals from substitute Paul Chalmers cancelled out the home side's two goal lead to secure a share of the points. At long last the celebrations could begin for the large travelling support! In the midweek prior to the match against Clyde, an interesting encounter took place at Bayview between East Fife and a Trinidad and Tobago select. No doubt the match, which finished all square at two goals apiece, was made possible due to the Fifers' international duo of Dwarika and Demmin, who both played for their country on the night. Club versus country matches are rare and, needless to say, this was the first time that East Fife had been involved in such a game. Only one win was recorded from the three remaining league fixtures, which meant that Champions Stirling Albion won the Second Division title by fully eight points.

Only days after the end of the season, the club received a huge boost when it was announced that the proposals for the construction of the new stadium at Methil Docks had been given the go-ahead by Fife Council's Central Area Development Committee.

Although one or two problems were still to be ironed out, it was anticipated that building work would commence over the coming months. In the event, however, several unforeseen stumbling blocks presented themselves and the development had to be put on hold once more.

Preparing for life in the First Division, rumours were rife during the summer of 1996 that a row had developed between Steve Archibald and the Board with regard to the club's decision to remain part-time during the coming season. News that full-time football would not be coming to Bayview was also received badly by the supporters, many of whom declined to purchase a season ticket. With almost every other club in the First Division boasting full-time players, many believed that one relegation place had been filled even before the season started!

Although a 2-0 win was recorded against a strong Dundee United side during the programme of pre-season friendlies, the supporters' fears seemed to be justified when the competitive games got under way. After fellow First Division club St Johnstone had inflicted a 5-1 home League Cup defeat on Tuesday 13th August, St Mirren visited Methil on league business four days later and scored four times without reply. The outlook started to look brighter following a goal-less encounter with Airdrieonians at their temporary home of Broadwood on 24th August and, three days later, the first competitive win of the season was recorded when Falkirk were beaten 2-0 at Bayview in the Challenge Cup.

When the points were then shared with both Clydebank and Morton, it looked like a brighter season might just be on the cards. At least the team were not at the bottom of the league!

Just when it looked like Steve Archibald's influence and wealth of experience were going to pay dividends, however, the Manager was sacked for reasons which were never fully explained. After having been knocked out of the Challenge Cup by Stranraer, Archibald was shown the door following a 4-1 home league defeat from St Johnstone on 14th September. The reason for the sacking was, according to Chairman Julian Danskin, *"for irreconcilable differences with the Board"*. Reading between the lines, however, it would appear that Archibald's departure was largely due to the fact that the club steadfastly refused to go full-time; a situation that the Manager believed would prove detrimental to the club's ambitions in the long run.

Flooded with correspondence from angry supporters, the *East Fife Mail* was forced to print just nine of the many letters received, most claiming that the Board had once again shown a lack of ambition by dismissing one of the most promising young managers in the land. The managerial vacancy was filled on a temporary basis by players Alan Sneddon and Gordon Rae and it seemed that the club could do worse than make the arrangement permanent after the following three league fixtures produced a creditable 2-0 defeat from Dundee at Dens Park, a share of the points with Stirling Albion and a convincing home victory over Falkirk.

Prior to the Falkirk game, the club appointed Jimmy Bone as the new Manager, although hedidn't officially take charge

One notable visitor to Bayview for the league fixture against Falkirk on 5th October 1996 was former England Internationalist Chris Waddle (Jim Corstorphine)

until the following week and watched the 3-1 win against the 'Bairns' from the comfort of the Directors' Box.

Bone's first game at the helm proved disastrous as Partick Thistle ran riot by scoring six without reply at Firhill. Anyone thinking that matters would surely improve over the following weeks was to be sorely disappointed, as the Partick game marked the start of a staggering run of sixteen league defeats in succession, which was finally ended with a 2-2 draw against St Johnstone at Bayview on 28th January 1997! As if the losing streak wasn't bad enough, the club's record home defeat of 7-1 was equalled when Dundee visited Methil on 17th December.

On the Saturday before the dismal sequence of league defeats came to an end with a share of the points against St. Johnstone, the Fifers managed to beat Queen's Park at Hampden in the third round of the Scottish Cup and were rewarded with a fourth round tie against Rangers. The 41,064 crowd that packed Ibrox on 15th February provided a much needed boost to the Bayview coffers and, on the day, the team did their bumper travelling support proud as they held the score to a respectable 3-0 for the home side.

As for league form, however, there was little improvement as the season wore on and the club were officially relegated following a 4-1 defeat from Stirling Albion at Forthbank on 15th March. Ironically, the best performance of the season was saved until the very last game,when Clydebank were beaten 4-0 at their temporary home of Boghead, Dumbarton.

The Fifers' venture into the First Division had proved nothing short of disastrous. Would the club have fared any better if Steve Archibald's wishes had been granted and full-time status adopted? We shall never know, but in hindsight the move to become full-time could well have inflicted untold financial damage on the club. With Fife rivals Raith Rovers and Dunfermline Athletic both enjoying Premier League status during East Fife's season in the First Division, crowds at Bayview had little chance of reaching the level required to pay full-time wages.

Following a two game tour of the north of England, during which Peterlee were beaten 5-0 and the honours were shared with Seaham Red Star, season 1997/98 started in earnest with a visit from Kilmarnock on 9th August for a League Cup second round tie. Despite playing quality opposition, a meagre crowd of only 963 turned out for the game, no doubt many having been put off by the announcement that there would be no concessions for the match and that ground admission was set at the ridiculous price of £11! For the record, the Ayrshire side won 2-0 although the Fife played well on the day.

The following midweek saw St Mirren make the trip through to Methil for a Challenge Cup tie. The home side eventually won a bruising encounter by a single goal, but exited the competition at the next hurdle thanks to a 2-1 defeat from Hamilton Academical.

The league programme finally got under way with a 3-0 home defeat at the hands of Stenhousemuir, but following wins against Caledonian Thistle, Clyde, Forfar Athletic and Clydebank the Fife were sitting at the top of the table by mid-September.

A slump in form then ensued and only one win was recorded over the following ten fixtures as the team slipped down to fourth bottom by the beginning of December.

When Stranraer dumped the Fifers out of the Scottish Cup with a 3-2 win at Bayview on 6th December, Jimmy Bone decided that enough was enough and ended his days as Manager 'by mutual agreement' with the Board.

Two days before Christmas, the supporters' prayers were answered when Steve Kirk returned to Bayview as Player/Manager. It was Stevie's third spell with the club and his popularity with the Bayview faithful had never waned since he first pulled on a black and gold jersey back in 1979. Although Kirk's first game in charge ended with a 4-0 defeat from Caledonian Thistle in Inverness, his first home game at the helm, on 11th January 1998, resulted in a win against Forfar Athletic. The only goal of the game was scored by 38 year-old former Swedish Internationalist Robert Prytz, an old colleague of Kirk's from his days with Stoke City, who had been signed only days before.

Wins in the next two games against Stranraer and Livingston saw the team climb back up to fourth place by the end of January, but the change in fortunes could not be sustained and once more the Fifers slipped back down the league table. Despite a promising run towards the end of March and into April, when convincing wins against Clydebank, BrechinCity and Queen of the South were complemented with a share of the points against Livingston at Almondvale, the Fifers never really looked like promotion material. When the curtain finally came down on season 1997/98, East Fife were sitting sixth in the ten-team league, twelve points off promotion and only eight points clear of relegation.

Bayview Stadium under construction during the summer of 1998 (Jim Corstorphine)

It was early days, though, for the new Manager. The Bayview faithful were convinced that, as time progressed, experience would surely bring rewards.

Meanwhile, there had been major developments regarding the re-location of the club to a brand new stadium at Methil Docks. At the beginning of April 1998, two years after the scheme had been initially approved, it was announced that agreement had finally been reached and that construction work would shortly begin on the new £2.25 million stadium. The initial capacity, however, was to be just 2,000 with all seats located in a single grandstand situated on the west side of the ground.

No time was wasted in getting the building works under way and, on 10th April, Central Fife M.P. and former East Fife player Henry McLeish had the honour of cutting the first turf. All through the close season, building firm Morrison Construction busily went about their duties and, by mid-October, the new stadium was complete and awaiting a safety certificate to allow the Fife to move in.

Whilst the finishing touches were being put on the new ground, season 1998/99 got under way with a four-team pre-season tournament at Links Park, Montrose, where the Fife

Long shadows to match the long faces! Visitors Livingston pressurise the home defence during East Fife's last match at BayviewPark on 31st October 1998(Jim Corstorphine)

lost to Dunfermline Athletic as well as the host club, but unfortunately didn't get the opportunity to play the against the third side, Preston North End.

The following week the pre-season preparations were rounded off with a three game Highland tour, during which wins were recorded against Balintore, WickAcademy and Golspie Sutherland.

The competitive season started well, with a 3-2 home victory against Partick Thistle after120 minutes play in the first round of the League Cup followed by a narrow home defeat, again after extra time, against Premier League Motherwell in round two.

A comfortable 2-0 win against Arbroath at Gayfield kicked off the league campaign, but only two wins from the following twelve matches saw the Fifers slump to second bottom of the league when the time finally came to quit BayviewPark at the end of October. The 2-0 league win against Queen of the South at Bayview Park on Sunday 27th September 1998 turned out to be the club's last ever win at the old Methil ground.

The last senior match played at old BayviewPark was lost by the odd goal in five to Livingston, a sad end to the club's 95-year association with the venue.

When the final whistle blew on the last day of October 1998, the players of both sides shook hands and headed off towards the pavilion. Slowly, the spectators made their way towards the exits. Some lingered a little longer and took one long, last look around the neat little ground. Uppermost on the minds of the slightly larger than usual crowd who had witnessed the game was not the fact that East Fife had lost an entertaining match by three goals to two, but the fact that this was the last time the men in black and gold would ever grace the Bayview turf.

The Livingston match was not, however, the last game to be played at the ground. On the day following the opening of Bayview Stadium, over two weeks after the Livingston game, an Under-18 match was played out at BayviewPark between Bayview Youth Club and Comrie, which finished 5-0 to the home side. For the record, the last goal scored at the old ground was a last-minute penalty netted by Chris King at the AberhillSchool end.

The Author claims a souvenir piece of Bayview turf from 'TommyAdamsTerritory'. (Bob Hunter)

Just days after the last match was played at BayviewPark, the bulldozers moved in and the stadium was razed to the ground. This view shows the west end of the ground, with the concrete steps and crush barriers already removed from the embankment. (Jim Corstorphine)

When the final whistle sounded at Bayview Park for the last time on Sunday 15th November 1998, the small band of East Fife 'die-hards' who attended the youth match made their way on to the park. Most had come armed with spades, intent on claiming pieces of the famous turf as keepsakes; others went home with various small souvenirs taken from the grandstand and the turnstile booths. Some youngsters even brought a ball along and seized the opportunity to have a kick-about on East Fife's famous old ground!

Just a few days later, the bulldozers moved in and, within a matter of weeks, BayviewPark had been completely razed to the ground.

Chapter Twenty-One: A Fresh Start in a New Stadium

Almost finished! Bayview Stadium is just days away from hosting its first match against Forfar Athletic, although the floodlights and goalposts have still to be installed. The foundations for one floodlight pylon can be seen in the foreground. (Jim Corstorphine)

On 14th November 1998, history was made when the first match was played at New Bayview Stadium, a league fixture against Forfar Athletic from which full points were taken thanks to a late Barrie Moffat goal. Most of the 1,422 who attended the game expressed their satisfaction with the new venue, not just for the comfort of the seating in the grandstand but also for the bar and lounge facilities which were enjoyed by many after the match.

One pleasing aspect of the post-match facilities was that most of the players, once showered and changed, happily mingled with the supporters in the lounge. It is a feature that is still enjoyed today and one that helps to give the club its relaxed and welcoming atmosphere.

Although three more games were played at the new stadium before the end of the year, full points were taken from only one match, a thrilling 3-2 win against Inverness Caledonian Thistle on Boxing Day.

The New Year brought a welcome break from league business, with a second round Scottish Cup tie against Forfar Athletic at StationPark on 2nd January 1999 which finished all-square. In the replay at Bayview Stadium a week later, the 'Loons' avenged their recent defeat at the same venue by scoring the only goal of the game.

The dismal league form continued and Assistant Manager Andy Harrow was sacked in mid-January. Days after Harrow's departure, Dave Clarke returned to the club after a twelve year absence to take up the position of Assistant Coach along with Dave Gorman.

At the beginning of February, Partick Thistle had the honour of participating in the first competitive match played under the new Bayview Stadium floodlights, which the home side won thanks to a Barrie Moffat goal. Although the next game produced a victory against fellow relegation candidates Forfar Athletic at StationPark, the anticipated improvement in form due to the change in coaching staff failed to materialise. Only one point was picked up from the following four matches as the Fifers slipped down to second bottom place in the league table.

Although a slight improvement in form did materialise with home wins against Stirling Albion and Forfar and a share of the points with Partick Thistle at Firhill, the team just couldn't lift themselves out of the relegation zone.

Going into the last game of the season against Clyde at Bayview on 8th May, a win was vital if the drop down to Division Three was to be avoided. Unfortunately, although all three points were won with a 2-1 victory on the day, the Fife took the drop as fellow relegation candidates Stirling Albion beat Arbroath by the same score-line.

Having suffered the indignity of relegation during the club's first season at their brand new stadium, Chairman Julian Danskin quickly pledged 'changes at all levels' in order to escape from the bottom league.

Danskin went on to say, *"the club wants the best possible organisation for their escape bid from Scotland's senior soccer basement. A positive outlook will be adopted and the changes will start at the top."*

Manager Stevie Kirk, citing inconsistency as the main reason for the demise, hoped that he would still be in place to lead the team but hinted that his own playing days were reaching an end. *"I love this club and I love my job"*, commented Kirk, *"and I will work as long as it takes to get a bit of success back. This club deserves better, and we have a stadium that merits Second if not First Division football."*

Three days after long serving kit-man Alex Doig had been honoured with a testimonial match against Sheffield United, Bayview Stadium was officially opened with a match against Kilmarnock on 21st July 1999. Former player and M.S.P. Henry McLeish performed the opening ceremony in the presence of several well-known figures including former referee Tom Wharton who, as President of the Football Trust, had taken a keen interest in the building of the new stadium. As for the game itself, the Ayrshire visitors proved to be too strong on the night and won comfortably by three goals to one, although home supporters were treated to a superb Steve Kirk volley from the edge of the penalty area which gave the Fifers a first-half lead.

Competitively, season 1999/2000 started with a thrilling first round League Cup clash with Stirling Albion at Bayview. With the score standing at 2-2 after extra time, the Fifers progressed to the second round following an incredible 8-7 penalty shoot-out during which all eleven players from each side were forced to take a kick. The match was eventually won when Albion 'keeper Gow blasted wide of the post.

The second round of the competition produced another entertaining game against Airdrieonians, who were also beaten on penalty kicks following another 2-2 draw.

The Fife were rewarded for their efforts with a home draw against Hearts in the third round but, following safety concerns allegedly highlighted by Hearts' Director Chris Robinson, the game was moved ten miles west to Stark's Park. Although the Edinburgh side eventually won an entertaining match 2-0 at the Kirkcaldy venue, the Fifers had several chances to score and held their SPL opponents to a single goal lead until well into injury time at the end of the match.

The future First Minister of Scotland, Henry McLeish, meets the East Fife team accompanied by Football Trust President and former referee Tom Wharton at the official opening of Bayview Stadium on 21st July 1999. (Jim Corstorphine)

Meanwhile, the campaign for a quick return to Division Two got off to a poor start with a home defeat from Berwick Rangers, but a two goal victory against East Stirlingshire the following week sparked off a five game unbeaten run from which full points were taken from four matches. With league re-construction looming once again at the end of the season, it seemed as if one of the three promotion places on offer would be won with ease!

When the unbeaten run came to an end, it came to an end in spectacular fashion. In what was the first league meeting between the local rivals for over five years, Cowdenbeath scored four without reply at Central Park on 18th September to send the Methil Men home with their tails firmly between their legs.

Within a few games the Fifers regained second place in the league table, but it has to be said that performances were far from convincing.

After losing by the odd-goal-in-five to Forfar Athletic at Station Park on 30th October, Cowdenbeath visited Bayview Stadium for the first time on the following Saturday, but home supporters expecting revenge in the derby encounter were to be sorely disappointed. Despite a Barrie Moffat brace, the second coming from a 20 yard volley that almost burst the net, the 'Blue Brazil' again took full points with a 3-2 win.

In the week that followed, major changes were made at the club. Vice-Chairman Gordon Dow took over from Julian Danskin as Chairman and Manager Steve Kirk was sacked and replaced at the helm by player Rab Shannon.

With confidence severely dented, things went from bad to worse in Shannon's first game in charge when bottom club Albion Rovers celebrated their first visit to Bayview Stadium with a shock 4-1 victory.

Following the humiliation at the hands of the Coatbridge side, however, all three league matches played before the end of the year were won, including a single goal victory against league leaders Queen's Park at Hampden thanks to a stunning Kenny Munro strike from all of 30 yards.

Kenny's 'wonder goal' may have been a pleasing way to end the Millennium, but disappointment was to follow in the first match of the new year. On 3rd January, Cowdenbeath recorded their third derby win of the season by a single goal at Central Park as East Fife struggled to hold on to second place in the league table.

The following Saturday saw the Fife knocked out of the Scottish Cup with a 2-1 defeat at Stirling. Although an early exit from the competition was disappointing, the main goal was to win promotion from Scottish football's basement league at the first attempt and hopes were high that the club could at least consolidate its league position over the coming weeks. What actually happened was quite different.

By picking up only two league points from the beginning of the year to the middle of February, the Fifers slipped down into the bottom half of the league table and, although a home win against Montrose brought a brief respite, the players' morale dipped even lower following further defeats from Albion Rovers and East Stirlingshire.

During this time, the club failed in an ambitious move to bring Ally McCoist to Methil on a short-term loan from Kilmarnock. McCoist was in need of match practice at the time and the Fife were desperately in need of a striker. The deal would have suited both parties as the extra gate money generated from McCoist's home appearances would have more than paid his wages! McCoist eventually declined the offer, although he later hinted that he had perhaps been a little hasty in turning down the move.

Results during March were of a more satisfactory nature, largely due to the loan signing from Hibernian of Tom McManus. Described as 'one of Scotland's brightest young prospects', McManus helped the Fifers resurrect their push for promotion with wins against Dumbarton, Berwick Rangers and league leaders Forfar Athletic.

Although the team suffered a setback with a single goal defeat from fellow promotion candidates Queen's Park at Hampden, the five games played during April netted three wins and a draw, including victory against table-toppers Berwick Rangers at Shielfield. With only one match remaining, the Fifers had managed to claw their way back into the top three. If Dumbarton could be defeated on their own soil on the last Saturday of the season, promotion was assured.

There was one major snag, however. The last game of the season was also to be the last game ever played at Dumbarton's famous old Boghead ground. East Fife were determined to win the match and return to the Second

Division at the first time of asking. The 'Sons' were equally determined to end their 121-year association with Boghead on a winning note.

A crowd of over 3,000 attended the final game, on 6th May 2000. The first half belonged largely to East Fife and, following early pressure during which John Cusick forced a great save from the home 'keeper, Raymond Logan gave East Fife the lead with a 25-yard lob. The second half, however, was a different story.

Dumbarton equalised seconds after the re-start and, after the 'Sons' went ahead midway through the half, the Fifers just couldn't force themselves back into the match. Third Division football was destined to remain at Bayview Stadium for at least another season.

On 14th June 2000, the club were dealt a blow when the influential John Cusick failed to agree terms and signed for Arbroath, only two days after defender Gordon Forrest had departed for Berwick Rangers. Arrivals at Bayview Stadium included forwards Steve Kerrigan from Brechin City, Murray Hunter from Clydebank, and midfield players Paul Mortimer from Stirling Albion and John Allison from local junior side Kelty Hearts.

Two other signings at this time were teenage strikers Steve Ferguson and Paul McManus, both of whom were destined to make a big impression at the club.

Preparations for season 2000/01 included a testimonial match against Hibernian for long serving fans' favourite Richard Gibb on 15th July, followed by a visit from a Rangers XI on the following Saturday.

On the competitive front, the season started with a single goal victory against Albion Rovers in Coatbridge and, when the following three games produced wins against East Stirlingshire and Montrose and a share of the points with league newcomers Peterhead, the future started to look a little brighter.

A good performance in the first round of the League Cup against Raith Rovers at Bayview Stadium on 8th August also helped to boost morale. In what was the first competitive meeting between the sides for over twelve years, excluding Fife Cup encounters, the Rovers were fortunate to record a narrow 2-1 victory. The Methil Men matched their First Division counterparts in every department and it took a late goal from the visitors to separate the sides.

Once again, however, the team was brought down to earth with a bump when the previous season's 'bogey' side, Cowdenbeath, came to Methil at the beginning of September and took full points with a 2-0 win. For the second season in a row, defeat in the local derby had an adverse affect on morale and only one point was taken from the following three fixtures.

Results during October were more favourable with two wins and two draws helping to resurrect the challenge near the top of the table. What was most pleasing about performances during this period was the emergence of young striker Steve Ferguson as a first team regular. Ferguson's first goal for the club came in the 3-1 home win against Montrose on 28th October and, over the following seven competitive matches, the youngster failed to find the net on just one occasion. Needless to say, Ferguson's talents attracted the attention of scouts from several big clubs, including Celtic, Liverpool, ManchesterCity and Tottenham Hotspur. On 12th December, Ferguson scored twice to knock Albion Rovers out of the Scottish Cup and, during the following midweek, Tottenham Hotspur seized the opportunity to take the promising teenager to White Hart Lane for a six-figure fee.

Even without their goal scoring talent, full points were taken from the two league games played before the end of the year and hopes were high that the club's bogey could finally be laid to rest when Cowdenbeath visited for the New Year

Derby on 2nd January. Once again, however, the 'Blue Brazil' took the honours with a 2-1 win.

Four days later, a single goal Scottish Cup win against Queen's Park at Bayview Stadium brought the reward of a third round home meeting with Livingston on 27th January. Despite taking an early lead through Barrie Moffat, the First Division pacesetters went on to dominate the cup-tie and eventually ran out 4-1 winners. Unfortunately, the game was marred by a shocking tackle by Livingston's Tosh on John Allison, which resulted in the East Fife player being stretchered from the field with a severely injured leg.

Back on league business, inconsistent form saw the promotion challenge all but disappear by the end of March and, following a dismal run of poor performances that included 4-1 home defeats at the hands of both Hamilton Academical and Brechin City, Manager Rab Shannon left the club 'by mutual agreement' in mid-April.

Following much speculation about Shannon's successor, the former Management team of Davie Clarke and Mike Marshall were re-instated during the last week in April 2001.

There was also a major change in the boardroom at this time, when Gordon Dow tendered his resignation as Chairman. Mr Dow was replaced by W. Bruce Black, a lifelong supporter of the club.

On 5th May the season finally came to an end with Clarke and Marshall at the helm for the first time in over fourteen years as the Fife demolished East Stirlingshire 4-1 at Bayview Stadium. Suddenly, the air of despondency was lifted, leaving the supporters frustrated by the weeks of inactivity that lay ahead during the close season.

Notable arrivals at the club during the summer of 2001 included James Herkes from St.Andrews United, Ross Graham from Kirrie Thistle and Grant Cunningham from

How's the leg, John? A concerned spectator chats to John Allison at Dumbarton on 3rd February 2001, a week after the player's leg was severely injured in the Scottish Cup tie against Livingston. In the centre is Tottenham Hotspur striker and former East Fife favourite Steve Ferguson, who had returned home for the weekend to see his old mates. (Jim Corstorphine)

Glenrothes Strollers. Unfortunately, despite some creditable performances throughout the campaign from the aforementioned players, the following season turned out to be nothing short of disastrous!

After sharing the points in a no scoring draw against Albion Rovers in the opening game, only one further point was taken from the following six league fixtures; a run which included an embarrassing 6-0 defeat from Brechin City at Glebe Park and a 4-0 home defeat from East Stirlingshire. A narrow defeat from Raith Rovers in the first round of the Challenge Cup during the same period did little to raise the gloom.

A ray of hope arrived in the form of a home win against Arbroath in the first round of the League Cup on 11th September, which was rewarded with a trip to play SPL side Livingston at Almondvale two weeks later. Not surprisingly, the home side won comfortably by three goals to nil, although the Fifers put up a brave fight.The first league win of the season came courtesy of a 2-1 victory against fellow strugglers Queen's Park at Hampden on 22nd September, quickly followed by a convincing 4-1 home win against Dumbarton. Despite losing the following game 3-0 to Albion Rovers, league form started to pick up and further wins were recorded against Peterhead, ElginCity and league leaders BrechinCity during October and November.

Once again, however, league form slumped and no further points were won before the end of the year, although progress was made in the Scottish Cup when Queen's Park were beaten at Bayview Stadium on penalty kicks following two drawn matches. By now the goal scoring talents of Paul McManus were coming to the fore, and the young striker's second goal in the cup replay against Queen's Park was voted the *BBC Sportscene* 'Goal of the Round'.

Behind the scenes, there were further changes at board level towards the end of the year when J.Derrick Brown was installed as Vice-Chairman following the death of Bob Stevenson.

A new Bayview Stadium record crowd of 1,658 paid to see the second round cup-tie with Partick Thistle on Tuesday 8th January 2002, which the First Division leaders won 4-2, despite going behind to a Paul McManus goal midway through the first half.

Home defeat from Peterhead on the following Saturday, the fourth league defeat in succession, resulted in the resignation of Manager Davie Clarke after less than a year in charge. Assistant Manager Mike Marshall took over at the helm and guided the Fifers to a 2-0 home success against Montrose a week later, but unconvincing performances over the following six games resulted in Marshall quitting as caretaker Manager at the end of February. Stirling Albion assistant boss Jim Moffat was appointed Manager a week after Marshall's departure and, after installing former Aberdeen, Dunfermline Athletic and Raith Rovers stalwart Craig Robertson as his assistant, the pair took control of the side for the visit of Stirling Albion on 9th March 2002.

With nothing left to play for, the new management team used the remainder of the season to experiment and only two further wins were recorded before the end of the campaign. One pleasing aspect about the run-in to the end of the campaign, however, was the promise shown by new signing Gordon Gilbert from Bo'ness United.

With the club finishing third bottom of the league, which in reality meant a ranking of 40th out of the 42 most senior Scottish clubs, it could be argued that season 2001/02 was the club's worst since being admitted to the Scottish League. Would new boss Jim Moffat and his assistant Craig Robertson manage to turn the club around? Only time would tell.

Almost as soon as the curtain came down on season 2001/02, Manager Moffat started to re-build his side for the forthcoming season.

In May, influential midfielder John Allison returned from Montrose, accompanied by experienced goalkeeper Jim Butter.

Defender Euan Donaldson and midfielder Craig Farnan were both signed from Forfar Athletic, along with defender Michael Hall from East Stirlingshire.

Arrivals at Bayview Stadium during the remainder of the close season included speedy attacking midfielder Gordon Love from NottinghamForest, defender Andy Rollo from Livingston, defender Gordon Russell from East Stirlingshire and striker Kenny Deuchar, a player destined to have a huge impact on the season that lay ahead, from Falkirk.

A terrific start was made to the new managerial team's first full season in charge.

The first league game of the new campaign, on 3rd August, produced an impressive 2-0 victory over Peterhead at Balmoor Stadium.

Following an early exit from the Challenge Cup against Dumbarton, who progressed to the second round courtesy of a single goal win on Tuesday 6th August, the Fife extended their unbeaten league status to seven matches. During the unbeaten run, which was halted in controversial fashion against Morton at Cappielow on 28th September, an impressive 5-1 victory was recorded against fellow table-toppers Albion Rovers in Coatbridge.

A week after the Rovers match, league newcomers Gretna were beaten 2-1 at RaydalePark in the first round of the League Cup. The second round of the competition brought Motherwell through to Methil on Tuesday 24th September, where the SPL side progressed to round three thanks to a 2-0 win.

Pole position was reclaimed when Gretna were beaten by the odd goal in five at Bayview Stadium on 5th October, a position which was not relinquished until Morton inflicted an embarrassing 4-1 defeat at the same venue in mid-December. The intervening matches certainly produced no shortage of thrills! An impressive 4-1 win against East Stirlingshire at

FirsPark on 19th October was followed by a nail-biting encounter with second placed Peterhead at Bayview a week later. With the Fifers leading by a first minute John Allison strike at half-time, the visitors struck twice midway through the second half to turn the game around. Gordon Gilbert then equalised, but the 'Blue Toon' regained the lead with ten minutes remaining. With time running out, James Herkes equalised once again to keep the Fifers at the top of the table, albeit on goal difference.

A week later, the team's promotion aspirations were dealt a severe blow when Albion Rovers gained revenge for their earlier embarrassment by inflicting a 4-0 defeat in extremely blustery conditions at Bayview Stadium.

The critics who voiced the opinion that the Fifers' bubble had burst were well and truly silenced a week later when Montrose were beaten 5-0 on their own soil. Craig Farnan opened the scoring and, when Grant Cunningham doubled the advantage early in the second half with a superb diving header, the result was never in doubt. Kenny Deuchar then added a third from the penalty spot before James Herkes notched a late brace to complete the scoring.

After ElginCity had been swept aside by four goals without reply in the following match, the points were shared with fellow promotion challengers Stirling Albion at Forthbank. Although the Stirling game had been a nervous, nail-biting affair, nothing could have prepared the travelling support for the following fixture against Gretna at RaydalePark. With the home side leading 2-1 with just a minute remaining, Paul Mortimer rifled home a free kick then, with virtually the last kick of the game, Kenny Deuchar calmly slotted home the winner. The lead at the top of the table had been maintained in the most spectacular fashion and, to put the icing on the cake, Jim Moffat was named Third Division Manager of the Month during the following midweek.

After pole position had been surrendered following defeat from Morton in mid-December, the two fixtures played out before the end of the year produced just two points, but included a creditable draw against Peterhead at Balmoor Stadium in which the Fife fought back from 2-0 down at half-time to square the match thanks to goals from Hall and Deuchar.

New Year's Day 2003 dawned cold, wet and blustery, putting the home fixture against Montrose in danger of being cancelled. After the referee had declared the park playable around an hour before kick-off, the game went ahead with just 519 hardy souls huddled together at the rear of the stand. The Fife regained their place at the top of the table thanks to a 2-0 win, but the adverse weather conditions made the victory far from convincing.

The weather continued to deteriorate during the first few days of the year, and the scheduled Scottish Cup tie against Hamilton Academical at New Douglas Park on 4th January was called off on the morning of the game. When the match eventually went ahead eleven days later, Accies broke the deadlock midway through the second half and it looked like the Fifers were about to exit the competition at the first hurdle as the game went into injury time. With virtually the last kick of the ball, however, Craig Farnan netted a deserved equaliser to force a replay at Bayview Stadium on Monday 20th January. The deciding game proved to be an exciting affair, with the full-time visitors taking the lead against the run of play midway through the first half. The Fife applied relentless pressure to the Accies goal for the remainder of the match and, following a second half equaliser from James Herkes, it looked as if they had won the tie when Ross Graham scored with just two minutes remaining. The visitors had other ideas, however, and equalised in controversial circumstances deep into injury time from the penalty spot.

Following a goal-less half hour of extra time, the Second Division side won through to the following round on penalties.

Back on league business, the unbeaten run was maintained with a single goal victory against Elgin, before the points were divided in two crucial fixtures against fellow promotion challengers Albion Rovers and Morton. With the side now strengthened by the arrival of utility player Barry McLean and left sided midfielder Chris Miller, maximum points were taken from the following fixtures with Stirling Albion, East Stirlingshire, Queen's Park, Gretna and Montrose before Albion Rovers travelled through to Methil on 15th March for their final meeting of the season with the Fifers. Another tense encounter finished all-square as the Methil Men maintained their position at the top of the league.

On the Sunday evening before the Albion Rovers fixture, a Century to the day since the club was founded on 9th March 1903, East Fife's 100th birthday was celebrated with a highly successful dinner at Dean Park Hotel in Kirkcaldy. Guest speakers included Scottish League Secretary Peter Donald, SFA President Jack McGinn, former goalkeeper Alan Blair and award-winning after-dinner speaker Willie Allan.

With the end of the season now clearly in sight, the table-topping Fifers now realised that they had a real chance of landing the Third Division title. Against Stirling Albion at Forthbank Stadium on 22nd March, a share of the points looked inevitable as the game went into injury time all-square at a goal apiece. Substitute Barry McLean had other ideas, however, and forced the ball home to win the match with virtually the last kick of the ball.

Scoring in the dying seconds had by this stage become the Fifers' trade-mark and, following a one sided demolition of Elgin City a week later in which Kenny Deuchar scored four, the feat was repeated against Gretna at Raydale Park on 12th April. After having come back from being two goals down midway through the first-half, the home side regained the lead with ten minutes remaining. Just when the travelling supporters were resigning themselves to the first league defeat since December 2002, substitute Gordon Love was sent crashing to the ground inside the penalty area. The referee had no hesitation in pointing to the spot and Ross Graham calmly stroked the ball home to tie the match at 3-3.

With the other promotion challengers dropping points on the same day, the Fife were now sitting four points clear of second placed Peterhead and five points ahead of both Albion Rovers and Morton. With just four fixtures remaining, three of which were scheduled for Bayview Stadium, it looked like the Third Division Championship was destined for Methil.

Standing room only! Bayview Stadium was filled to overflowing for the visit of Greenock Morton on 19th April 2003. (Jim Corstorphine)

Unfortunately, two of the remaining home games were against fellow contenders Morton and Peterhead, but general opinion was that if the honours were to be shared in both of these fixtures, the league title was as good as won.

Over 2,000 spectators were shoehorned into Bayview Stadium for the visit of Morton on 19th April, where a win for the Fifers would have put them in easy street. Instead of going all out for victory, however, defensive tactics were employed throughout the game in order to secure at least a share of the points, a scenario which would have suited the home side far more than their guests. Unfortunately, after having contained the Greenock side for 75 minutes, the Fifers conceded the only goal of the game when 'keeper Jim Butter attempted to fingertip a speculative shot around the post, but only succeeded in touching the ball on to the upright, from where it squirmed agonisingly over the line.

A win against Peterhead at the same venue a week later would have maintained pole position, but on the day the north-east side were the better team and deservedly won by two goals without reply.

Chris Miller is on hand to clear against Morton on 19th April 2003. The East Fife players looking on anxiously, from left, are Craig Farnan, Michael Hall, Ross Graham, Paul Mortimer, Jim Butter and, far right, Gordon Gilbert. (Jim Corstorphine)

Unbelievably, from being in the driving seat just a fortnight earlier, the club now found themselves in fourth place with the prospect of remaining in Division Three for yet another season a distinct possibility. One thing in the team's favour, however, was that the two remaining fixtures, against East Stirlingshire at FirsPark and against Queen's Park in Methil on the last day of the campaign should, in theory, produce full points. Fellow contenders Peterhead, Morton and Albion Rovers, on the other hand, had to play each other, so it was inevitable that these clubs would drop points over the following two games.

The first hurdle, against East Stirlingshire, was overcome with ease on 3rd May as Farnan, Hall, Herkes and Deuchar all found the net to record a 4-0 win. On the same day, Peterhead shared the spoils with Albion Rovers, which once again meant that the Fifers' destiny was entirely in their own hands with one game to go. If Queen's Park could be defeated, then promotion was assured as the top two teams in the table, Morton and Peterhead, were facing each other at Cappielow and at least one team would have to drop points. If the top of the table clash ended all square and East Fife won their fixture, then the Third Division Championship would be on its way to Methil!

Once again, Bayview Stadium was packed to overflowing for the final fixture against Queen's Park. Some exiled Fifers even travelled home from overseas for the event, with one former Leven resident, Peter McCue, arriving from California on the morning of the match before flying home the following day! For the most part, the game against the 'Spiders' was instantly forgettable. For ninety minutes the home side struggled to string two passes together and, from the chances that were created, woeful finishing presented few problems for the visitors' 'keeper.

Then, with the referee about to signal time up, came one of these utterly magic moments that makes following the beautiful game so worthwhile. Substitute Gordon Love lobbed the ball across the face of the goal to the far post, where Kenny Deuchar was perfectly placed to bundle the ball over the line. The biggest roar ever to emanate from the Bayview Stadium grandstand filled the air as the players raced over to the crowd to soak up the applause. Seconds later the referee signalled the end of the contest and hundreds of jubilant supporters invaded the pitch to congratulate their heroes. In keeping with form throughout the season, East Fife had won promotion with virtually the last kick of the ball. But had they also won the Championship? Unfortunately not. Minutes later the news filtered through from Greenock that Morton had beaten Peterhead by a single goal and, in doing so, had secured the title. If the truth were told, however, the destination of the League Championship was of secondary importance to the masses of black and gold clad supporters who continued to dance around on the park long, long after the match was over. The main thing was that the Fifers had finally managed to escape from the Third Division.

Magic moment! With only seconds to go, the ball is in the net, the players run towards the crowd and East Fife are on their way back to Division Two! (Jim Corstorphine)

The events of the afternoon of May 10th 2003 will be talked about for years to come. It was a fitting way to complete the club's hundredth season, with victory in the dying seconds securing promotion after four miserable years in Scottish football's basement.

Will promotion in season 2002/03 signal the start of a turnaround in the club's fortunes? Will East Fife ever return to the standards set during the late 1930's when the Scottish Cup came to Methil; will we ever again see the Scottish League Cup held aloft by a team Captain wearing the famous black and gold?

The answers to these questions, of course, lie in the years ahead. I will therefore conclude by expressing the sincere hope that future historians will have similar stories to relate when commemorating the club's 200th birthday!

Goal hero Kenny Deuchar is lifted high on the shoulders of goalkeeper Jim Butter after the victory against Queen's Park on 10th May 2003 secured a return to Division Two. Closest to the camera is Gordon Love, who supplied the cross for Deuchar's last gasp winner. (Jim Corstorphine)

Acknowledgements

Unfortunately, there is insufficient space on this page to list every single person who has assisted me in producing this book. During several years of research, many people have provided information and items of interest connected with the history of East Fife Football Club. Some have shared memories of great moments they personally witnessed dating back as far as the 1920's, without which it is doubtful such a vivid picture of the club's early days in the Scottish League could have been painted.

Regular contributors to the official East Fife website forum were also of invaluable assistance, particularly with helping to identify certain players in various team photographs dating from the 1950's, 1960's and 1970's.

As for supplying the photographs, sincere thanks go to Ben Supple (*Dundee Courier*), John Brown (*Dundee Evening Telegraph*), Peter Smith, Alan Brotchie, Stephen Mill, Ernie Mackie, John Ross, Bob Hunter and former match programme photographers R. Janetta and R. Valente. Several photographs, particularly those from the club's early days, were obtained from private sources where it simply was not possible to identify the original photographer and have therefore been credited to the 'Author's Collection'.

Sources and Bibliography

By far the greatest source of information relating to the history of East Fife Football Club is the collection of local newspapers held on microfilm in Methil Library and Kirkcaldy Central Library. The publications referred to more times than I care to remember at these locations were the *Leven Advertiser and Wemyss Gazette*, the *Leven Mail*, the *East Fife Mail* and the *Fife Free Press*. At Cupar Library, bound volumes of the *Dundee Courier* also proved to be invaluable.

Other publications referred to were:

Scottish Football Records *(Gordon Smailes, Breedon Books, 1995)*

The Football Grounds of Great Britian *(Simon Inglis, Willow Books, 1987)*

The First 100 Years of the Scottish Football League *(Bob Crampsey, Scottish Football League, 1990)*

Rothmans Book of Football Records *(Jack Rollin, Headline, 1998)*

Scotland: The Complete International Record *(Richard Keir, Breedon Books, 2001)*

Scottish Football League Review, 1980 to 2003 *(Scottish Football League)*

The Methil Maverick *(Dominic J. Currie, Methil Heritage Centre, 1996)*

Black and Gold Heroes *(Andrew Wilkie and Jim Stewart, Artigraf, 1988)*

Diary of a Season *(John Ross and Jim Stewart, Scottprint, 1997)*

Black and Gold All The Way *(Jim Beavers, Cupar Print & Stationery Office, 2001)*

Through the Years with East Fife F.C. *(William Phenix Jnr., Simmath Press, 1948)*

Printed in Great Britain
by Amazon